Embodied Wisdom

Embodied Wisdom

What our anatomy can teach us about the art of living

Joy Colangelo

iUniverse, Inc.

New York Lincoln Shanghai

Embodied Wisdom
What our anatomy can teach us about the art of living

iUniverse, Inc.

For information address:
iUniverse, Inc.
2021 Pine Lake Road, Suite 100
Lincoln, NE 68512
www.iuniverse.com

ISBN: 0-595-29551-7

Printed in the United States of America

CONTENTS

Introduction 1

Chakra One—STABILITY 15
Legs, Base of the Spine, and Immune System 15
How to Evoke Stability 36

Chakra Two—CREATIVITY 48
Lumbar Spine, Pelvis, Hip 48
How to Evoke Creativity 67

Chakra Three—CHOICE 78
Thoracic Spine, Abdomen 78
How To Evoke Choice 96

Chakra Four—LOYALTY 105
Chest, Diaphragm, Shoulders, Hands 105
How to Evoke Loyalty 127

Chakra Five—FAITH 135
Throat, Neck, Mouth 135
How to Evoke Faith 157

Chakra Six—TRUTH 166
Brain, Nervous System, Eyes, Ears 166
How to Evoke Truth 190

Chakra Seven—HARMONY 199
Muscular System, Skeletal System, Skin, and Fascia 199
How to Evoke Harmony 226

Bibliography 241

Index 249

ACKNOWLEDGEMENTS

I am thankful for the many researchers and deep thinkers whose work fills these pages. There is barely an original thought included in this text—what is mine is merely a way of telling the story from a different point of view. If I have misused the words of these authors and merged them with concepts that were never intended, I take full responsibility for the error. The idea for the book originated after reading Neese and Williams landmark text, *Why We Get Sick*. They inspired me to view rehabilitation through the eyes of evolutionary medicine and view my work in a new light.

Thank you to the librarians at the Pacific Grove Public Library and Monterey Public Library. Also to Ian Stevens, PT (Scotland) and Matthias Weinberger, PT (Germany), who always seemed to send pertinent articles at just the right time. Also Nic Lucas, DO in Australia for his thoughtfulness. A huge thank you to NOI Group (Neuro-Orthopedic Institute) for their web site discussion group especially David Butler and Israel Zvulun—I am so appreciative of the intellectual community you facilitate.

Thank you to Community Hospital of the Monterey Peninsula, especially Vice President Jim Jenifer for his counsel and tolerance, and Vice President Laura Zehm for her enthusiasm and untiring optimism. Thanks to my co-workers who teach me something everyday, especially Amy Britton CHT/OT, Alain Claudel PT, Baron Vanhonsebrouck OT, Marta Lynch OT and Katherine Stephenson PT. Also, to the many nurses and dietitians who have inspired me with their knowledge and kindness, especially Trina, Barbara and Christine. Thank you to Dixie and Lauren who kindly find an audience for my talks.

Thank you to Dr. Terry Moran for his writing support, advice and pep talks that always came at the right time. Thank you to the many physicians who trust me with their patients, especially the inspired Dr. Cathy Petronijevic.

Thank you to Professors Neill Cooney and the late Norman O. Brown who always thought I had something worth saying. They were instrumental in laying the foundation in my thinking about word play, metaphor and the philosophy of the body.

Thanks also to my patients, some who see pain as a brick wall, some who see it as a screen and some as a mirror. You have all taught me invaluable lessons about living in a body. Thank you for letting me be a part of your experience.

Thank you to friends who have walked and ate dinner, lunched, taken tea, kayaked, listened and were interested when I mentioned "The Book"—Helen and Rick, Jayne, Mary W., Michael and Mary, Kristen and Quinn, Gwen, Elizabeth, Emily, Janice, Leila, Kitty, Val, Roberta, Kendra, Patrick and Normi.

Thank you to Diane Jacobs, a constant source of comfort and encouragement. She was a tireless reader and opened her home in Vancouver during the last week of editing. And to creative consultant Diana Claire Douglas in Vancouver whose techniques allowed the final editing to be enjoyable. My mother was the last marathon reader to find errors—if any linger, it was I who did not take her advice.

Thanks finally to my family. My mother who always set an example and my twin brother Jay, who is the most courageous person I know. To my sister Susan for her steadfastness and loyalty and to my brother Jim for his uncommon sense and wit. This book would not have been written were it not for my husband Britt and children, Dakota and Allie. Their patience, advice, and support makes life worth living. You are why I do what I do.   **Joy**

INTRODUCTION

"From my earliest years as a surgeon, I have been forced to
confront the difference between health
and lack of disease."—Mehmet Oz, heart surgeon

"The operation was a success but the patient died."—Maxim of physicians

"To believe in medicine would be the height of folly, if not to
believe in it were not a greater folly still."—Marcel Proust

"The witch doctor succeeds for the same reason all the rest of us succeeds.
Each patient carries his own doctor inside him. They come to us
not knowing that cure. We are at our best when we give the doctor who
resides within each patient a chance to go to work."—Albert Schweitzer

Medicine is a science of ironies. Terminal patients vow they will live each day to the fullest, while healthy people spend ten years of their life watching television. Medical professionals greatly underutilize medical services in their personal lives, while their patients demand a prescription for the sniffles. Studies warn us to avoid a certain food or drug one week only to tout the healthy effects of the same food or drug the next week; and scientists study disease while all of us just want to know how to be happy. In addition, medicine's most powerful tool is the body's ability to heal itself yet most of us have lost hope that we can change ourselves from the inside. We overestimate the occurrences of rare dangers like plane crashes, murder, or shark attack and show an "optimistic distortion" of the real risk of over-eating, addictions, and a sedentary lifestyle. We long for more connection but media assures us that we should fear each other with murders down by 25% in the U.S. in 2002, but television and newspaper reports of those murders up 600%. Automobile exhaust is killing the planet yet we drive to the corner store for organic produce. And finally and most ironically, we are built to walk upright to perform meaningful work but sit 80% of our day performing repetitive jobs. How can we be healthy when television determines how we think, automobiles determine how we move, and chairs determine how we work? What if the answer to our question was right inside of us?

Recent texts have linked revolutionary brain science with the ancient wisdom of Buddhist psychology and immune function. But the body in mind/body medicine is more than immune function; it is movement. The work of many researchers and sages are gathered in these pages in an effort to re-member parts of us we may have forgotten existed. In linking those parts together, we might become more of who we really are. *Embodied Wisdom* unveils our great capacity to transform brain function through movement and links the way we move with the way we think.

Let's start with what you did today. Did you awaken at dawn to witness the first light that begins a day, or did you awaken to the shrill of an alarm? Did you choose a light breakfast of fruit and grains to pace the day's activities, or did you skip breakfast making the body wonder whether there might not be a famine? Did you walk five miles by the day's end or did you sit all day and drive yourself home only to sit some more? Do you know how to live but fail to do it? Then, join the club.

Many of us, when it comes to doing something about our lives, are paralyzed into a state of apathy especially when our bad habits may eventually lead to illness as measured in decades. Instead of flight or fight, we freeze, as if no response is better than the wrong one. Yet, we know our feelings of apathy and emptiness are not the right response. We can feel it in our aching bones.

Our temporary comfort in doing nothing eventually becomes uncomfortable and as a Buddhist teacher once said, we realize we are "licking honey from a razor's edge." But might we choose clarity rather than apathy, or insight rather than a sharp, albeit symbolic, cut to the tongue? How would we go about finding that clarity? Well, just as we might untie a complicated knot, we know enough to look carefully at first before gently undoing the tangle. We know a hard yank will only make the knot tighter. Likewise, yanking on the body to make it understandable is like using logic to understand a song—it just isn't the most appropriate way to go about it. We can't yank on bodies that feel as if they have lost their minds or use logic on minds that have forgotten they live in a body.

So instead of taking the world by storm, let us take it by calm. But let's also remember that half the struggle in learning a new way of being is unlearning the old one, or as Freud said, "If you want to understand something, look closely at it when it is broken." As we look at what makes our hearts and our muscles ache, we might find that discomfort is simply our body's way of announcing its inability to adapt to a lifestyle habit—something we could easily alter once we have new information. We might find that discomfort is exactly "what the doctor ordered," after all, if hunger were not uncomfortable, we would starve to death. Our discomfort can lead us to its cure.

While scientific studies can offer measurements, numbers, and expected outcomes, it is time to seek broader answers—answers as broad as nature itself. To uncover these answers, we might have some redefining to do. What we term success and failure, or health and disease, might become blurred. As Joseph Campbell warns, the myth of achievement and success is "climbing the ladder only to discover it was against the wrong wall." Let's put the ladder against a wall that matters. Perhaps what we desire in life is something more than health; more than knowledge. If you are like me, you have a deep longing for a life well-lived. For that we shall start with the genius that is the body.

*   *   *   *   *

"A few of us have lost our minds, but many of us have
long ago lost our bodies."—Unknown

"Men go abroad to wonder at the height of mountains, at the huge
waves of the sea, at the long courses of the rivers, at the vast compass
of the ocean, at the circular motion of the stars; and they pass by
themselves without wondering."—St. Augustine

"It is our natures that are the physicians of our diseases. We must
not meddle with or hinder nature's attempt toward recovery.
First do no harm."—Hippocrates

Most of the time, we are unaware of our body unless it hurts. We adaptively block out the feeling of our shirt collar on our neck, the hair tickling our ears, and the tight elastic of undergarments around our waist. We block out our surroundings in an effort to pay attention to only what is an immediate priority, skillfully not noticing every piece of furniture whenever we walk through our living room or ignoring the noise of traffic when we listen for a bird cheeping. We wouldn't have enough energy or time in the day to notice every object, listen to every sound, feel the act of digestion, or attend to every breath we take.

In fact, data that is always present is often perceived as nothing. Air, gravity, and even good health are ignored by the brain's filters. Forgetting then becomes as important as remembering and blocking sensations are as important as feeling them. But that ability to block sensations can work for or against us depending on the culture we live in.

For instance, members of a mobile society can disregard the slight twinge in their wrists as they dig to plant seeds because they will soon stop to water or rake weeds. When their back fatigues from chopping wood, they will sharpen the blade, stack logs, and sip water. The tasks are paced throughout a day; tasks that will occupy a physically demanding but just as physically varied day. Some cultures stop for siesta, others for numerous prayer times or tea times, and many dance or socialize for hours after work. The key lies in the variability of work and rest throughout the hours of a day.

What about the sensation of pain in a sedentary society? What about the pain in our wrists from the prolonged use of a computer mouse or the fatigue in our backs after loading a truck for eight hours, working by the rhythms of a clock bent on productivity? What if we shut down or take medications to hide those sensations? In the case of repetitive motion injuries, the body has become so good at ignoring sensations that disregard turns into neglect. If we continually over-ride pain sensations and also fail to vary our tasks throughout a day, actual damage can occur. Instead of siesta, we drink coffee at mid-afternoon, accelerating the system instead of resting it. Instead of dancing or playing at night, we work harder to buy larger television screens in order to watch other people dance or play sports. So how much physical and psychic pain must occur before we take notice? How much pain must occur before it is the only thing we can think about?

Dr. Paul Brand notes in *The Gift of Pain* that "pain must be persistent and it must be unpleasant or we would shut it off." The body uses the language of pain because it is the most effective way to get our attention, but unless the pain is relentless, we have learned to ignore its early ranting and raving. As we become more and more oblivious to early warning signals and as we take more and more medications to block our body's signals, we will fail to see the forest for the trees and soon find ourselves oblivious about how we got into the forest of pain at all. Additionally, as we become adept at over-riding pain in exchange for productivity and material acquisition, we stray further from our true work in the world.

As we will see in upcoming chapters, attention is a scarce resource of the mind and energy the body's only currency. Understanding how we move will help us use our resources wisely and offer valuable insight into the art of living in a body. Unfortunately, many of us feel a great debt when it comes to this "art of living," especially when it occurs to us that what we want and what is happening to us are often two different things. We might feel that motors have replaced muscle, our objects own us, that we are passengers instead of pedestrians, and that we work only to buy what we just got paid to make.

So what of this "shutting off" of our senses, our attention, and our life's work? What about the "language of pain" as the only way to get our attention? Might there be another language, even a few mumbled sentences we could use to understand our body before pain, regret, or disease has to shout at us? Rollo May in his book, *The Courage to Create*, proposes an idea he calls "courage for the body." He suggests using the body not for the development of musculature but for the cultivation of sensitivity stating, "This will mean the development of the capacity to listen with the body. It will be as Nietzsche remarked, a 'learning to think with the body'."

Such a view is emerging in America through the research and writings of dozens of scientists who are linking emotions with immune function and healing. Feelings in the mind are in fact, senses in the body with nature and nurture occurring at the same time. The influence of ancient body work such as yoga, acupressure, and pranayama breathing are rapidly finding a home in many U.S. hospitals in an effort to link the content of thought as it influences the harmony of the body. Instead of opting only for technological advances, hospitals are returning to simple, centuries old remedies for our modern illnesses, realizing that what the brain has always learned cognitively, the body might learn kinesthetically. Listening to the body and watching how it learns becomes an act of translation.

Author Wendell Berry notes that, "It is impossible to prefigure the salvation of the world in the same language by which the world has been dismembered and defaced." The language he proposes would not attempt to "figure everything out" or even understand it but "to suffer and rejoice in it as it is…To treat life as less than a miracle is to give up on it." We need the language of metaphor where we discover something new by leaping between two seemingly unrelated thoughts. This book might serve to leap between science and art, to mix them up so that they both become more or as Leonardo Da Vinci urged us, "We must study the science of art and the art of science."

While science may be easily measured, might there also be an "unevident reality," a way that speaks of unmeasurable things like the dreams we have for our future, of inspiration, of innovation, courage, and compassion? Might there be more than just a narrow strategy of survival encoded in our genes? Might we become citizens of a culture that is awake with curiosity and energy? Wendell Berry in *Life is a Miracle,* suggests there is a knowledge that cannot be proved, demonstrated, and explained. He states it is, "as far as possible unlike what we now call 'information.'" He likens it to religious faith that is not in any respectable sense a theory but a different kind of knowledge. He notes that although there may be no statistical proof of the existence of many theories, there is also no statistical disproofs. Carl Sagan said it best when he noted, "Absence of evidence is not evidence of absence." We need to use science the way it was meant to be used. It was meant to offer beautiful and compatible ideas that tell us of our relationship with the laws of nature.

What is keeping us from experiencing this new science of living? What keeps us from fully understanding the tension between our ideals of a healthy lifestyle and our current reality? Why is it so difficult to live the way we know we should live? The answer lies in the word "meme," which rhymes with the word "gene."

You've perhaps heard of the selfish gene but we really live at the mercy of the selfish meme.

A meme is a powerful process, a driving force that is more powerful than genes. It is so powerful that it can trigger the expression of a gene. It is culture. Richard Dawkins coined the term "meme," a word combining 'memory' and 'imitation' to convey the replication of ideas and cultural habits. He says that cultural memes can be as important as genes noting that the success of an egg depends as much on the nest as it does on its DNA.

While our genes may be dictating our selection preferences, our cultural habits create their own ecology with natural selection at work. Stephen Jay Gould writes in *Full House* that, "The obvious main difference between Darwinian evolution and cultural change clearly lies in the enormous capacity that culture holds—and nature lacks—for explosive rapidity and cumulative directionality. In an unmeasurable blink of a geological eyelash, human cultural change has transformed the surface of our planet as no event of natural evolution could ever accomplish at Darwinian scales of myriad generations."

Stephen R. Palumbi explains, "There is a big difference in the evolution of the Beatles and the evolution of beetles." The high concept of the Beatles evolved quickly through cultural transmission, appearing as an idea whose time had come and turning the music industry literally on its ear. Beetles, however, show very slow alteration through genetically transmitted evolution. Both change the world as we know it. But only one can change the world in the blink of an eye by appearing on the Ed Sullivan Show.

As we've noted earlier, our brain pays attention to incoming sensation, not like a machine or computer, but like an ecosystem. Information comes from the skin, eyes, nose, and the ears while the brain processes which piece of information is relevant and which can be ignored. This system of constant competition within the brain is a process Nobel Laureate Gerald Edelman called, "neural Darwinism," where each sensation from the outside world vies for attention to inhabit a neuron and become a thought. Every single event has the potential to upset the balance of sensations and thus, to change every subsequent sensation. It is survival of the fittest sensation.

Candance Pert researches peptides that are active when we pay attention to something and notes that what we attend to becomes the framework in which we think. Our choices shape our bodies and shape our picture of the world as our actions become habits. The "mu" opiate receptors, she says, are activated during attention and are triggered by exercising choice. Most abundant in the frontal cortex, they are the "bliss" receptors, steering us toward what is most pleasurable and rewarding. And it is the cultural memes appearing before us as choices that invade the frontal cortex, competing for attention. These choices become engrained and are the pattern our lives take. If they are seen as something that may threaten our survival, the amygdala, the portion of our brain that registers fear and unrest will be activated. If we practice reflection and pause between sensation and response, the pre-frontal cortex is activated. Therein lies the difference between bad habits and good habits; negative emotions and positive emotions. In other words, synapses get stronger only if they are used. For neurons, it is survival of the busiest. If the busiest thoughts are based on fear, one might feel as if they are merely surviving instead of thriving. If we choose among the good memes, we might feel as if we are engaged in a life well lived.

Each mind has a limited capacity for memes in that we cannot remember everything we read, hear, or have been taught. But since the ideas themselves have no need for real space (like a gene would), millions of ideas can assault the brain, trying to gain access. Those memes that are imitated and passed on are the survivors. Unfortunately, memes do not need to be true to be successful, as false or meaningless memes can sneak into use under the protection of true ones. Such a feat is evident in the meaningless and awkward dimensions of the space shuttle, which as we shall see in the first chapter, was ushered into reality by the functional and elegant dimensions of two horses standing side by side. Or a meme could simply claim to be true as in the statement "energy-saving appliances." You can't use energy at the same time you are saving it. Memes could even start their lives as one thing and evolve into a use never condoned by the inventor as is the case of Thomas Edison and his phonograph. He wished to record the last words of the dying and it was ten years before he acquiesced to use his invention to record music, which he called "dead music." He had wanted to preserve something that was dying, not deaden something that was alive.

Researchers offer that conscious selection, that is the selection of one meme over another, is vastly different than natural selection, in that we can imagine the outcome and thus question the validity of our choices. We can make a judgment and anticipate the future. The trouble arises when we are faced with too many choices. When a cultural idea is passed on that is good and fit (like reading bedtime stories to our children versus watching TV), we are pleased. When we succumb to a suggestible meme that is not so well thought out (watching a TV show and calling it "family time") we are ambivalent. And when we succumb to a memetic suggestion with no thought whatsoever to the outcome (allow our children to watch a violent TV show), we are oblivious. It is the oblivious and ambivalent feelings that haunt us.

One of the contentions of this book is that we have succumbed to self-serving memes which make us feel as if our body is out of its mind, while our mind feels as if it has lost control of the body. Nature's wisdom has been replaced by human cleverness in ad campaigns, societal pressures toward success at any cost, and inventions that dictate the way we behave. We simply don't know what is good for us anymore. Richard Brodie in his book *Virus of the Mind* says, "the effect of…mind viruses is the same: you unwittingly have a portion of yourself divided from what you might otherwise be doing with your life, and instead devoted to doing the work of the mind memes." Passing on a naturally arising cultural meme (the innate ability for language or music) or a "designer" meme (such as soft drinks or the use of automobiles), might benefit the meme, the user, or both.

The meme is like a symbiont says J. M. Balkins in *Cultural Software*, and is an organism that lives off its host. But in the case of a meme, it is an informational symbiont and may be one of three kinds. In mutualism, the host and the meme are enhanced by each other's fitness—for instance, playing musical instruments for enjoyment. In commensalism, the guest benefits but at no cost to the host—as in language which can spread lies and truths at a sum gain of zero. When the guest, in our case a meme, benefits at the expense of the host, it is a parasite—for example, the automobile. In thinking about symbionts, we must remember that things which interest people (cars and television) might not be in the best interest of those people. As Balkin notes, watching television helps the TV critic but not the law student facing finals.

Education is one of the only cures for parasitic memes. Education can mimic the body's immune system, a fluid central nervous system that decides what is an invader and what is of benefit. Just as our immune system might recognize a cancer tumor as an enemy and destroy it, we might be educated that something as seemingly innocuous as a chair offers only short term comfort and long term disability. An immune system might also overreact and try to correct a harmless invader, as in an allergic reaction to benign pollen. Education might overreact and try to correct non-scientific faith in a higher being, a benign and oftentimes comforting invasion on our thinking and attention. By looking at memes as symbionts, we can educate ourselves on which are self-serving and which might serve The Self.

This book will look at biological theories which display an ecological perspective where the workings of the human body suggest the fittest lifestyle. In finding out what is good for us, we will identify common themes in nature that suggest memes which can bring value to our lives. We will re-member the body and watch it become whole again. But first, we need to know where theories about the body went wrong.

*   *   *   *   *

"Scientists…may lead us—to put it in extreme terms—to the Buddha or to the bomb, and it is up to each of us to decide which path to take."—Fritjob Capra in *The Turning Point*

"The world has achieved brilliance without wisdom, power without conscience. Ours is a world of nuclear giants and ethical infants."—General Omar Bradley

"The means by which we live have outdistanced the ends for which we live. Our scientific power has outrun our spiritual power. We have guided missiles and misguided men."—Martin Luther King Jr.

"Yoga is one of the greatest things the human mind has ever created."—Carl Jung in *Psychology and the East*

Theories of physiology are dominated by models drawn from physics and engineering. Scientific descriptors of the human body are seen in accordance with the most typical machine in use during a certain period and that has never been truer than today when the brain is described as working like a computer. Unfortunately, such analogies do more to elevate the machine than to encourage a holistic concept of our bodies. As machines become more complex, their inner workings deeply hidden from those who operate them, any analogy likening the body to the machine will serve to further disconnect us from ourselves. Not only are we unable to fix our own car due to computer chips for every function, we are led to believe we cannot fix our own body as well. We suffer "cognitive lock," the behavioral phenomenon witnessed during mechanical disasters wherein the operator is frozen, unable to decide on a course of action. While alarm buttons or lights signal "all is well," the operator can clearly see evidence to the contrary, yet is paralyzed with indecision. Cognitive lock was responsible for the Chernobyl disaster and is often behind many airline disasters as well as tanker oil spills. In *Inviting Disaster*, author James R. Chiles notes that linking our lives with ever complex machines is inviting "extraordinary disasters from ordinary mistakes."

James McAllister, in his book *Beauty and Revolution in Science*, outlines the link between the body and machines. He notes that in the 17th and 18th centuries, the body was likened to a clock with analogies from dynamics theory wherein our bodies functioned merely as an arrangement of rods and wheels. In the 19th century, theories of thermodynamics were used to understand the body more as a heat engine with cooling systems and caloric energy expenditures. Twentieth century theories brought electronic engineering as a model.

In the 1940's, the nervous system was thought of as a telephone switchboard (information theory) which is a passive network of electrical impulses where there is no response unless there is a stimulus. By 1950, the nervous system was seen more as a feedback mechanism like that of a thermostat (cybernetic theory), an active system which constantly changes according to deviations from chemical equilibrium. In the 1970's, computer science brought the nervous system into the realm of a central processing unit, reading programs, offering up multitudes of pathways, and serving to code information. Today, the brain is likened to the internet with its information links, and the networking between cells according to receptor sites. This is a long way from Renaissance times where anatomy was explained according to alchemy and magic. Or is it?

Magical theories attributed powers to plants and minerals that would affect the body from afar. For instance, wounds could be healed by applying a salve to the weapon that had inflicted the injury. Ridiculous we might say, but gravity is a theory of action at a distance, as is the spread of infectious disease by the "carrying power of air." Both speak of an abstraction in physical theory that requires a physical distance between the observer and the object and the energy between them, whether it be mechanical, magical, or physical.

The French psychiatrist, Jacques Lacan, noted that when medicine began to look in the body for the machine, the idea of energy disappeared. He suggests it was Freud who attempted to return energy to the body by introducing the concept of libido as an energy around which the body organizes itself. Today, longevity studies tell us that social connection, faith, and our ability to find meaning through disappointment are the critical determinates in not only how long we will live, but in our ability to heal from disease. What these studies are attempting to do is derive a theory of connection that enhances energy.

Nei Jing, a second century medical classic notes "maintaining order rather than correcting disorder is the ultimate principle of wisdom. To cure disease after it has appeared is like digging a well when one already feels thirsty." In fact, Western medicine is thought to detect the last two stages of disease development. It is late in "digging the well" since it treats signs and symptoms but, so often, neglects the underlying cause of disease. This narrow definition of disease, and thus, of health allows only a narrow connection with life itself.

A narrow view of life might explain our pervasive feeling of knowing there must be more. If we continue in our narrow viewpoints, how will we connect our aspirations with our lifestyles? Goals will go unmet, our bodies will feel unconnected to our mind, and we will succumb to the most apathetic of diseases, TATT (Tired All The Time), or what has been called a spiritual vertigo. Sociologist Karl Weick coined a phrase "*vu jade*" to describe the opposite of "*déjà vu.*" Rather than feeling as if everything is strangely familiar, *vu jade* is the profoundly frightening impression that the world no longer makes sense. It is as if you have blundered into a circumstance so alien, no one has ever been there before. It might be a world where ecology has been replaced by economy and gardens replaced by groceries. We have new kinds of disappointments—there is a distance between who we are and who we want to be.

We need to rely on the phenomenon of cognitive dissonance, the psychological given that humans will work to reduce the dissonance, or distance, between two conflicting ideas. We dislike things that are incompatible. We dislike the fact that we sit for eight straight hours when we know we should be moving more. The idea of holding those two incompatible viewpoints brings on unpleasant consequences. We are unhappy. I am unhappy when I think of myself as intelligent but sit and watch television. I am unhappy when I should do my "life's work" and instead spend my days doing mundane tasks. To be happy, we require connection, a calling that affords us a sense of unity. To do that, we might have to deconstruct our lives and investigate our lifestyles. As the poet David Whyte suggests, "There are giants slumbering inside us. Often in order to stay alive, we have to unmake a living in order to get back to living the life we wanted for ourselves."

We need to explore a science with an allegiance to nature and a connection to the wisdom of the body. We need to foster generosity instead of generators and compassion instead of competition. It will, by necessity, be a science that embodies an "unknowing" while carefully moving toward what we know deep in our bones.

Nobel winner Richard P. Feynman, notes in an essay entitled, *The Smartest Man in the World*, "The thing that's unusual about good scientists is that while they're doing whatever they are doing, they're not so sure of themselves as others usually are. They can live with steady doubt, think 'maybe it's so' and act on that, all the time knowing it's only 'maybe.' Many find that difficult; they think it means detachment or coldness. It's not coldness! It's a much deeper and warmer understanding."

A warmer understanding of the body can be gained from a practice like Yoga, one of the oldest systems of bodywork in the world and a meme that perpetuates wholeness. Yoga teaches us to listen to and observe the body rather than forcing it toward a goal. Much like another ancient type of bodywork, Qigong, the foundation is in relaxation where instead of making an effort to do more, one does less and gains more. Spiritual bodywork practice like Yoga or Qigong are distinguished from religion in that we are not expected to believe anything until we experience for ourselves which is why we "practice."

Yoga is a verb from the Sanskrit word "*yuj*" meaning "to join or yoke together." It is a practice of joining what is fragmented, of finding the relationship between two seemingly disparate entities. For joining to occur, a number of things must happen. First, there must be movement; one must move two things closer to each other. So Yoga is a movement which brings the self together by pointing to the body as the essential means of unlocking the brain's mysteries. By mastering a steadiness of posture in Hatha Yoga, one can master a steadiness of mind. Hatha, too, implies a joining and is a balancing act in its very name. "Ha" means "the energy of the sun" while "tha" means "energy of the moon." Incongruencies become partners.

By giving movement to the different parts of ourselves, our hips, our knees, or our shoulders, each part reaches its full potential. If our shoulder can move to its greatest potential, we become less fragmented because of its wholeness. If we put our body in a difficult yoga position, we may be able to handle difficult situations. By making our bodies fully connected, our insides will feel like our outsides. We will embody harmony and will be closer to being 100% ourselves; unfragmented, strong, confident, and clear about who we are and the direction of our lives. Yoga can be seen as a determined effort to become all we were meant to be.

Another way to develop a warmer understanding of our nature and our connectedness is to remove ideas from our head that the body is like a machine. Rather, we should return to memes wherein the body is likened to the forces of nature embodied in fire, water, air, and earth. How much better it is to think of ourselves as stable as the earth below our feet, as propelled forward like the gentle energy of a breeze, as creative as a river finding its sure way around rocks, and as passionate about living as a fire is about burning. We are forces of nature. Nothing less. Deane Juhan writes in *Job's Body,*

> "Indeed, since we have left the water and have become terrestrial creatures, subject now to the special forces of gravity, we have become miniature earths in the same way that we first became miniature seas; we have added more and more solid features to support our containers of fluid upon the ground. We have river channels and reservoirs in our circulatory systems, meadows and forests in our hair; we are mountains of flesh riddled with the caves and fissures of our pores and orifices; like enclosed valleys, we shelter our ancestral cultures, and like the open hillsides and plains, we teem with a microbial bustle of new citizens and migrants. We have become an ecology of earth and air, as well as one of water."

In his profound work entitled, *The Architecture of Life*, Donald Ingber notes that the form of living things "has less to do with chemical composition than with architecture." Nature, it seems, applies common assembly rules which are evident and implied by their recurrence in the micro—to the macroscopic. All matter, from small to large, use the same pattern as the rules for assembly. He notes, "If we are to understand fully the way living creatures form and function, we need to uncover these basic principles that guide biological organization." The way we think also borrows from the assembly rules of nature—we use motor pathways in the brain not only to move, but to think. We borrow them.

The influence of the body on the organization of the mind is evident when we say that we feel up when we are happy and down when we are sad. Abstract thoughts like happiness and sadness have borrowed the body's awareness in space. Cognitive linguist, George Lakoff, notes that our most basic cognitive models derive from our experience of living in a body. When we talk about "improvement or success models," we say "things are moving forward." We talk of "understanding models" with vision metaphors as in "I see what you mean," or "I have a clear view of what you mean," and "I can see right through that logic." When we talk of "comprehension models," we liken the brain to a container but not just any container; we liken it to the first container which was our hands when we say, "I've got an idea," "hold onto that thought," "I've a good grasp of that concept," and "I can't handle the thought of it." We use the body and only the body as a building block to understand all other concepts. From cell to self to society, the body constructs our world.

This book will explain the architecture of the human body using examples to uncover these natural patterns. For ease in discussion, body parts will be grouped from the ground up which coincides with the Indian chakra system, areas of energy that affect our health. Each area of the body represents a potential power that we have a right to develop. The third chakra, for instance, is located in the stomach and is the energy center for the power of Choice. To bring awareness to this part of the body is to bring the power of choice into our behavior—to decide what is nourishing and what is toxic in our lives and to choose between the two. Linking our physical and mental energies, and joining each chakra with the power of the other, is to link our physical bodies with our spiritual well-being. We will find that our anatomy can teach us about the art of living.

Offered at the end of each chakra section are holistic solutions in the form of Yoga postures which are noted with the sun/moon symbol, ☉. These postures allow our bodies to practice what our spirits need to learn. Natural metaphors are symbolized by, ☍, and will help us connect to a larger concept of our place in nature. Buddhist philosophy and psychology lessons are symbolized by, ☯, and offer words of wisdom in language so simple, we might wonder that we didn't think of it ourselves. We will understand the body in all its metaphorical qualities in order to better understand the world we live in.

As we reform our behaviors by re-forming our body, we will come to know more about the musculoskeletal system, the largest and most metabolically active organ in the body. We are going to learn what moves us and how movement can influence how we move through our lives. Survival tactics might come from the inventions of our minds but *thrivival* tactics will come from a reality that is shaped by our body. The good news is—there is an embodied wisdom.

CHAKRA ONE—STABILITY

LEGS, BASE OF THE SPINE, AND IMMUNE SYSTEM

"Body and spirit are twins: God only
knows which is which."—Swiburne

Regarding the nature versus nurture debate: "Indeed
the question is no more meaningful than asking
whether the wetness of water results mainly from the
hydrogen molecules or from the oxygen molecules
that constitute H_2O!"—V. S. Ramachandran, MD

"If you hesitate with each step, you will spend your
life standing on one foot."—Chinese Proverb

This area of the body represents our connection to the earth, with our feet having near constant contact with a planet. We are very literally grounded here. It is in standing that we are oriented in time and space and in walking that we move through time and space. Our erectness can be recognized as an attempt to connect to a higher state of being—our feet are on the ground and our head is in the clouds. We are body and spirit incarnate.

Our legs connect us to tribal dynamics in that our species evolved to be upright. There is a collective willpower to move with the tribe, to act like the tribe, and to find dignity and integrity in the tribe. This physical stability, survival of the species, safety in numbers, and code of conduct are the drives that make up a tribe. A tribe can be likened to the role our immune system plays as it seeks homeostasis in each individual body. In the same way, a tribe becomes strong as it identifies and fends off enemies and finds allegiance in a common goal. Finding stability in a tribe can also prepare us to stand on our own two feet while blind allegiance to a tribal way of thinking can lead us down a path that hampers the development of our individuality.

When Dawkins coined the word "meme," he linked imitation and memory into a unit of cultural transmission. A meme is a contagious information pattern that replicates itself by infecting human minds and altering behavior. It is the opposite of standing on our own two feet as an individual's will is subverted into the life of the meme. It is a cultural inheritance wherein the cultural event replicates, not the individual. And it can just as easily be beneficial to the individual as it is likely to be detrimental. It can even use individuals as tools of propagation.

In Lee Alan Dugatkin's book, *The Imitation Factor,* he notes that a "membot" is an individual whose entire life span is given to the propagation of a meme. Such individuals as evangelists, missionaries, politicians, or advertising executives would find themselves constantly converting other people. Objects can convert people for their uses as automobiles and chairs become more comfortable, inviting us to use them more often. It has been cleverly suggested that even plants make themselves attractive or edible in an effort to convince us to plant more of them, to trade them across cultures and to improve them through hybridization. Tulipmania, then, becomes the tulips' seduction of man, and marijuana's skyrocketing potency becomes a plant's rebellion against legal attempts to restrict it. We humans are merely pawns.

Individuals can be immune to brain-washing memes if, and only if, they are good judges about which memes are beneficial and which ones fail to contribute to a meaningful life. Psychologist David Perkins studies high IQ personalities and finds they have immunity to new ideas and tend to remain loyal to a prevailing theory. Those with high IQ tend to correlate with an inability to consider other alternatives, as they filter out novelty and squelch attempts at real innovation. Old memes would prevail, or be slightly "improved upon" until lo and behold, we might all find ourselves believing advertisements telling us we are delighted with the evolution of small cars into SUV's. This dilemma is called "The Planck Problem" after physicist Max Planck who said, "An important scientific innovation rarely makes its way by gradually winning over and converting its opponents…its opponents gradually die out and…the growing generation is familiarized with the idea from the beginning."

There is a tension then in meme identification, just as there is an essential tension in science between the total commitment to the status quo and the blind pursuit of new ideas. Do we follow the tribal instinct or think for ourselves? Is there, perhaps, a middle ground? The middle ground could be that we cooperate with memes, sifting out useful features and abandoning the non-useful; acting like our immune system when it detects a feature detrimental to the system as a whole.

It could be the difference in looking at a chair, a designer meme that adversely affects the anatomy and a rocking chair that is responsive to the body first and to its status as a chair second. The rocking chair is the lesser evil in that it moves, strengthening the walking muscles in our calves and thighs. Blood moves by way of constant muscle contraction, the rocking provides a calming effect and the ankle pump mechanism prevents blood clotting while keeping the sitter off the ground, away from germs and insects. Good features are highlighted and bad features are reduced.

Oftentimes, we lack the knowledge to know a detrimental meme when we see one. Once an idea has evolved and changed forms, the unadvised are at the mercy of memebots or out of control and out of context memes.

How far can memes go if left to their own devices? Let's talk about the criteria we use to transport ourselves across the planet. Rather than retain a culturally healthy tribal meme like walking, we have given our mobility over to cars that emphasize our independence. To allow cars to move, we need roads. This offers individual freedom in movement, and freedom, it turns out, is a key feature of our highway system. President Eisenhower, who wanted paved roads wide enough to allow tanks to travel across America in case of a Russian invasion, initiated the National Freeway System. Ironically, freedom is the last thing you think of when you are stuck in bumper-to-bumper traffic on our nation's freeways today. Bad memes quickly lose their original meaning and modern users find themselves feeling out of sorts because the meme is out of context.

Let's look at the story of the railroad gauge and see where it takes us. The U.S. Standard railroad gauge, which is simply the distance between the rails, is 4 feet, 8.5 inches. It's not an even number because that is how the rails were built in England. We built the rails the same way they did in England because the workforce was made up of English expatriates. They got that gauge from the people who built the tramways and they used the same jigs and tools that were used for building wagons, which of course were restricted by the geometry of wheel spacing.

Wagons used that odd wheel spacing because the axle would break if the wheels didn't fit into the decades old wheel ruts. Where did the rutted roads come from? The first long distance roads in Europe were built by Imperial Rome and the roads have been in use ever since, with the first ruts made the width of Roman war chariots. Since chariots were horse drawn, the unit of measure used to design them was the width of two horses back ends. So when any of us ride the railroad, two horses standing side by side have determined the width of that railroad car. The meme gets further out of context when we note the kinds of supplies that are shipped by rail.

The Space Shuttle lifts into the air by its two big solid rocket boosters (SRB's), which come from a Utah plant and travel in one piece by train to the launch site. Tunnels in the mountains then dictate how wide the SRB's can be and tunnels are only a tad wider than the railroad gauge. So a major design feature of the most technologically advanced transportation system, the Space Shuttle, is determined by the width of two horses' backsides. That is a replicated meme and it is a meme that finds duplicity in the ancient history, and the modern look of China. They too mandated that all roads meet the width requirements of ancient wheel ruts.

How flexible is our thinking when it comes to moving across the earth? How far have we come from transporting ourselves by horseback? Well, we've come so far we can propel ourselves to the moon and yet not so far that we don't measure it by a pair of horses.

The automobile, one of the most corrosive memes in our culture, is by far the most powerful tribal meme in America. Its danger is also the most discounted. In the year 2000, 115 people were killed each day in auto accidents and over three million a year are injured just in the U.S., the meme birthplace of the car. In 2002, a single parking space is estimated to cost $10,000 in each new construction and an inestimable amount of ecological value is lost making space for our cars when we aren't even using them. Millions and millions of miles of U.S. land is paved with no area farther than twenty miles within access to some type of road and yet, locally, our city planners work tirelessly to limit foot access to beaches or refuse bicyclists entry to dirt roads citing erosion concerns. What are we thinking?

At hospitals around the country, there are strict policies requiring newborn babies be carried by mothers only if they are seated in a wheelchair. She is not allowed to walk and carry her baby at the same time as every precaution is taken to ensure that the new baby will not be dropped as it is transported to the front door. Once outside, the baby is placed in the waiting car, and strapped in a car seat for "safety." The door is shut, the nurses wave good-bye and watch the car turn onto the highway. The car, traveling at speeds of over 60 miles per hour, is now sharing the road with cars driven by people whose behavior could have included drug use, alcohol consumption, hurriedness or inattention. That's how we get the babies home and once home, we tell everyone, "be careful when you pick him up; he's only a day old." Human beings aren't capable of carrying the baby but a bunch of metal barreling down the road is. Welcome to our world.

If cars have done one thing (and unfortunately they have done much, much more), they have separated us from our primary occupation as human beings: walking. Forget the pollution, the run-off from the paved roads, the noise, the mined metals, the accidents and the new baby's only way home, cars have usurped the reason we look the way we look. Every bone, muscle attachment, placement of our vital organs and position of our facial features is located in space to allow us to walk upright. We are walkers; the only upright walking animals on the face of the earth and the only animal that refuses to do so. Walking is a holy occupation. Nomadic journeys, pilgrimages and crusades are the calling of an inspired people. Even Jesus is hailed as the ambulatory God, walking among us like other men.

In the Middle Ages, the custom of declaring sainthood eroded away from sainting people and toward the sainting of objects such as Santa Cruz (Saint Cross). From the sainting of the earth, St. Terre, we gained the word "saunter" and we would be wise to remember its etymological source—sauntering is the act of walking on earth with a reverence for its holiness. We were made to saunter and every step taken in our external world awakens primitive neural pathways that the brain recognizes as "self." By awakening this powerful internal space, we become more sensitive to our surroundings, and the cycle repeats itself. We move through space externally, recognize it internally as we translate movement into sensation and in turn, sensation enhances and allows us to appreciate external information. It is in going for a walk that we might recognize the damage the automobile meme has done to our walking space.

One of the ways walking changes the brain is that it generates alpha waves, characterized as creative brain waves that spawn new ideas out of old material. Alpha waves are not generated during driving, a physically passive task. If we are to break the membotic idiocy of the automobile in our lives, we are surely going to require a fair amount of alpha waves to help us. We cannot rely on our high IQ's to get us to a meaningful version of successful living on this planet. High IQ's seem only to make better cars.

City planners and civil engineers need to hear the message that we want to re-design our congested cities back into walking cities. The average American family takes fourteen car trips a day according to the author Tony Hiss (son of Alger Hiss). In the Sierra article, *Man About Towns*, he suggests the designation of traffic reducers like bulbouts, and sidewalks that are wider at corners for pedestrians to safely cross streets. Roundabouts, where an intersection circles a middle landmark, reduces the potential collision points to eight, down from the thirty-two possible conflict points in a four-way intersection. In other words, there are thirty-two opportunities to get in an accident at each intersection we cross. Despite these mincing statistics, most of us refuse to walk and instead assign status, signs of intelligence and evidence of wealth to the cars we drive. Alpha wave thinkers will have to design roads to out-think intelligent drivers.

Road dieting, where lanes are shrunk from four to two can slow traffic, as can boulevarding, which is the beautification of roadways with landscaped median strips. In Tacoma, Washington on University Place, a traffic experiment was conducted owing to the need to reduce accidents. While the speed limit was 35 miles per hour (mph), cars usually traveled at an average of 44 mph. Police efforts were increased and in a two-week span, thirty speeding tickets were issued in order to slow traffic. And in fact, traffic did slow to 40 mph for a few weeks until it gained momentum and returned to its prior 44 mph. The solution was to place the street on a "diet," where the road was narrowed and a bike lane added along a tree-lined sidewalk. The speed has been kept at 31 mph with no police work.

This "road diet" meme is changing our behavior for the better but the question is, should it have to? Why do we resort to placing objects on a diet? In *Making Safer Roads*, Jim Bohen interviews Clarke Bennett, former director of the office of Highway Safety in the Federal Highway Administration, who notes that we can change the behavior of roads. In the 1960's, highway engineers thought their primary mission was to make a safe roadway. Bennett says, "Their job was to provide a good roadway; your job was to stay on it. Once you were off the roadway (that is, you had plunged off the side of the road), you were on your own. It was up to you to get out of a perilous situation." Bohen writes, "Luckily that attitude changed and a new concept developed dubbed 'the forgiving highway'."

Not only is there no mention that motorists might have a responsibility to avoid perilous situations, or drive at reduced speeds, but now the road is responsible for forgiving us our trespasses. Forgiving highways allow drivers to make mistakes and recover. They are wider, have smoother curves and a "generosity in design." What is needed to create a generous road? Remove more trees along the side, pave larger swaths of land, erect more barriers, and clear huge widths of landscape to create "clear zones" that allow a driver to regain control if they leave the road. The road is made to correct our behavior. It makes the choice, but it is the earth that suffers when we assign choice to objects and shirk personal responsibility.

Additionally, programs are being tested to reduce tailgating that involves painting dots in the center of highway lanes and signs (yes, more signs) that read: "Keep 2 Dots Apart." Road signs and guardrails will be coated with "micro prisms" that reflect headlights back into our eyes to get our attention. The future, the author says, belongs to "intelligent transportation systems" with built-in sensors controlling the vehicles and the ability to perform lane changes with no driver input. The road will be the only thing exhibiting any behavior at all; the driver will be ever more passive.

It appears that the road must not only be forgiving, generous, sensitive, intelligent, and on a diet, it must at all costs keep us from exercising any of those human traits ourselves. In Minnesota, the state's legislature turned off all 430 Twin Cities' freeway ramp meters for six weeks in the fall of 2000 due to budget cuts. These are the stoplights found on freeway ramps that hold excess vehicles out of the traffic flow, signaling in one or two cars at a time depending on traffic conditions. An independent survey firm found that freeway travel times increased 22%, speeds declined 7% and sideswipe crashes increased 200% while "run off the road crashes" increased 60%. Yet freeway volume was down 9%. We had fewer people on the roads, traveling at slower speeds and yet we couldn't stay out of each other's way without lights telling us what to do. The article decides that it is the slow evolution of the highways that is to blame stating, "Highway improvements can move at glacial speed compared to changes in vehicles." So highways evolve slower than automobiles and automobiles evolve faster than human consciousness.

If you take a very close look at the automobile, the whole memeplex of it, there is not one redeeming feature. We've mentioned some of the environmental atrocities, but what about the fact of sitting in a car, even if it weren't to go anywhere? Well, as you might have guessed, there is nothing inherently natural about sitting with one leg extended forward, our foot pressing on a lever for hours at a time, and our arms up over our heart to grasp a steering wheel. Our eyes don't understand information coming at us at speeds over 40 mph until we are 17 or 18 years old and yet 15 year old children are legally allowed to drive and a year later, able to drive freeways with speeds exceeding 80 mph. The vibration, the prolonged attention, the constant alerting intrusions into our visual field, the flight or fight mechanism used at a maintenance level, the unnatural posture, and the lethality should serve to keep us out of cars. Yet we are driving to the corner store for a loaf of bread and wondering, truly perplexed, why our knee, hips or back hurts and why we always feel as if we are on "overload." We don't need to make generous highways. We need to walk and smell the roses.

Steven Pinker in *How the Mind Works,* suggests that natural selection favored those who noticed flowers. The gatherers who took the time to notice the timing of flower blossoms and returned when the fruit would be ripe, were the survivors. The favored genes that were passed on were the sauntering genes and genes that caused us to really look at our surroundings. Modern memes are about speed, efficiency and becoming more oblivious. In *User's Guide to the Brain,* the author Ratey notes, "The clear message you should derive from the benefits of mental and physical exercise is that the worst thing you can do to your brain is to be content living a passive life. The habit of passivity is pervasive in our culture, from longing for miracle cures to watching television for hours to being politically apathetic."

I would add, "And from sitting in a chair," as Americans spend nearly 80% of their day sitting. Watch a child as they move through a day—they have little to no inclination to sit in chairs whereas adults cling to their chairs like barnacles. If you have children, you've no doubt heard yourself say dozens of times, "get up off the floor," "sit up here with us," and "don't eat down on the floor, come to the table," all efforts to get a child to sit in a chair rather than respect his own instincts. In this instance, our parenting instincts are wrong; our children are correct. It's on the floor, ideally on the ground, that we learn about our bodies. For an occupational therapist like myself, it is a constant struggle to convince new parents to allow their baby "floor time." Parents have purchased plastic carriers, swings, jumpers, walkers, strollers, play gyms with hanging mobiles, noise makers, and flashing lights. The list goes on and on and parents wonder why their child needs so much entertainment once they are older. The appropriate play position requires that we simply lay a blanket down, put the baby on top of it and presto, the baby has their favorite learning device—their body. Babies need to move their arms and legs. A properly supported head and spine is gained only in lying down; not reclined in a seat. They need to chew on their bare feet to prepare them for weight bearing during walking. They need to roll and get frustrated and finally crawl. They need to solve these early, basic problems; not have them solved for them. If they don't learn how to use their body well early on, they won't learn how to do anything well later on. If you've solved all the motor problems for a child, you might find yourself with a young adult who can't make any decisions for themselves.

The primary motor cortex, basal ganglia, and cerebellum all coordinate physical movement but also, not coincidentally, coordinate movement of thought. So it is in movement that we are provided with the physiologic release to think clearly and calmly. When we freeze with apathy, depression, or anxiety, we are without a motor response while the physiologic push to move remains. This only serves to increase anxiety. In brief, if we think without moving or move without thinking, we are out of balance.

In *The Tibetan Book of Living and Dying*, Sogyal Rinpoche suggests that all of life is a symmetrical, "continuous, unnerving oscillation between clarity and confusion, bewilderment and insight, certainty and uncertainty, sanity and insanity. In our minds, as we are now, wisdom and confusion arise simultaneously, or as we say, are 'co-emergent.' This means that we face a continuous state of choice between the two, and that everything depends on which we choose." And choose we must, for as Dr. Steven Berglass notes, baby boomers are suffering from "*akedie*," a Greek word meaning apathy. He notes, that they are suffering "from the struggle to make life worthwhile." They are indifferent to life, showing a paralysis of the soul; a permanent non-caring state. It must be true if a highway is more forgiving and generous than we are. So how can we get better acquainted with our human features? Let's start with the knees and see what they can teach us.

First off, the knees love to walk. They like to bend. Although they are a true hinge joint in that they bend and straighten, they prefer to be bent. In standing, one would think we should have our knees straight, like an open hinge, but our knees should be slightly bent at all times. In walking, although it appears to an untrained eye that our knees are straight during the heel strike (forward leg position), they are slightly bent at about fifteen degrees. In the mid-phase, where one leg is in full weight bearing, the knee is still bent. Knees are about continuously putting one foot in front of the other and once we have chosen a path, knees insist that we stay on it straight away. Knees don't side step the issue; they move us forward. In fact, we will "tweak" our knees when our feet go one way and the body goes another. It is similar in building character; when we say one thing and do another, we tweak our integrity. Our knees then, in the way they move, teach us a great lesson about integrity.

In rehab medicine, we know that sitting in a reclining chair with the knees straight out in front of us can exacerbate low back and sciatic nerve pain. The pressure of sitting on the sciatic nerve, which runs through the buttocks and is the width of your thumb, is constant as the straight leg pulls the nerve through the hamstrings. If you insist on a reclining chair (which is probably better for you than an upright chair), place a pillow under your knees to slacken the nerve.

The reality about the chair, any chair, is that, while it may be comfortable, it is physiologically harmful. It is thought that the number of back problems directly correlates with the increased number of hours spent seated, according to Galen Cranz in *The Chair: Rethinking Culture, Body, and Design*. If we are seated in a regular chair, feet on the floor, the ninety degree sitting angle of the hip exerts pressure on the diaphragm and restricts the internal organs. Blood flow slows, oxygen to the brain is reduced and we tire more quickly. Sitting in a chair to rest only serves to tire us out with chair sitting considered an athletic endeavor without the cardio-vascular benefit. The body has to constantly work to sit upright and it soon works at a deficit, working harder and harder in the name of relaxation.

The Australian physician Colin J. Alexander, suggests that only chair sitting cultures have varicose veins. The static angle of the leg and foot opens the saphenous vein in the ankle to the maximum so the walls of the vein are under constant pressure. Eventually, they lose elasticity and are dilated so long, they rupture.

Deep vein thrombosis (DVT's) can be a life-threatening blood clot lodged in the legs, that can break loose and travel to the lungs as a pulmonary embolism. It is showing an increased occurrence during plane travel due to the cramped seating on a long flight, coupled with high altitude and the likelihood of dehydration. The medical journal, The Lancet, found such blood clots in 10% of airline passengers. In an attempt to assure airline passengers, Dr. John Scurr, a vascular surgeon at London's Middlesex Hospital said, "I don't believe this is a problem related to the airplane or the airline…sitting in front of your computer for hours does the same thing." Reassuring? Sitting still for long stretches implies stretches in time, not stretches of the legs and it is known that pumping the ankles or stretching the legs can reduce DVT's by 50%. Signs on long airline flights now remind passengers to move their ankles but perhaps we need such a sign imprinted on all our computer stations.

The ankle has a little known biomechanical feature called "the ankle pump" which is a series of veins and muscles taking up the space of about the size of a fist. The fist, as we will learn in a later chapter, is about the size of our heart. So in each foot and at the end of each arm, there occurs a pumping mechanism, the ankles flexing and pumping with each footstep and the hands flexing and pumping with any movement of the fingers. They are all heart helpers strategically placed at the greatest lengths away from the heart. Unfortunately, we spend far too much of our time being sedentary and these "heart helpers" are grossly underemployed. A rocking chair would put the ankle pumps to good use.

Gordon Heves reports in *The Anthropology of Posture*, an article in Scientific America, that there are over 1,000 postures assumed in the world. Variations are not anatomically determined, but rather culturally determined. It turns out, less than 1/3 of the world's population sits with the hips and knees at a 90-degree angle, the posture required for a chair. A chair is not only detrimental to our anatomy, it serves as a cultural dictator, telling us where in a room it is appropriate to sit. A German philosopher and historian, Hajo Eickhoff, argues that the chair is a sedative and creates a docile population, a "population not inclined to criticize or become politically active." What he is referring to is that a sedentary populate is sedate, a Latin word meaning, "to calm."

Maria Montessori would agree with him and in fact, based her theories of schooling on the elimination of furniture in the classroom. She described traditional classrooms as places where "children were reduced to immobility." Montessori warned of the socialization toward passivity that begins in school where the first task is to sit still. Ask any kindergarten teacher and they will tell you their mission is to teach the children how to stand in line, to sit quietly for "circle time" and to wait at their chairs and desks for the bells to ring. Cranz echoes those thoughts when she says "In schools, children learn to regulate their bodies first and foremost by the chairs they are given to sit on."

What we do know about chairs is that they increase the pressure in the disc of the spine by 30%—more than any other position we assume. So, it is true as Cranz says, "Chairs in and of themselves are the problem, not poorly designed chairs." New York design consultant, Ralph Caplan says in *How Chairs Behave*, "Designers who will go to any investigative length to learn about materials neglect such elementary material as flesh and blood—although the flesh is weak and the flow of blood has been greatly impeded by a succession of prize winning chairs." And if you don't believe that chairs behave, as suggested by his title, remember we have anthropomorphized them. Chairs have legs and feet, seats, backs and arms just like we do. L. R. Caporael, an evolutionary psychologist, points out that our default mode for dealing with ambiguous or troublesome things is to interact socially with them. We personalize them. If we aren't busy treating humans like machines, we treat machines like humans. We talk to our cars, expect computers to be "friendly," yell at the copy machine, use the arms of a chair, and make our roads generous. And it seems we are likely to make a chair more comfortable than our own bodies.

The height of window openings is dictated by our sitting in chairs, being that they are not at standing height, but seated height. We even put chairs in the Space Shuttles, so bent on the fact that humans must sit, yet they were found useless in zero gravity and were later dropped from future missions. Look around your living room. Are the chairs arranged for your comfort? For instance, are they near a window so you can sit in the sun and read? Or are they positioned for the best view toward the television? Are you craning your neck to see the television because it is located in the only place it looks good in the room? In other words, does the television and its best friend, the chair, deserve the best spots in the house, or do you?

It's a pretty sure bet your chair is more attractive and comfortable than you are, especially if you are sitting in it. The diaphragm, the large muscle we breathe with, is at a mechanical disadvantage when sitting. In sitting, the diaphragm must count on some of the chest and neck muscles such as the scalenii, to assist with breathing. The increased respiratory load on the scalenii results in overuse, which restricts the blood flow to the muscle. The muscle tightens, pulling at its lower attachment to the first rib and impinging the nerves of the brachial plexus that go down the arm. This refers pain into the arms, wrists, and fingers, contributing to diagnosis such as carpal tunnel, cubital tunnel, tennis elbow and thoracic outlet syndrome. Ergonomic furniture brings its own problems, oftentimes more detrimental than helpful in the long run. Comfortable chairs allow us to sit for longer periods and condone postural fixity. We would be wiser to participate in "autonomous sitting," which is sitting upright without external support. Stools, benches and even therapy balls require our postural muscles to continually work to keep us from falling. Rocking chairs, invented around 1760 in the U.S., at least allow "active sitting."

All in all, it is good to remember that our postural habits can rearrange the relationship of our bones to one another, whether it is the scalene muscles pulling the first rib toward the clavicle or the lax abdominal and back muscles allowing the rib cage to rest on our vital organs. Continued misalignment can alter the shapes and articulations of individual bones so that sitting in a squat position, one of the three primary positions so loved by the human body (standing, lying down and squatting), enlarges the facets in the hip joint. A slumped, seated position in a chair alters the contours of the rib cage and wears a ridge onto our hip joint that serves as a breaking point. Squatting cultures do not need hip or knee replacements. Our 600+ bones were suspended in space in the womb in the presence of balanced, fluid forces, not shaped by gravitational and muscular stresses. Thus, the genetic make-up and alignment inherent in our bony structures can be easily overwhelmed by cultural conditions (sitting in chairs vs. squatting, lack of exercise vs. movement). Weak muscles result in weakly supported joints and weak joints place compression stress on the long bones, leading to the dreaded words "no wonder you're in pain, your knee is bone-on-bone."

Deane Juhan in *Job's Body*, a must read for any bodywork practitioner, notes "bones can only go where muscles pull them, and muscles can only respond to conditions which prevail in the nervous system." How do we create healthy "conditions which prevail in the nervous system?" We move. We expose the nervous system to varying stimulation from the senses. We walk and in walking, we see flowers we didn't know were blooming and grasses that insist on peeking up through asphalt. We hear birds and notice puddles. It is up to us to use our muscles in ways that enhance the alignment and spacing required for joint and bone integrity and in so doing, witness what is aligned and finding space on the earth. John Napier in the Scientific American article, *The Antiquity of Human Walking*, notes "Human walking is a unique activity during which the body, step by step, teeters on the edge of a catastrophe....Man's bipedal mode of walking seems potentially catastrophic because only the rhythmic forward movement of first one leg and then the other keeps him from falling flat on his face." He calls walking "flirting with falling," and it seems, the less walking we do, the more we flirt with falling flat on our faces.

Stiff muscles become weak and we literally splint ourselves, the tissues hardening with waste materials. The fear of falling is heightened, and we are pushovers—afraid of losing status, fearful of falling flat on our face, falling apart, or falling down on the job. The more energy we spend trying not to fall, the more energy we deplete that could be used for other activities. As we choose to be overburdened or out of balance, every muscle, joint, bone and cell will see life as a struggle.

Being sick is a powerful veto over activity. When ill we will not only refrain from taking risks, we will find ourselves unequal to many tasks. Illness may even serve to legitimize our fears of performing. For some, it might be an excuse not to do difficult things, as if being sick isn't more difficult. Those who concentrate their efforts on documenting or micro-managing an illness may absolve themselves of the requirement to be in charge of their full lives. All of us have illnesses at some time and most of us have aches and pains if we are over fifty, but more and more of us are labeling ourselves disabled by pain. In an industrial society, if you are not watched over by several medical practitioners, you are considered non-compliant. We live as Marcel Proust declared when he said "Illness is the most heeded of doctors. To goodness and wisdom we make only promises; pain we obey."

Having a narrow definition of health and illness binds us to either/or thinking. If we think we should have immunity from depression and illness and that every ache and pain should be eliminated, we are inoculating ourselves from living a whole life. While we should refrain from asserting that people cause their own sickness or that their thinking can make them well, we need to remember that sometimes illness can be overcome, sometimes it is just part of our journey and sometimes it is there to teach us something we need to learn. As we will see in later chapters, the hands might hurt when we spend a couple of hours at the computer. They are the messengers, these painful hands, telling us to get up and do something else for a while. If we allow the pain to continue, because we continue at the task that is making them painful, soon our entire life will feel painful. Pain always demands action, hopefully in a direction away from the object causing pain. The body is always the messenger, and the message is always to move. And to move, we need to listen to our body and understand it in all its languages.

Savion Glover, a tap dancer who describes his art in the book *My Life In Tap*, says, "I know my feet, all about them. It's like my feet are the drums, and my shoes are the sticks. My left heel is stronger than my right; it's my bass drum. My right heel is like the floor tom-tom. I can get a snare out of the right toe, a whip sound, not putting it down on the floor hard, but kind of whipping the floor with it." Susan Faust, a critic who reviewed the book said it beautifully when she wrote, "Obviously, a foot is not just a foot."

Most of us coax our feet, not into sounding like musical instruments, but coax them to assume the shape of fashionable footwear. If we tilt our heels up, as in wearing high-heeled shoes, we cancel all the effects of the foot's balanced design. As the large tendon at the back of the heel tightens, the ankle stiffens, throwing the whole body out of balance. Nerve conduction to the foot is impaired and circulation is weak. Wounds can go unnoticed, because they simply aren't felt—the warning signs dampened and defeated. Correcting stiff heel cords has been shown to substantially reduce diabetic foot ulcers and resultant amputations.

Should the ankle stiffen, the knees will have undo stress. Couple this biomechanical strain with an inactive lifestyle, which allows the quadriceps to weaken, and you have *genu recurvatum*, a common stance of the de-conditioned body where the knee bends backwards in standing. The quad, which would fix the knee during extension and allow it to go no further than straight, allows it instead to curve backward. Strengthening the quad is easy with walking, sitting in a rocking chair, squatting and getting up and down from the floor. Sitting in a chair weakens the quad by shortening the hamstrings in the back of the thigh. Interestingly, tight hamstrings can promote tight quads which have the same effect as weak quads; they curve the knee backwards as other muscles like the sartorius and the iliotibial bands (IT bands) take over.

Once one muscle has to do the job of another muscle, fatigue overtakes it. It would be like working someone else's job for which you are not trained; you wouldn't last long in the position and you'd complain the entire time you were doing their work. When the substitute muscle fatigues, another muscle has to do its work and the vicious cycle continues. A weak quadriceps will inhibit the gluteus medius which then calls on the quadratus lumborum and the IT bands to support the pelvis and we find ourselves standing with a forward tilt; our backs in bitter pain. When we lock our knees, it's as if we are saying, "this is the last resort to hold myself together."

To test tightness of the IT band, look for the Ober sign by lying on your side. The knee of the top leg should be able to reach the floor without you twisting your back. If it does not, you may display what looks like a shortened leg on that side as the IT band sucks the leg up into the hip. Thus, when you walk, you would show a slight limp or a side tilt. Either way, you will move through space in an asymmetrical pattern.

Weak legs and feet can make us feel as if we are fighting gravity, which is a phrase that should be eliminated from common usage. We are in no way at some kind of war with gravity and in fact our bones require its force to set calcium. Zero gravity, which would be experienced by astronauts, will cause significant bone loss after 90 days. Gravity is, in fact, a weakling among the natural forces, as science writer K. C. Cole reminds us. Gravity is "a trillion, trillion times weaker than electromagnetism. A few electrons rubbed off the surface of a balloon creates an electrical force big enough to hold the balloon on the wall in defiance of the pull of gravity from the entire earth." When we say we are "fighting gravity," we are giving in to a weak authority. We should have more passion for standing than that.

Interestingly, the knee and the sacrum have spiritual connotations. Although the words "knee" and "know" both come from the Old English "*cneo*," they are thought to have etymologically evolved into two separate meanings, with "knee" taking on its meaning from "angle." Leonardo da Vinci theorized that the knee promoted religious thought, or what he called "knowledge of God." He noted in an autopsy that the sciatic nerve went the full length of the body, connecting us from the earth to heaven above. The sciatic nerve, he ventured, was stimulated as it passed through the large, mobile knee joint and must account for why so many cultures kneel on their knees to pray. Leonardo's theory always elicited a slight snicker from modern, levelheaded scientists, sure that a nerve in the knee couldn't make you think about God. That is, until scientists tested nerve conduction in the brain with Functional MRI (fMRI). Moving each joint, they measured brain activity and found that different joints lit up different areas of the brain. The knee, it turns out, heightened a very precise section of the tempo-parietal lobe, an area where we store religious and spiritual thoughts. Some schizophrenics for instance, who have a heightened sense of religious ecstasy, or even believe they themselves are God, show constant stimulation in this portion of the brain. Leonardo wasn't far off when he thought the knee brought knowledge of God—getting down on bended knee enhances the area of the brain that houses spiritual thoughts, and spiritual thoughts might be comforting enough to prompt man, throughout time, to kneel in prayer. It is an example of genetic makeup finding expression in behavior and behavior placing our genes in situations where they can be expressed.

In Greek mythology, the knee is linked with god-like powers. Chiron was half man, half horse who taught heroes medicine (Chiron means "hand healing touch"). He learned the secrets of medicine after having been shot in the knee with a poisonous arrow and while he could not be cured, he could not die and was granted immortality. Without his knee, he was unable to move on like other mortals and was granted some of the gifts of a God. Again, the knee is linked with the human occupation of moving forward.

Sacrum, the bone we sit on when we sit cross-legged on the ground, literally means "sacred bone" and reminds us to sit in connection with the earth and take in the sounds of the universe. In sitting on the ground, we might feel the vibrations of the earth, be part of the cosmology and be a part of the whole ecology of living. This sacred bone, the holy bone, reminds us to listen to all that is holy.

How far can we get from the earth's ecology if we fail to listen? Let's take the example of the toilet, a favorite sitting spot of people in industrialized nations. Witold Rybcyznski, in his book *One Good Turn: A Natural History of the Screwdriver and the Screw,* explains that just as the world "is divided into those who wrap and those who button up, those who eat with their fingers and those who eat with utensils, it is divided into craftsmen who work kneeling, squatting, or sitting on the ground, and those who work erect—or sitting—at a bench." He could have added, "those who squat on the ground to eliminate and those who sit on a toilet." Even toilet training, or the time when children learn to control their bowels and bladder, turns out to be a cultural variable. Children do not "naturally" grow to control their sphincters at two years old as is thought in the U.S. In fact, in the 1930's, American children were easily "toilet trained" at one year and great variation in bladder control can be found across cultures.

What is a fact is that none of our bodies appreciate eliminating on a toilet. To fully open the sphincters of our bowel and bladder, our knees should be placed higher than our hips. A toilet places the knees even with the hip joints, essentially "telling" the sphincters to remain slightly closed. For the bowel, it discourages easy elimination and for the bladder it discourages full emptying. In a rehab incontinence clinic, a quick solution for leakage upon standing from the toilet is to place your feet on a small stool while you sit on the toilet. By placing your knees above your hips and wide apart, the bladder can fully empty. Essentially, you are mimicking a squat position.

Another rehab "trick" to help incontinent patients, is to teach them how to apply pressure to an area that will close the sphincters for about thirty seconds, enough time to rush to the restroom. There is an area on the back of our legs, about mid-thigh, that is the pressure point for the bladder sphincter. Children instinctively know of this area—you can see them pressing it as they cross their legs and yell, "I've got to go potty." They uncross and cross, alternating legs and giving themselves minutes to save grace as they engage the pressure points. Oddly enough, a toilet, if you'll picture it in your mind, is a hole we sit on where the only pressure applied to our body is on the back of our legs, about mid-thigh or the natural pressure point that tells our body to close the sphincters.

There is another odd design feature of the Western toilet—it contains clean water. It's doubtful there is a species on earth that defecates in its clean water supply like we do, with each of us effectively contaminating 13,000 gallons of water a year to move a mere 156 gallons of body waste. We take a clean resource, mix it with waste (actually a potentially valuable resource if treated and used as fertilizer) and then use additional resources and energy to separate them again. If we were good listeners to the earth's ecology and the body's inherent wisdom, we would understand that everything about a toilet is telling us not to go to the bathroom.

We've chosen to use toilets because we have voted for hygienic solutions over ecological or physiologic solutions. We don't want cholera or dysentery. It is worth noting though, that in avoiding diseases that arise from waste products, our solution is not beneficial for our overall anatomy. We "vote" in these ways all the time, depending on the cultural factors at the forefront of society.

If you look at the history of children's furniture, cultural dictates jump out at you. In the 17th century, the first children's apparatus stood the baby up and propelled them as it was thought the parent should be freed from the baby. Prior to that time, children's furniture was nearly non-existent and babies were carried. In the 18th century, physical correction forced erect posture by placing babies in walking stools, as rigid rules on behavior was culturally accepted. The 19th century began a long period of holding babies down to ease care giving. Babies were contained in one spot with playpens and leashes. In the mid-19th century, barriers that separated adults from babies came into fashion with highchairs, swings, carriages, and gates across doors. The 20th century focused on safety with car seats but also promoted hyper-entertainment by placing small babies in bouncies, jump-ups, rompers, swings and walkers.

As we will see later in this book, we essentially decided to addict our children to constant movement only to become perplexed when they won't sit still for school. In an agrarian culture, such movement-minded children would find an advantage as their families constantly moved homesteads. But the purpose of American life is getting ahead, not moving ahead. It is evident that children's furniture has been marketed to get a child moving in a certain direction as soon as possible, even before their developing spine is ready to hold them upright.

The idea of temporary gain (hygiene over anatomy, entertained baby over hyperactive child) is seen in lifestyle habits across the board. Using alcohol to increase our sociability has to be weighed against the increase it brings in aggression and early dementia. The focus cocaine can foster has to be weighed against the increased startle reflex and eating away of the sinuses. The security overeating offers has to be literally weighed against the health problems obesity brings with it. When we live for short-term benefits, our life feels out of balance and we stand ignorant about what is making us so miserable.

The motor units we use to perform any task are fixed in infancy. We are never allotted more motor or nerve cells or synapses from the motor nerve to the motor cell. The synapses, or the communication between cells that tell them what to do, get larger and stronger only by synthesizing more myocin and actin filaments within each cell. So habits take the form of increased chemical signals to the muscle. If our habits are gained in distorted patterns, say by placing a child in a walker before their legs and spines can naturally support them, the distortions will be incorporated into the activity or function. If our habits "make sense to the body," that is, we walk when the body is naturally ready to walk and not before, we will learn to utilize patterns with greater subtlety and variety.

These habits will dictate what in the future is easy for us to do and what is difficult. If we have "learned to walk" at 8 months old in a walker that spreads our hips, bowed our knees and caused us to bear weight on ankles and feet before they were ready, we might find jumping rope, running and skipping difficult as a six year old. Habits are the way motor development works and can have positive or negative results. Placing our babies in apparatus that promote the too-early gain of motor skills will lead to degenerative habits. It will be easier to sit as an adult if you've been placed in a walker as a child but it will be more difficult to climb stairs. Early parental choices will determine what is painful and tiring later; what is possible and not possible in the future.

Balanced and reciprocal development of our musculature leads to healthy interactions with our own body, which in turn leads to healthy interactions with our parents. This reciprocal relationship allows us to interact in a healthy manner to others in our tribe and as a healthy tribe, interact with the earth that sustains us. Without these reciprocal relationships, we are doomed.

If one were to look back on the history of mass production, or producing for the tribe, early consumer goods tried to inhibit individuality. Mass produced shoes were called "straights" and made to fit either foot so that not only were you identical to your shoe wearing neighbor, there was no difference between your left and right foot. Early cars were all black and Thomas Edison fearing that the phonograph would be "trivialized as a toy," wanted his invention to erase any characteristics of the individual. At first, he wished it to be used to record the dying words of great men, noting that the phonograph would give a permanent and persistent quality to the voice. It would be the same every time it was replayed, just as moving film was termed "persistence in vision" with the picture the same for all time. However, after ten years of languishing as an innovation, Edison offered the phonograph as a mechanical device that would "establish music on a scientific basis," but he would only record clear diction—what he called the straight tone. His violinist in residence, hired to record to Edison's exacting standards, called his own playing "dead sounds." Edison required that no names of artists be used in recordings, and that there be no contemporary music and no vibrato or any other flair that would highlight an individual singer's dramatic personality. He didn't want us to enjoy listening to recorded music—he wanted us to play musical instruments and sing for ourselves.

We've really not come that far from deleting signs of individuality when we can walk into nearly any home in the U.S. and see furniture arranged around a television. In middle class homes, you might even see the same Martha Stewart bedspread with the same Land's End bathrobe hanging from the same Pottery Barn hook as in your own home. Ultimately, we bristle when we suddenly notice that we are like everyone else, causing us to start all over again and redecorate. This striving to have something different than what others have, or at least more of it, actually goes against our genetic make-up, leading to the horrific feeling of living a life on the outside that doesn't match our insides.

Hunter-gatherer societies "work" far fewer hours than farming and consumer societies. They are free of possessions or signs of wealth because in their societies, to accumulate too much is evidence of a refusal to share. To them, the concrete evidence of material wealth is not nearly as important as the abstract value of being seen as generous. Their insides are more important than what is outside. Our effort to accumulate more in order to incur jealousy is dead-set against their effort to have little in order to show reciprocity. An added benefit: If you want little, little is easy enough to achieve and there is more time for play.

It was John Nash, the scientist portrayed in the movie, "*A Beautiful Mind,*" that formulated the equilibrium theory that so many hunter-gatherers, not to mention, all social animal kingdoms, live by. He called it "Nash Equilibrium," an evolutionary stable strategy wherein each player's decision is an optimal response to those adopted by other players and nobody has an incentive to deviate from their chosen strategy.

This theory would eventually explain why animals rarely fight to the death, why even non-kin vampire bats will share their blood meal with bats that weren't successful that night, and why ants have what is called a "social stomach" wherein they feed every other ant in the colony until all have the same amount of food in their stomach. It turns out most wasps have social stomachs, some wild dogs, and all ant species (ants make up the largest, most successful biomass on earth, far outweighing the biomass of even our 6 billion human beings). Nash came about his 1974 Nobel Prize winning idea after an insight in how he and his colleagues could all be assured of a date when faced with one beautiful blond amidst a sea of brunette girlfriends. He suggested that all of them ask the company of one of the brunettes, forfeiting the blond. If all were to pursue the blond, only one fellow would win her hand. Since the brunettes would now know they were thought of as second rate, they would refuse all requests. Only one fellow and the blond would end up with a date leaving most of the players out of the game, causing instability. The important feature of the theory is that the game has to be played more than once. It's the second chance at a date that is the deciding factor. If you weren't nice to the brunettes the first time, they would not be nice to you when you searched for a date the second time. He proved that selfishness is not the rational thing to do as long as the game is played more than once.

Fascinating studies on his findings come in the form of "game theories" wherein a computer scientist named Robert Axelrod held tournaments where one computer "animal" is pitted against another vying for screen space. In the first tourney in 1979, 14 entries of varying complexity were entered in this game exploring the logic of cooperation. The only rule was that the game had to be played 200 times between the two competitors. The "animal" had several choices in dominating the screen: it could try to kill competitors, be nice to them so they would be nice in return, or allow the help of a nice animal but never return the favor. The shocking results were that the "nicest" animals did the best with none of the top 8 programs ever resorting to "defection" or "not returning the favor." The winning program was not only the nicest program, it was the simplest one. Anatol Rapoport, a Canadian political scientist, was the winner with his program called Tit-For-Tat (TFT). It began by cooperating and then did whatever the other guy did in the last turn. In other words, if the other animal was mean, he was mean. If nice, he was nice. Once word was out, the next tourney brought 62 programs trying to beat TFT. None could. TFT was a nice program, but also a very clear program. It was always nice its first turn, forgiving of those who were mean their first turn but nice their second turn and quickly retaliatory with those who weren't nice even after two tries.

As Axelrod said, "Its niceness prevents it from getting into unnecessary trouble. Its retaliation discourages the other side from persisting whenever defection is tried. Its forgiveness helps restore mutual cooperation. And its clarity makes it intelligible to the other player, thereby eliciting long-term cooperation."

When Axelrod changed the rules a bit and asked for survival of the fittest strategies, software creatures could now vie for space at all costs. Unsuccessful or weak strategies were quickly consumed and the most robust program was in charge of the field. The nastiest strategy survived at the expense of nice ones. Retaliator programs, like TFT, kept pace with the mean ones. But once the nasty ones ran out of easy victims and met up with other nasty ones, TFT was again the sole survivor. Axelrod says, "TFT does not envy or wish to beat its opponent. Life, it believes, is not a zero-sum game: my success need not be at your expense; two can 'win' at once. TFT treats each game as a deal struck between the participants, not a match between them."

Axelrod then took the concept of Tit-For-Tat to biologist William Hamilton of the University of Michigan, looking for biological evidence of the strategy. Hamilton recalled a 10 year old paper, written by then graduate student Robert Trivers showing animal cooperation due to reciprocity. The paper predicted the success of TFT as it found that the longer animals interacted, the more likely they were to repay favors. Trivers would become stellar in the field of altruism and Axelrod and Hamilton would author *The Evolution of Cooperation* wherein even unrelated animals are aware of social debts. An example was found in social ants and bats, as mentioned before, and a beautiful example in the ecology of coral cleaning. Fifty-one fish species offer cleaning service to the coral, yet not one is ever eaten. The cleaning fish are the correct size and the right taste, yet they are spared as a meal, while other similar, but non-cleaning fish, are eaten by the coral. The coral never defected, never ate one of the cleaner species, as a good cleaner is more valuable as a future cleaner than as a present meal, according to Matt Ridley, who documents these extraordinary theories in his book *The Origins of Virtue*.

This is where we stand today; we're out of sync with the rest of the planet's animals. We're jeopardizing a clean future for a meal today. We are living out of balance, fallen from grace, so dizzy from all the opportunity that we choose to do what is easiest. Instead of doing something meaningful, we sit down and think about it.

Imbalance in this area of the body, known as the first chakra, affects all the six chakras above it, and poor health here can set a certain pace for the rest of the body. It is thought that by not having your feet squarely under you, you will perpetually reside in your own prison, the door of which can only be unlocked from the inside. We must raise our consciousness regarding the valueless memes we have left our lives to. To gain balance, sometimes we have to get off our feet and sit squarely on the ground, rooting ourselves like plants. In fact, the cross-legged pose in Hatha Yoga is called the Lotus wherein you sit like the lotus plant, a single flower surrounded by a sea of water but whose flower never gets wet. There can be watery chaos all around you, but you do not have to let it touch you. Further it is thought that sitting like the Buddha, on the ground, is creating the Buddha in you. Therein, you may unlock the prison.

Muladhara is the name of the first chakra and its lesson is "The Call To Be." Muladhara means "root" in Sanskrit and implies the act of vibrating with engagement—it is what grounds us and connects us to the depth of things. Modern physicists know that every atom vibrates. We need to awaken to the simplest way for a system to behave—to vibrate. The first chakra is where a mature person walks toward their destiny. Key words are stability, cohesion, survival and reciprocity. We honor gravity and take full responsibility for the vital, tribal part of our lives. We remain upright by virtue of the downward pull and we are grounded enough to move in any direction we choose.

The muscles and joints enact the will, embodying the option of movement. If we become tight or loose our balance, our purpose on earth will be confused and we will cower to social directives that are ill thought out. It is in this chakra that we are supportive of each other, just as both feet support our body. And it is where we find the greatest support as we sit in meditation in order to think clearly about where we are going to go.

Sitting in meditation, one watches the mind wander and is privy to every discomfort the mind or the body advertises. A crick in the knee comes and goes, followed by the bruised feeling of the sitting bones, which is immediately replaced by the itchy nose. Let them come and go. Short term discomfort will eventually evolve into a healthier pair of knees, ankles and hips. Anger enters the mind and is met with compassion. With graded exposure to minor pains and destructive emotions, we can gain strength through good habit.

Martin Luther King Jr. noted that, "The ultimate measure of a man is not where he stands in moments of comfort and convenience, but where he stands at times of challenge and controversy." Finding your balance in standing and being stable enough to venture forward in walking, is what this area of the body is all about. Its lessons warn against a half-formed self, one that wanders aimlessly, one that follows blindly or one that fails to move at all.

Our best strategy for living will involve finding a balance between what is good for us in general and what is good for us as unique individuals. We must pursue actions that lead to harmony. Living the way we do, consuming the earth's resources faster than it can replenish them is at the heart of a deep dissatisfaction. We have not learned how to make ourselves do what is good for us. We have forsaken reciprocity. We have not taken a stand and pretty soon, there will be nothing to stand on.

HOW TO EVOKE STABILITY

❖ If this chakra is unbalanced it can skew your whole perspective. Your life will always feel topsy-turvy. If energy is high here, you might always resort to "geographical solutions" to your problems. You might walk away from conflict, leave the room if challenged, move to another state when your life begins to fall apart, change jobs or constantly leave relationships. If energy is low here, you might be stuck in dead-end jobs, relationships that never grow and you might feel an overwhelming sense of stagnation. Aim for the middle ground. Stand up to your responsibilities and know when it is time to move forward. Seek healthy social contact and work for the betterment of the community.

❖ When is the last time your feet touched the earth? I mean where your skin touched grass or soil or sand, without shoes between you and the earth, without carpet or pavement between your feet and your planet? Count how many layers of man-made materials lie between you and the earth (socks=1, shoes=2, carpet=3, insulation=4, floor board=5 and so on counting pipes, plastic, and concrete). Appalled at the lengths we've gone to separate ourselves from dirt? Three quarters of the land in Los Angeles, California is paved over. Nearly half of Portland, Oregon is paved. We should find this wholly unacceptable. Right now, we willingly keep ourselves from touching the earth, but soon, we may be unable to touch it. Go barefoot and get reacquainted with the textures of the earth.

❖ Sink your roots into a situation. Connect to it deeply. See creations in their entirety.

☙ Buddhist elder Jocelyn King says, "Rest on the firm ground of emptiness." Don't try to fill your day up with entertainment or more material goods. And don't do it to your children.

❖ In a temple, there is a sign "Remove your shoes—you are standing on holy ground." Is there any ground you know of that is not holy?

❖ Eat root plants like carrots, potatoes, leeks, and onions. Grow a garden and get reacquainted with the earth. You might just re-root parts of yourself that long for attachment and contact. Once you feel grounded, you can safely uproot parts of yourself that need to see the light of day.

❍ Asana, the Sanskrit word for all Yoga poses or postures, means, "seat" with its Sanskrit synonym found in the word '*pitha*' meaning "sacred place." Likened to a plant or a sacred statue, an asana is the effort to construct the divine body while relaxing in the pose to honor that body as a temple. An asana is cultivated properly if it yields the sensation that the body is loosening up or widening out. As the joints, muscle attachments, and ligaments lengthen and widen, a widening of consciousness follows, merging with the environment. This play of dualities inherent in Hatha Yoga asanas (literally translatable as "Sun Moon/Yoked/Sacred Seat") crystallizes the vital forces within us. Each asana roots us to the earth with the pose acting as a hero who comes to the rescue of the legs, the part of us that take a stand for long periods of time. You are on a heroic journey when you seek to become fully embodied and conscious at the same time. Remember that in Yogic tradition, failure is treated lightly while curiosity and courage are held in the highest regard. Yoga philosophy appreciates the hero in you.

○ In Virasana, or hero pose, the decision to relax is courageous. It is brave to relax in the face of fear. A hero "shows up for life," faces his demons, confronts a challenge, and sees it through even with imminent failure. A hero is resilient. Joseph Campbell notes that a hero's life begins when every man living a mundane existence is called upon to discern wrong from right. A hero stays present, stands in the here and now and chooses the fire of transformation.

❖ Advance children only when a task becomes easy, compelling them to always make an effort. Moshe Feldenkrais taught that children need the slight strain of pushing the limits, not for the task itself, but for the increase in confidence found in "positive learning." Don't push children before they are successful with the first steps.

❖ Do you believe you can embody opposites? Watch your foot do two opposite movements at the same time; lift your foot off the ground and flex your ankle. Your toes come toward the knee and the heel slides away from the knee at the same time. Many of us loose this sliding motion that counterbalances ideal flexion. If the ankle flexes without the heel sliding, excessive strain is placed on the shin. All joints are wrapped with connective tissue, which works to provide stability when called for. But when movement is called for, that connective tissue has to slide enough to ease off the joint. If there is no play in the connective tissue, excess "bandaging" causes the joint to regress. It does less and could therefore be called "an immature joint." Make sure you can do two things at one time. With mature joints, might you not feel more mature?

❖ Notice how many of the Greek myths are obsessed with the foot. Oedipus, literally meaning, "swollen footed," was tied to a tree by a hook in his heel when left by his parents as they tried to outwit destiny. Achilles had his heel pierced and numerous myths talk of women who were turned into trees so they could no longer be chased on foot. Also, read the beginning of many of Plato's dialogues—Socrates always begins a discussion by asking his nemesis to walk with him. Thus starts the debate. Take a walk and start a conversation with yourself. Don't allow yourself to become lame.

❖ Many words show the Greeks obsession with the symbolism of standing. Words like stancheon, status, staunch, steadfast, statute, statue, and constant use the word 'stand' as its root. Beautiful standing metaphors are found in stallion (standing alone in the field), star (standing in the sky), stare (eyes standing still), stank (standing water), restaurant (place where wanderers stand still), distance (stand far away) and even prostate (stands in front of the rectum). Perhaps the most beautiful is ecstasy, to stand outside oneself. What brings you ecstasy and when is the last time you did that activity?

❖ Ask yourself "What parts of myself are buried?" What parts can be dug up to see the light of day? What can you loosen from the grips of your history? Wilhelm Reich said, "I compared the stratification of the character with the stratification of geologic deposits, which are also rigidified history." Longevity studies show that people live longer who can disclose past traumas. Unearth what has hurt you and tell a friend.

❖ Nikolai Bernstein, a Russian physiologist used the term "degrees of freedom" to describe how the body organizes itself to accomplish a task. When performing an unfamiliar task, we freeze the amount of movement allowed, limiting the degree of freedom. This keeps the task rudimentary so the brain does not have an overwhelming amount of motor information to organize. Repetition is the only thing that will "thaw" the strategy of freezing. In that way, a cold and clumsy attempt at playing the piano for the first time can thaw into a series of fluid motions with practice. And as a monk once said: Practice means someday you will make the mistakes of a master and not the mistakes of a beginner. Have you remained frozen in familiar tasks? When might you thaw?

❖ Moshe Feldenkrais said, "Just like a person who adopts a crippling use of her body when confronted with a task for which her previous experience has not equipped her, so does humanity as a whole adopt crippling methods of achieving security." Ask yourself "In what way am I crippled?" What part of your life are you limping through? Is there a part of life where you are choosing to just "sit it out?"

❖ Antaeus, son of Poseidon, could not be defeated in battle. If he were wounded, he would lie on the earth and be filled with its vitality again. Hercules conquered Antaeus by holding him aloft, out of touch with the earth and draining the life out of him. What kind of Herculean effort is keeping you from your vitality?

❖ Thomas Aquinas said that despair tears charity out by the roots. He encouraged one to live a life of zeal, intensely loving the lovable things of the earth. What virtues have you allowed to be pulled out by their roots? Replant them and watch yourself grow.

❖ Derek Bok, past President of Harvard University, criticized the massive diversion of students with exceptional talent into pursuits that add little to the growth of a resilient economy, to the pursuit of culture, or to the enhancement of the spirit. He suggested law school was an example of wasted talent. Most businesses are concerned with the economic bottom line. We need to re-root our talented students and design businesses with the triple bottom line in mind—the economics of business, the ecology of the Earth and the enlightenment of the community. Contribute rather than destroy.

❖ Try jump roping for exercise. Lift your feet off the ground and delight in their return to the ground after each jump. Nicolas Mosley notes a mathematical theory called Catastrophe Practice, which suggests that evolution happens in sudden jumps rather than infinitesimal gradations. "So—could not humans practice to be ready for such a jump?" Whether you agree with his theory or not, it's an attractive metaphor.

❖ Psychological research on happiness offers us unlikely conclusions. Theories of what drives human behavior usually assume that humans are motivated either by the need to eliminate unpleasant conditions like hunger and fear, or by expectations of future reward like money or status. But in truth, happy people devote a large amount of time to tasks that are inexplicable. They can't explain why they do what they do, only that the tasks are enjoyed for their own sake, offering a sense of timelessness. Activities like listening to music, reading, socializing, creating, and playing offer "flow." Develop a flow personality where the ability to engage your skills matches the opportunities. Find yourself "lost" in the here and now. Don't be afraid of losing yourself for a spell.

❖ Never resist an authentic challenge that tests your strength of character. Engage in daily acts of courage. Test your character next time you shop. Buy organic or refrain from buying things you don't need. Take a stand against blind consumption.

❍ Practice Savasana; Corpse Pose. Establish the true ground of your being and feel your body's full contact with gravity. Surrender all effort and let yourself die to the old way of thinking and doing. Melt all of your muscular effort into the ground and imagine your body sinking into the floor like a puddle. Soften the eyes, the tongue and your mind. Surrender. This is considered the most difficult pose in Hatha Yoga; difficult because we are asked to imagine our death when we spend so much of our energy struggling to prove our existence. It is the easiest physical posture and the most difficult spiritual posture in Hatha Yoga.

❍ Try Twisting poses. If you are trying hard to keep things together or feel like your life is just a constant struggle to keep things from falling apart, sit in yoga postures that wrap you up into tight twists. Cowface pose balances the left and right brain while opening the shoulders to let go of joylessness and open the heart. Eagle pose finds our arms and legs wrapped around each other representing the eagle's wings just prior to unfolding. It is that moment before deciding and it is that moment where choice is gathering energy. Seated Twist allows us to get tangled up in a tight knot yet brings on relaxation breathing. Relax, it tells us, and pull it together. Lao Tsu writes in the Tao Te Ching, "To remain whole, be twisted!/To become straight, let yourself be bent,/To become full, be hollow./Be tattered in order to be renewed."

❍ Try Kandasana: root pose. To sit in this pose is to fully realize our rooted-ness.

❍ Try Merudandasana: Mountain staff pose. In this posture, we trust in the support we feel beneath us. By becoming the staff, or cane, we are both the one on the journey and the one who will assist us in our journey. We know the way may be uneven, even risky, but we have thought to bring a walking stick.

❍ Try Eka Padasana: One-legged pose, which tells us that we cannot feel supported if we cannot find balance. In this pose, we explore the full space around us and admit that sometimes we must rely on slender things to get us through a crisis. It is faith in the almost impossible.

❍ Try Utthita Hasta Padasana: Hand to foot extension pose shows us that all resources are involved in keeping upright and the effort of the pose awakens us from slumber.

❍ Try Garudasana: Sacred eagle pose, shows the eagle that is earthbound. It is readying itself for the spiritual journey or the world beyond that which it can see today.

❖ Survival can often look like a struggle. When emotions arise, we may habitually double the trouble by linking one emotion with another. We are angry that we are angry, sad that we are sad, and we struggle at the struggle of it all. Allow yourself to feel anger and sadness when it comes. Don't fight with it as it will only learn to grow stronger like a resistant strain of bacteria. Give the mind one thought; one emotion at a time. Conserve your energy. Find spaciousness in your path that didn't exist before when so many emotions were crowding the way.

❍ Practice Trikonasana: Triangle Pose. This is a play of opposites wherein we establish a solid foundation in order to learn to fly. Stand firmly on your feet in order to reach away from the earth. Find muscular support in order to become lighter and less serious. Rest into the back of the body in order to liberate the front.

❍ Practice inversion poses like Shoulderstand, Plow, Woodchopper, and Fish. Shoulderstand puts our feet where our head used to be and our head where our feet once were. It turns the world upside down. The plow reaches back and reconnects the feet to the earth, ready to plow a new furrow, and plant a new beginning. Woodchopper allows us to see behind ourselves to gather fuel for the road ahead. Fish shows you that sometimes there is another world with new air to breathe. Fish pose has us reach up for air and sink back into the watery world below.

❖ Learn the beautiful grouping names for animals. Read *Exhaltation of Larks* and the next time you see a group of Bluejays, remember they are called A Party of Jays. Delight in an Ostentation of Peacocks, a Cloud of Gnats, a Gaggle of Geese, a Charm of Finches, and a Parliament of Owls. What would your breed be called? Be someone special in that group; be someone you would like to meet. There is a healthy way to separate yourself from a clan and an unhealthy way. Those who feel victimized and ostracized become different and then there are those who, with their lives, make a difference. Which one do you want to be, hero or victim? A victim might say "I can't stand it" or "I keep tripping over my own feet." A hero knows what they stand for and goes forward knowing there might be failure and hardship. How do you want to walk on the earth?

❖ The Chinese Encyclopedia of the 10th century classifies plants and animals in the text *Celestial Emporium of Benevolent Knowledge*. The list is as follows: a) those that belong to the Emperor; b) embalmed ones; c) those that are trained; d) suckling pigs; e) mermaids; f) fabulous ones; g) stray dogs; h) those that are included in this classification; i) those that tremble as if they were mad; j) innumerable ones; k) those drawn with a very fine camel hair brush; l) others; m) those that have just broken a flower vase; n) those that resemble flies at a distance. These categories once prioritized the world. What priorities, worries and behavior patterns have you set in stone? Would they sound silly five years from now?

❖ Think of someone in your life who "takes a stand." Now visualize that what they are doing is putting their whole self in the same place at the same time. They have condensed their energy and are standing up for an idea. What is so important to you that your whole life could be about making it happen? It's doubtful that it is something you need to learn; it is most likely something you just need to remember.

❖ Be prepared for at least silence or most likely noisy cackle from the crowds should you choose your own path. David Whyte, poet and soul bringer to large corporations reminds us that the truer we are to our own creative gifts, the less likely there will be outer reassurance or help in the beginning of that journey. He notes that we will sometimes be met with silence from others when we follow our heart. This is where we need the element of fire. He tells of an "alchemical wedding" where the more internal world of the individual meets the soul of the world. The hero will tend the flame so that the elements of each melt together and create something anew. These elements, he tells us, would fall apart at room temperature. Meet silence and apathy with fire. Create something new.

❖ Maya Angelou once said that the greatest virtue is courage, because you must have courage to enact all the other virtues. "You need courage to tell the truth and courage to stand up for yourself."

❖ Winneap Shosone, an Indian medicine man could feel his ancestors walking inside him; that is what the memory of them felt like. He said, "If the dead be truly dead, why should they still be walking in my heart?" Will the memory of you be enough to walk in the hearts of those left behind?

❖ Take a walk in the forest and note how it rests. Instead of noticing the green leaves and the blur of a skittering animal, notice the dead branches, the bones, and the crunch of dried leaves. See how the earth uses all its resources so it never becomes exhausted. Notice how animals are remarkably good at sitting still. It is a survival strategy.

❖ Consider what might be the root of all evil. Violence and apathy perhaps? Apathy sees no gifts in life and violence destroys the gifts the earth offers. Conquer evil with gratitude. Meister Eckhart said, "If the only prayer you say in your whole life is 'thank you,' that would suffice."

❖ Slow down. Many of us secretly know that if we slow the busy pace we keep, we will be forced to reassess our lives. A simple way to reacquaint yourself with your true needs is to walk to the grocery store. You will buy only that which you can carry home and you are unlikely to choose to carry a package of cookies along with all the fruit and vegetables you need. If you must drive to the store, act as if you had walked and buy only that which you would be willing to carry home. The automobile has made us too efficient and expanded what we can carry—we aren't made to think about what we buy as there are no immediate consequences for our poor choices. If you had to walk, you would make better choices.

❖ Be wary of "surface sanity." In our capitalistic culture, insanity has taken a different twist. Insanity is no longer reflective of losing our minds or the absence of reason—it is reason gone amok. Fail to be one of the working wounded; those who work hard, are rewarded, acquire possessions and are tranquilized. Ask yourself if you are adapting to the work environment at an emotional or spiritual or even an ethical cost. Have you become a frozen version of yourself, having only the traits required for work? Are you in suspended animation, a sort of willful autism wherein you are pre-occupied with a narrow part of the world, ignoring dreams, hopes and community? Envision yourself paired with a company that allows your unique contributions to improve the organization toward cooperation with the environment. We can be open to such situations or shrink from them. We might close down for an eight-hour day or for a lifetime.

❖ Be wary of the "megabyte mistress" also known as the computer. Computers are attractive not only because of their huge knowledge base, but because they feed an exaggerated sense of control and mastery. They do not criticize or counsel us. But remember, the time we spend with machines depletes the time we spend in real relationships. With people. With nature.

❖ Nature refreshes our sense of being fully human. Throughout this book, look for the sections at the end that ask you to imagine you are earth, air, water or fire. Understanding the elements in you can be powerful. Nature metaphors are vitality filled memes; ideas that make you feel alive and unified. To feel the powerful support from the planet under our feet, to feel inspired by a gentle idea that breezes into our minds, to witness the depths of a pond, and to feel a fire of passion for living, are all offerings to us through the visualization of nature's elements. We want our insides to feel like our outsides. We want our lives to make sense. We want to connect, to find union, to find value. We simply want our bodies to permit us to fully live our lives.

❖ The smaller a structures' foundation, the more likely it is to fall over. Remaining upright requires near constant adjustments in muscular activity. Exercise can never create balanced musculature if the muscles are not used properly the rest of the day. Function is continual exercise and most cultures never have to think of their fitness. They live fit. The more functional an activity, the more accepted it is by the brain. In rehab, therapists should be modifying activity, using large mindful movements with the goal of easing into patterns that were once thought of as painful by the brain.

❖ The bottom of our foot is called the plantar surface. We get the word "plant" from plantar, as the foot was the first tool used to cover seeds with soil. In the ancient Hindu scriptive, *Veda*, the caste system was embodied in each person. The mouth is a Brahmatic priest and our arms, a warrior. A tradesman is found in the thigh and, in sticking to the etymology of plantar, a farmer was found in the feet.

❖ The telephone company now charges you to move. How many of you pay roaming charges?

❖ Successful novels and fables that have stood the test of time create an "attractive hero." The hero might be incredibly flawed so that many of us can relate to him. The story plots to take something away from the hero; something they will miss which sets off an energy. The story, or journey, awaits some sort of completion to remember the hero. The main plot device is a "call to adventure" with the possible refusal of the hero to listen to the call. If he refuses, the job is given to another character. If the hero answers, the job of refusal is given to a character that represents the "can't do it energy." Further in the story, the hero is stopped from completing the journey and must overcome obstacles. There is often "mentor energy," a character that guides the hero with advice, training, and even maps on how to get from one place to another. The test finds the hero facing their greatest fears and reconnecting to the journey with courage. So, what is your story? Should it be told? What makes up your calling? Have you answered the call or will it be passed on to someone else? Do you merely give advice and not live by it? I have a small embroidered piece made by one of my clients that says, "Take my advice, I'm not using it." It reminds me to live the life I teach others to live.

❧ Imagine the earth with many paths where others have gone before you. Choose one and walk on it for a while. Once you are comfortable, realizing you are safe as you go farther into the woods, decide on another way. If there is a clear path where you have chosen, you are still living someone else's life.

❧ Imagine a fire inside you that relies on a constant fuel supply from the outside. Once it is burning hot, prepare to relinquish that need and stoke your fire from inside. David Whyte translates Pablo Neruda's poem *"La Poesa."* "I went my own way, deciphering that burning fire, and I wrote the first bare line…and suddenly I saw, the heavens, unfastened and open." In his own poem called *"Out on the Ocean,"* Whyte writes "And the spark behind the fear, recognized as life, leaps into flames. Always this energy smolders inside, when it remains unlit, the body fills with dense smoke." Both poets tell us that we feel most alive when we stoke the fire inside us and if we don't, we will feel only a smoky version of what it means to be human.

Imagine the water inside you creating waves. Watch a piece of driftwood bobbing on the surface. The wave gathers energy from below as water moves back into the ocean and the ocean pushes another layer of water atop it, creating a swell. The wave breaks yet the driftwood has barely moved a few inches. Going back and forth with the crowd will not move your life forward.

Imagine the air inside you creating a cloud of warm and cool air mingled together. My joining the energy of opposites, lightning can lash out and ignite. Realize that we are all part of a community but must find where we stand apart. Strike out and light your own way. Don't allow your eyes to cloud over in blind allegiance; make sure you can see for yourself. Mingle wisely.

Stanley Keleman in *Emotional Anatomy* tells us that our emotions follow the rules of water. When we brace ourselves for shock or a blow or when we harden to confine pain, our liquid state is like ice. When we convert strong feelings into action, we might shed water in tears or share bodily fluids. Depending on our ability to display emotions, we might find ourselves shrinking with shame, stiffening with pride or frozen in fear. In that way, we are stuck in our body instead of the creative process of action. It is in our muscles, either fluid or stiff that we dance or guard ourselves.

Practice non-stealing. Never forget to return goods borrowed, and never forget to return favors. "Give without remembering and receive without forgetting."

Although we are unable to discover new lands or settle a new village, we can become moral pilgrims. We can break new ground or break from the pack. We can do the right thing even though other people settle for less.

Our brains are designed to enforce conformity. Our limbic brain is an intense and constant monitor of others as we keep track of which behaviors earn praise and which earn blame. This enforcer is so strict we will alter reality to comply. Elizabeth Loftus discovered the phenomenon of False Memory in the 1970's wherein hints leaked to people by authorities during an experiment, overrode what they saw with their own eyes. When all but one of the tested reported that the purple object was blue, the one experimental tester would change his response to blue to match the other's answers. Compliance tyrannized both the visual system and the speech center. The tester "decided" he saw blue AND failed to speak up that the others were wrong. Think of ways in which you dutifully comply even if the task goes against your grain. What don't you say at work even though you notice practices that are wasteful or unethical?

❧ Kundalini is Goddess Energy and not to be compared with energy in physics. It is our Divine Nature that cannot be coerced or controlled. While our primitive brain wants to conform and reshape events, Kundalini is more graceful and is the part of us that will not be tyrannized or shared with others just for the sake of sharing. Its energies must be matched.

❖ The first step is the most important as it embodies intention. That is why goal setting is so important. Properly framed goals can decrease the probability of disappointment. The simplest way to decrease the frequency of negative thoughts leading to negative outcomes is by selecting moderate expectations. Instead of saying you will lose 50 pounds, lower the expectation to 5 or 10 pounds. Instead of saying you will get your Masters Degree, make a goal to return to school. You should out-perform the goal, not the other way around. Never have your goals out-perform you.

○ In Hatha Yoga, a particular pose is held in a relaxed manner and you stretch the pose. The pose does not stretch you. Do not attach blame saying, "my hamstrings are tight," or "I can't balance on one foot." Stay mindful of the shape of the experience, not the shape of the pose.

❖ Do not allow yourself to be humiliated but do show humility. From the Latin, 'humus' meaning "ground or soil," having humility is to return to the ground of your being.

❖ Chaos is a technical term in mathematical theory designating non-linear dynamics. It is not synonymous with disorder but means the sensitive dependence on initial conditions. The area of the feet, our contact with the planet, can be considered our initial condition. It is here we begin our chaotic journey either toward enlightenment or misunderstanding.

❖ The most important talent is the talent for practice. It may be part of our nature to cling to stability and to static self-concepts but the human body is dynamic and likes to create patterns as short cuts for the next time. Practice does make perfect.

❖ Remember, many features of old age are just the static representations of what was once dynamic: squeezed arteries, stiff joints and inflexible posture. Since the body and brain are going to create patterns no matter what, why not make sure you create flexible ones?

❖ Conceive of something that is moving in the same direction nature is moving. Walk that way.

❖   A monk was asked what the difference was between illness and wellness. He walked to the chalkboard and wrote the two words: ILLNESS/WELLNESS. He took the chalk and circled the "I" in illness and the "WE" in wellness. That is the difference, he said. Perhaps we have an "affiliative neurocir- cuitry" or some biological basis for turning to others, but we must be aware that blind allegiance to social constructs is not the same as establishing meaningful social contacts. Who makes up your "we?" Who brings out the wellness in you?

CHAKRA TWO—CREATIVITY

LUMBAR SPINE, PELVIS, HIP

"Be not afraid of growing slowly, be afraid only
of standing still."—Chinese proverb

"I see people stuck because they keep getting in
their own way."—Barbara Bailey Reinhold

"Nothing happens until
something moves."—Albert Einstein

To understand this part of the body, one must understand how stability generates mobility. This area of the body reminds us that our foundation exists to allow us the creative business of moving. Each muscle is a sense organ according to Deane Juhan, author of *Job's Body*. Muscles are attached on each end to a bone (except some of the muscles in the face which are attached from bone to skin), the stability of the bone acting as a fulcrum to move against. While we think of muscles as lengthening and shortening according to the workload requested of them, there is a portion of muscle that does not actively move. This stable portion of a muscle is the spindle, a bundle of fibers that do not have striations in their central portion and so cannot contribute to movement, but are passively moved along with the rest of the muscle. The central region is home for a sensory ending wrapped in a spiral arrangement around the spindle. When the spiral is either widened or narrowed, the muscle moves accordingly.

Thus the muscle spindle bridges the gap between what is stable and what moves. In the same way, it bridges the two halves of the nervous system where sensation becomes movement, and movement is sensation. The spindles, by housing the motor and sensory fibers, merge the two physiologic features into one and as Juhan says, "movement and sensation are joined directly together in a firm embrace, where no intervening barriers exist and no intermediary messengers are necessary." In other words, they feel themselves. This part of the muscle does not need the higher centers of the brain or consciousness. It does not need to be told to move. This static portion is movement.

Interestingly, this blurring of definitions is inherent in mobility itself. Walking, it turns out, is just a cousin of falling down. As we age, we become more and more aware of the daily possibility of falling, a possibility not afforded a tree or a plant during their immobile lives. Few of us are aware that we are just experienced toddlers, a word that literally means, "to have an unsteady gate." The physics of walking, or as researcher Giovanni Cavagna from the University of Milan likes to call it, the physics of falling forward, attempts to save energy much like an inverted pendulum. The problem, Cavagna notes, is that "we do it badly."

A pendulum transforms the kinetic energy of motion into potential energy and back again. At the bottom of the arc, kinetic energy reaches its maximum. At the top, the pendulum slows to a stop where potential energy is at its peak. There, potential energy is converted back to kinetic energy. A pendulum anchored from above converts energy at 100% with only a tiny bit lost to friction. However, our body is "attached" to the ground where our foot pivots off the planet, thus inverting the pendulum. Dr. Heglund, a physiologist at the University of Louvain in Belgium, notes that humans convert energy at 65%, with 35% of the energy of each step having to be supplied afresh from food. He notes that birds do a better job with movement, even though they must defy gravity and fish are more efficient even though they swim through a dense liquid.

Cavagna finds the energy loss at the top of the stride, where we start to fall into the next step. What happens is that most of us pause, imperceptibly for a few milliseconds, falling forward. It is there we lose potential energy and fail to convert it into increased speed as the muscles in the leg contract in order to fight the fall. But Cavagna found an African tribe that does convert at nearly 100%. How do they do it? They carry objects on their heads, changing their center of gravity and becoming in the process, an efficient energy converter and a model pendulum. It is an example of a cultural habit or meme that allows full human potential instead of wasting it.

There is a science to falling, one that can be taught in any rehab clinic, or during martial arts classes—tuck and roll. The strategy holds that even though you are falling; don't stop moving. There is a consolation, I tell my patients, in falling—it implies you were moving. In other words, you can't fall if you weren't moving and just as there is an art to falling, the same art applies to failing in life— if you are going to fail, fail reaching despite the uncertainty. It has been said that the single most powerful secret to unleashing your creativity is to keep your mind open in the face of uncertainty.

Herein lays the power center to establish a life full of personal choice and the creativity to strike out on one's own. It is a secure person who decides to take a different path from the tribe in order to find wholeness. Once we have found our own way, we can return to the community where we can share with others in a healthy way, adding to the tribe's wisdom. It is this area of the body where the solid parts of us branch out to connect and relate to a partner, whether that partner is another person, a commitment to an idea, or interaction with the physical environment. Healthy attachments find their energy here whereas unhealthy attachment can lead to addiction, fear of losing control, and misdirected life energy.

Our sexual organs live here, as do our bowels and bladder and their functions resonate with the actions of taking in, storing and eliminating. Too much power here and these functions morph into physical or symbolic forms of betrayal, rape, constipation, loss of continence, and impotence. We might keep too much in and brood or hoard. We might let too much out and be excessively emotional or waste too much. We might stifle our creative abilities by failing to give birth to new ideas and new commitments or we might turn our creative abilities into toxic ones by forcing our ideas on to other people. Healthy attachments can be viewed spiritually and emotionally as well as anatomically. Let's take a small muscle on either side of our back to prove our point.

The quadratus lumborum (QL) is a muscle that attaches from our last rib to the lumbar spine (L1-2-3-4) and finally to our pelvis, connecting our trunk to our legs. Without it, our vital organs would not go where our legs led them. It connects our insides to our outsides. The QL has many jobs: it functions as a brake in side bending, stabilizes the lumbar spine and stabilizes the last rib for inhalation and forced exhalation. It elevates the hip, works as a lateral flexor of the spine and can extend the spine. If this muscle were paralyzed, walking would be impossible. Janet Travell M.D. writes, "The quadratus lumborum muscle is one of the most commonly overlooked muscular sources of low back pain." QL tightness can cause the 'pseudo-disc syndrome' and the 'failed surgical back syndrome.' Patients with a tight QL note a loss of vitality because of the energy expended in suppressing the pain. Lying down relieves the sense of heaviness in the hips, cramping of the calves, and burning in the feet. This change from vertical to horizontal has literally and figuratively turned your world on its side just as back pain has turned the medical field upside-down.

Dualities present themselves in the medical field and if not anticipated, can lead to misdirected energy in the form of funds, medical personnel and even diagnostic testing. Low back pain (LBP) and its disability are considered to have reached epidemic proportions only in countries with Worker's Compensation benefits. Many LBP patients find themselves stuck in the disability system, reliant on small monthly pensions and seemingly inadequate lifetime medical coverage. Seemingly, for they receive a stipend and medical insurance coverage that appears adequate excepting for the fact that this particular population experiences an on-going search for medical solutions and often resorts to complex interventions. Patients seeking the next X-ray, MRI, CT Scan, rehabilitation therapies, pharmaceutical prescriptions, surgeries and psychological support create a distinct burden on an already burdened medical community.

Medical personnel find themselves faced with incongruencies as well. Health care workers feel redirected away from patients struggling with acute diseases such as cancer, stroke and heart attack and beleaguered with chronic pain sufferers whose problems and solutions to those problems remain elusive. Medical personnel may feel impotent in their ability to help chronic pain patients and resort to dispensing medications, even though they know that reliance on pain medications occurs most often in low back pain patients. This only adds to the sense of "loss of control" on both sides. Chronic pain patients also serve as an uncomfortable mirror for the medical team. They tend to exhibit exaggerated behaviors that are more subtle, but nonetheless, present in all of us. Their lack of direction in their lives, their complaints about small details, their shifting areas of discomfort, and their lack of gratitude are displayed on a grand scale and appear ugly to us because we do those same things ourselves.

It is not unusual to find an emergency room heavily populated with chronic back pain patients utilizing the ER for "break-through pain," crisis events where the pain has broken-through the effects of their daily medication. Such patients might be labeled "drug seeking" as they request stronger or heavier doses of narcotics, "help rejecting" when they fail to comply with exercise or behavior programs, and "system manipulators" or "doctor shoppers" when they secretly obtain narcotics or opinions from several doctors at the same time. Suspicion, betrayal and manipulation then skews the physician/patient relationship with the patient suspecting the doctor of not understanding or even believing the pain and feeling betrayed by medical personnel who have taken an oath to help. Patients might feel manipulated by a worker compensation system that replaces loss of livelihood with inadequately eked out stipends. Health personnel in turn, suspect the patients of drug addiction or the secondary gain of being off work. They feel betrayed when they have attempted to ease the pain with carefully written prescriptions only to find a patient has duped other physicians into writing the same prescription. Doctors might feel manipulated into prescribing the next MRI or surgery, knowing full well that back surgeries show little benefit and will only lead to signing off permanent and stationary disability claims. Both sides find themselves in unsatisfactory relationships, each with varying insight into the irony of a system that, while seeking to avoid addictive behavior, plunges both caregiver and patient into addictive behaviors with each other and the system.

The word, "addict," shares it's etymology with "dictator" and means, "to allow someone or something to tyrannize your life." If a dictator rules your world, whether that dictator is a person, a drug, or a destructive and compulsive lifestyle, you are not in control. As pieces of your life are given over to someone or something else's control, you settle for mere fragments of your former life, rarely making decisions for yourself, and allowing other people or things to tell you what to do. If you use a drug to be happy, shop when you feel depressed or eat when you feel lonely, you allow a drug or an activity to dictate how you feel, what you do with your money, what you do with your time and even how you look. It is not living as a whole person but rather as one that has been overruled. We should ask ourselves what it would look like, how would we feel, how would we spend our resources and time if we were to become our own authority and control our life's energy?

There are many addictions and betrayals to the self that engage us, most of them innocuous when compared to what we think of as truly self-destructive behaviors like drug use, alcoholism, and inactivity. Whenever our lives feel stuck, in a rut, going nowhere, or spinning in circles, we can bet we are addicted. We are addicted to thinking and not doing. Addicted to daydreaming and not initiating. Addicted to patterns of behavior, relationships or activities that we know are meaningless and futile. We know we are going nowhere fast. Nowhere-fast energy can be symbolized in back pain for you literally cannot get up and go anywhere. You're stuck.

The lumbar spine connects our body to our hips and legs. It is the supportive structure that allows stability to the parts that get us moving. And without the stability, there is impaired mobility. Without mobility, you're stuck in one place over and over again, addicted to going nowhere. LBP patients are often the toughest challenge a rehab therapist will encounter, for more than any other disability, they are immobilized by their pain. They seem to be lost in the "now" of the pain, hooked on the feedback loop circulating from their back to their brain, unable to evaluate what to do next. They are stuck in the muck. Success in rehabilitating these patients lies in graded exposure to pain-free movement, specifically using nerve glides to initiate more creative movement that can challenge the brain. LBP patients require a reintroduction to movement and activity. Even migrainers show more activity than LBP patients. Are debilitating headaches a "lesser" pain that LBP? It's doubtful. Is it because headaches are not covered by Worker's Compensation? It's possible.

Why do we have a so-called epidemic in low back pain? What makes low back pain so debilitating that the idea of future work and employability is lost? What is the advice from rehabilitation experts that might break the disability loop and get a growing number of our population back on its feet? The answer—we are entirely too sedentary, even for those of us without back pain. Those of us who are able to get up and go, don't. We should all heed the advice, "Take your dog for a walk everyday, even if you don't have one."

A sedentary lifestyle is considered an activity rate of less then 10,000 footsteps (about five miles) a day, everyday. Most of us know of course, that we should be more active—it certainly doesn't take a rehab expert to tell us that. We tell ourselves we'll start a walking program tomorrow, knowing how good it will make us feel. Yet, if we know it to be true, what keeps us from doing it? What allows us to betray our own logic, our own expertise, and our very word to ourselves? What makes it so easy to commit to lying to ourselves yet fail to commit to that walk we promised to take every evening?

Put simply, you can't have a bad life unless you have a lifestyle that supports it. One of the premises of this book is that the body has a wisdom we fail to appreciate only because we have failed to realize that simple, seemingly innocuous lifestyle habits are profoundly detrimental. Our lifestyles, our furniture, the food we eat, and the things we give value and the values we choose to ignore, are body and soul-snatchers. Much of our bodily pain and feelings that "something is missing" can be attributed to our lifestyle and cultural conditioning, a culture we are so immersed in, we fail to see our problems clearly.

People often wonder about the validity of the theory of evolutionary change. If the world is designed and adapted through evolutionary alterations, why do we not see adaptation before our very eyes? If our low back and hips cannot tolerate sitting at a 90 degree angle, yet we have sat that way for generations, why haven't we lost the genes that would produce such an anomaly? The reason is that evolution is not always a change in biologic form since change in biology can take millions of years. The evolutionary changes we can see can be intellectual alterations, clever distractions and inventions. The only way we have become better "sitters" is not by means of a more tolerant anatomy, but by becoming better at entertaining the higher centers of our brains with television, computer software, and stereo equipment and by designing more comfortable chairs.

Evolution is at work when a culture defines and places value on a certain set of skills and then offers early training and educational manipulation to produce and improve those skills. Once a meme has a value attached to it, it allows it to spread. The evolutionary gains seen in music shows piano players more proficient than in prior decades. The same goes for sprinters and swimmers. It is survival of the fittest individual every time we subject our children to a piano recital or sporting event. It is survival of the fittest meme every time we subject our children to an ad on television telling them they are not worthy without the next generation of athletic shoe or a blue ribbon from a competition.

Our culture decides what to punish or reinforce which reconstructs our physical and intellectual make-up without a change in our genetic make-up. Dissatisfaction occurs when a culture places a narrow definition on success or survival (i.e., a child is successful at school only with straight A's, whether or not he has good friends. Or we are successful if we earn $100,000 a year and not if we have a balanced life). But adapting to value-lacking memes might just be an individual's, or even a civilization's, downfall.

Take something as simple as television viewing, simple in the minds of most industrialized citizens—we have one, we watch it, it doesn't make us a better or worse person. It's entertainment. It keeps us company. It keeps us up on the world news. It's a cheap baby-sitter and it is harmless relaxation. But television viewing is nothing less than a culturally accepted addiction. It's what could be called a "parasitic meme," a meme that seeks survival for its own benefit and without benefit to our survival. Were we to walk as many hours as we watch television, low back pain might be non-existent.

Statistics from "Television and the Family" from the *Journal of Family Issues*, tells us that we spend 10 years of our life watching television and that more households have a TV than indoor plumbing. While the purpose of technology is to reduce or augment the time we spend in labor, television occupies time and in fact, consumes time with no resulting product. Are we really willing to acknowledge that we spend ten years of our lives watching sit-coms whose plot we can't remember two days later? Were we that entertained? Are we so stressed that we want to be oblivious and numb for ten years of our lives?

Some of us suggest that we view more and more television simply because it has been made so attractive and easy to do. More channels, excellent educational programming, large as life viewing screens, surround sound and affordable prices are such a lure, none of us could resist. However, statistics point to an interesting fact about improved technology as it occurs in television viewing—there has never been an appreciable increase in TV viewing from improvement in the technology. Not with the advent of color TV nor with the increase in the number of channels. More than one TV in a household does not increase the amount of time spent watching (just like two bathrooms does not increase the number of times someone goes to the bathroom). Cable hook-up doesn't increase it. Conversely, the advent of VCR's did not decrease TV viewing as was thought nor did it increase viewing. The only variable that has increased the number of hours we spend watching TV is the increase in hours of leisure time. If we have more time, we choose to give it to our television set. It's as if time is a stressor in and of itself, something we don't know what to do with so we "veg out." We might feel differently about TV viewing if we stated, "Last night, I acted like a vegetable for three hours."

J. P. Robinson in an article entitled, "*I Love My TV*" cites a study out of the University of Maryland that found for every hour of leisure gained, we watch at least one hour of television. Madison Avenue bets their bottom dollar that we will be glued to the TV set. They know *not* to place the bulk of their ads in magazines, on highway signs or on the radio. They know television is the primary source of commerce in the United States. Television commercials carry the largest, most expensive ad revenues, so much so that commerce has become television's purpose. The goal of a commercial is to make us want an item we didn't even know existed ten minutes ago, and they usually succeed.

Even without ads that manipulate the way we spend our money, television executives are manipulating our time with what they call "appointment TV,"— shows that are so alluring, we will essentially make an appointment with the television. If you hear yourself say, "I can't go to dinner with you, I always watch West Wing on Wednesday nights" then you are keeping the appointment. That appointment with the TV means you have forfeited being with other people.

These same executives know what ad executives know—TV's biggest competitor is not magazines, not books, and not the movies. It is not even our leisure time for we will forfeit it without a thought. It is the family. If we spend time with our family, it will automatically usurp TV time. Unfortunately, many of us gather the family around the television, claiming it as "family time." By doing this, it not only dishonors genuine family time, but allows the television to assume a role by becoming, itself, a member of the family. Our challenge, if we cannot relinquish the TV, is not to allow it to become a dominant family member.

We can further explore the oftentimes hidden influence television has in our lives by taking a look around the living room. Notice how the furniture is arranged. Is it arranged for socialization with chairs facing couches? Or are they arranged solely in the direction of the television? Is there a built-in cabinet just perfect for a television set? In other words, have you bought furniture for your furniture? If so, TV is dictating how we design and populate our living spaces. Its mere presence in the room, whether it is on or off, has dominated our space. Another question to ask ourselves is whether the television is of such a size and shape that there is only one place for it to reside, forcing the chairs or bed into uncomfortable arrangements? Do you have to crane your neck to see the television? If so, you have adapted your body position in order to make the machine more comfortable or the room more attractive. As is often the case with culturally defined adaptation that is bad for us, our body will attempt to "put the brake on," trying to tell us that we are on the loser's end of the struggle to survive. It's called pain and it can come in the form of a bad back, a stiff neck, buckling knees or even insomnia. If we succumb to the cultural allure of watching television, we should sit squarely in front of it, our eyes, neck and shoulders held in midline. Our knees should not be straight out in front of us on an ottoman or a recliner footrest. The extended leg pulls the sciatic nerve downward toward the knee, stretching root sheaths and nerve roots at the spine. The lumbar disc must then "borrow" relaxed tissue from the pelvis by drawing part of the dura, nerve roots and spinal ganglia further into the spinal canal. If we were aware of how much harm our body experiences from the positions we get into to watch television, we might just watch less.

Furniture that makes for easy television viewing is just that; geared for prolonged television viewing, not your body's health. Soft, squishy and overly supportive furniture allows for hours of "passive sitting," passive in that none of our postural muscles have to work. Hip and low back pain can emerge from overstretched and lax muscles habituated by the chairs we sit in. Hip and sciatic nerve pain can be perpetuated by sitting with straightened knees, the position often afforded by reclining chairs that prop your knees and feet out in front of you.

As you sit in your favorite chair, take inventory of what muscles have to work. Are your legs making a rocking chair rock? If not, the valves in the arteries and veins of your ankles are less active than they should be. Are your hips adjusting to keep you from falling over sideways? If not, they are shut down. How about the back muscles? Are they holding you upright, or are you slouched forward or to the side? If slouched, the ribs are pressing against your stomach and confining lung space. Are you propped on one arm, leaning to one side of a chair? Then, muscles are asymmetrical, shortened on one side, and over-stretched on the other. If you have a head rest, your neck is also lax which could be the wisest part of the position so far. If all parts of your body are not working, that is, over-supported and overstretched in a chair but your head remains unsupported, then the only working muscles are that of your neck. This could be a perpetuating factor in headache and neck ache. If you are seated in a straight-backed rocking chair, you legs working, your pelvis square, your back muscles holding you upright, then your unsupported head has help. Furniture contributes to much of a "civilized" cultures' pain syndromes. Remember, 70% of the world squats and they are right—we are wrong.

If the mere fact of having a television in our living space combined with the furniture choices we make to view television is deleterious, imagine how the actual content of the shows is influencing us. Let's suppose we are naive enough to believe that the content of television, whether it is violent, sexual, exploitive, or just what we call "a dumb show," does not influence us. Perhaps, then, the primary damage of television is not in the behavior it produces, but in the behavior it prevents. Talking, preparing meals, playing music together, playing games, meditating, going for a walk, dancing and a myriad of other activities both individual and communal are impossible if time is given to the television. If we tell ourselves that we are watching television as a family, we should make sure it is not adult programming we are "sharing" with our children. I doubt many of us sit down and watch cartoons with our children but instead, have them sit with us while we watch "our shows." If we are saying that TV time is "family time," then shame on us. If we are sitting with our children and shush them to be quiet so we won't miss the next bit of dialogue, then what message do we give our children? Who would we rather listen to? It may be no small wonder when we lament, "My teenager won't talk to me," after we have conditioned them with 15 years of, "Shush, I'm trying to listen to the TV."

Television also threatens another area; that of our attention. In 1969, the program Sesame Street used child psychologists to ascertain how best to focus children's attention. Laborious research studies placed children in front of a test TV and monitored their eyes to note when and why they would look away from the screen. It was found that they were most attentive with 10-second scenes that involved both a real person and a puppet. Scenes with only puppets or only people failed to interest them. The psychologists warned the producers that it might be harmful to a child's sense of reality to have fantasy mixed with reality (puppets with people) and far too hypnotizing. The producers ignored the advice and had a huge hit on their hands. As warned, children were glued to the screen.

Other producers found another part of the study more to their liking. The group found that children who veered their attention away from the screen tested as high or higher in recall of the scene than children whose attention was stuck. It seems distractibility signals that the information has been processed and the child seeks another stimulus. They "get it" quicker. To work with this distractibility, and to ensure the child was not distracted enough to go play with toys or people off screen (their family for instance), scenes shortened in duration and shows like MTV, which came out thirty years after Sesame Street, now have scenes that run three seconds per slot.

Studies with Attention Deficit/Hyperactivity Disorder (ADHD) children flashed an image on a computer screen and recorded reaction times. The ADHD kids were no faster in their identification of the picture, but they were slower when the signal demanded that they inhibit their response. They couldn't stop reacting to novel stimuli. Dr. Kenneth Blum from the University of Texas defines a new syndrome called "reward deficiency syndrome," wherein the sufferer fails to recognize that a reward is enough due to low dopamine levels in the brain. Such people are susceptible to anything that will release dopamine such as distracting novelty and immediate gratification both because they fail to calculate that the reward they got is enough, but also because they cannot hold the idea of a long-term reward or goal in their mind long enough. Thus, they would be addicted to more and more novelty and riskier behavior that keep the level of alertness elevated enough to sustain the release of dopamine.

Television is the perfect medium for programming distractibility into our children's brains. Try watching a soft drink commercial. Adults, who were programmed with sustained camera shots, get dizzy with the speedy images while our children can tell us whether the Pepsi drinking pop star has a pierced belly-button. Interestingly, when these same children, whose brain we have adapted to faster and faster images, enter school, the world has slowed down. Now we expect them to sit still with one "talking head" in front of them, using teaching methods that haven't changed since our parents were in school. Slow, repetitive, static information is in opposition to the wirings of their television viewing brains. What do we do for these children? We call them hyperactive. And what do we do then? We medicate them with a stimulant that, in overly stimulated people, serves to sedate them.

Meanwhile, television is speeding up, causing us to spend more sedentary viewing time because we are less distracted. Our children, out of shape and addicted to a sedentary lifestyle at earlier and earlier ages, are the future work-force. A study out of the University of San Francisco finds that children are experiencing medical conditions once seen only in people over the age of fifty. Muscle-fatigue syndromes, high cholesterol, obesity and repetitive motion injuries are occurring at such high rates, the study predicts that once children reach the workforce, they will only be able to work a four hour day. They will work half days not because they will have values that promote rest and relaxation, hobbies and caring for the elderly. They will be physically incapable of working a full day without resultant disability and work injury.

It is amazing the lengths a culture will go in order to promote a sedentary, comfortable lifestyle, which in turn promotes destructive patterns that lead to pain and discomfort. John Robbins in his book *A Diet for a New America*, notes that "Yankee Stadium was originally built in the 1920's to accommodate the great crowds who wanted to see Babe Ruth play baseball. When it was renovated in the 1970's, the seating capacity had to be reduced by 9,000 seats. The seating reduction was necessary because, in the 50 years since the Babe swung his bat, the average American fanny had increased in width by four inches. And so the ball park seats had to be widened from 15 to 19 inches." The seats evolved and a meme evolved, because our size had changed due to poor eating habits. It is thought that the genes for obesity only survive if people with the obese gene pass it on. But there is another way to pass it on—memes are making it more comfortable to be obese and thus they carry the gene along with them.

It's not that memes need to be especially alluring to tap into our willingness to waste our time, divert our attention and choose comfort over reason, for we are a society in competition with time itself. People who are addicted to work, register in our minds as their own diseased population with the term "workaholics." In the medical field, they are called "Type A" personalities, people with rapid firing emotions, outbursts in behavior, irritability with the slow workings of others and obsession with fast acquisition and upward mobility despite their downward nobility. Type A's are considered "over adapted" to work, addicted to adrenaline and acquisition despite the lack of value in their work. They work for money, power and a high level of activity only for activity's sake. They possess a poverty of thought and a lack of values when it comes to working at "green ideas," business practices that are mindful of minimal pollution, maximum kindness and true service. They have an unbound interest and commitment to success for successes sake, never realizing that if success in our pursuits were all there was, a baby would be content to walk and never run, a millionaire would stop earning money after the first million and athletes would quit after they won their first race. We are failing to see what really makes us tick.

Our addiction to working and living hard can be seen in how we view growing old. Older adults are respected to the extent they can behave like young people: capable of working, enjoying sex, running marathons or lifting weights into their eighties. They are not valued in our culture for wisdom, experience, having time to themselves or in moving slower, driving slower, and enjoying a nap after a morning of gardening.

We can even view illness as it relates to time. Dr. Jeffrey Bland, a nutrition expert, notes there are two types of physical disease. There is vertical disease, such as backaches, headaches, high blood pressure, fatigue, weight gain and indigestion. We can go through the motions and remain upright with these symptoms since they are not immediately life threatening. We'll deal with them when we get the time. Horizontal disease however finds us making priorities and often having to be bed-bound for a time, forcing us to be horizontal. Cancer, heart attack, and stroke all signal down time with no time to put off the future. But what if we were to view the "vertical" signals as warning signs, something we should pay attention to early before we are forced to confront a "horizontal" crisis? How many headaches are unreasonable? How much obesity finally gets our attention? Why doesn't our body deserve our time when it has a headache or is just tired? What illness or disease would make you stop and set priorities? A headache? Migraine? Migraines every month; every week? Vascular spasm from a migraine resulting in a stroke? Which one?

Disease or dysfunction is the body's way of saying we have failed to adapt to the situation. It might also mean we have engaged in "negative coping," where we have changed or adapted but at the price of physical or mental disturbance. We might also engage in "negative solutions" which make small matters worse. For instance, if our body is unable to adapt to a small virus, we might get a fever. If we adapt by taking medicine, we might stifle the symptom but set ourselves up as a better host for the virus to grow. If we take medicine to stifle the heat generated by a moderate fever, we stifle the activity of phagocytic neutrofils that will kill viruses. The fever can worsen or the bugs can grow more virulent. Treating fevers is now known to postpone recovery, increase the probability of secondary infection and deprive us of clues about worsening symptoms.

Likewise, ingesting extra iron in a healthy body is probably harmless (and needless) but in one with infection, can be deadly. Anemia in the presence of an infection is the body's way of "stealing" the food bacteria love to eat—iron. Iron-binding proteins wrap themselves around the iron, starving the bacteria. During infection, our gut suppresses the assimilation of about 80% of dietary iron, neutrophils release chemicals to bind iron at infection sites, nitric oxide is sent out to disrupt the iron metabolism of the bacteria and the liver works toward the further binding of hemin and hemoglobin. All of these anti-bacterial systems are at work to keep iron levels low. We interfere by adding iron, making it freely available, thus facilitating bacterial growth. E. coli, a potent bacteria found in undercooked meat, shows an increase in virulence 100,000-fold with added iron. What this tells us is that we don't know our solutions from our problems.

We might also use any number of methods to keep ourselves from knowing what is good for us. Negative coping can take the form of consuming caffeine to mask our true condition of feeling tired. Excessive food, alcohol, shopping, work, and television all keep us from paying attention to our body and our true thoughts. If we shop every time we feel unrewarded, we might never seek more rewarding activities, better relationships, or meaningful work. If we watch television every time we need to "just zone out," we might never understand what is draining our lives of energy.

Ironically, many of us take pride in our stress and fatigue. Arthur Kleinman noted during the proceedings of the CIBA Conference on Chronic Fatigue that, "In our times, the metaphor of being exhausted by the multiple, competing demands of work, family and play is a badge of success and achievement, a lifestyle that demonstrates that one has prestige, position, and power." In the 1870's, the neurologist George M. Beard argued that life in the fast lane precipitated mental and physical fatigue with organic causes beyond the diagnostic capacities of 19th century medical science. He noted, over one hundred years ago, our great capacity to suffer from "American nervousness," NE or "nervous exhaustion," and what he called, "Hysteria of the Elite." Mark Twain had it. Thomas Edison and his wife suffered from it as did many of the "greats" who "invented the century."

If we continue to be oblivious about our fast paced lives, our body may one day rebel, attempting to talk to us in the only language it knows will get our attention—pain. Pain and illness, then, can actually become the cure for what ails you—the paradoxical "God that comes through the wound." We should think twice when we silence defense mechanisms as we are failing to recognize the adaptive significance in our symptoms. When illness breaks us apart, making us pay attention to one part of the body, we just might become aware of life itself. This intense appreciation for the simple things in life, and the once overlooked or taken for granted pleasure, points to a new way of life. But we shouldn't have to appreciate life by contracting a life threatening illness. We must ask ourselves, "Am I waiting for illness to point the way or am I willing to listen and make choices before I have no choice?"

Larry Dossey says in *Beyond Illness*, "illness leads health onward, makes it perceptible…the silver behind the mirror without which the mirror is nothing more than a transparent sheet of glass." We must be willing to look at ourselves honestly without all the masks and listen to earlier warning signals that can point the way. John Ratey writes in *Shadow Syndromes* that, "the mildly depressed are quite possibly the most accurate observers of life in our midst. They perceive with crystal clarity that, when the glass is half full, it is also half empty." It seems we would be healthiest if we were cultivated in the Yogic tradition and have the inner discipline to choose the good over the pleasant and comfortable. Or as a wise person once said, "There are a thousand ways to place your comfort ahead of your growth."

When we develop our abilities only for material reward, and stifle our instincts that tell us we are on the wrong track, or are too stressed, or are in any way not living the life we know we should be living, we bring forth the negative side of normalcy. Feelings of guilt in having betrayed our true self, failure to find our true calling, trading off contentment for money and material goods, and trading joy of life for safety in retirement plans are all aspects of the down side of "normal." This is the crux of the word anxiety, which literally means to be tied in knots. Anxiety is the emotional effect of compromise.

We become the "worried well" or the "working wounded," suffering from non-problems. We are the have-it-all's who are less and less tranquilized by the material rewards of work. We are healthy people having trouble adapting to our own cultural niceties and are in psychic pain as we pay the emotional and spiritual costs of working, and living without value.

While we are openly troubled, we show no neurosis or irrational tendencies beyond normal. Many of us will make unhealthy adjustments within the work force, adjustments somehow tolerated by institutions. Some will have a work injury, justifying a release from work. Others will become whistle blowers, grievance writers and gripers justifying their workday around some trivial issue. Others will give up, abandoning hope that work will provide meaning and value to their lives. Some will develop alternative interests outside of work, doing volunteer work or pursuing individual interests. Worse yet are those that "retire on the job." We can all identify some person where we work who is going through the motions, taking long breaks, accomplishing little "real" work but who remains on the payroll. All of these scenarios reflect workers with "psychic pain," and like pain in a knee might make the knee freeze up, these people become emotionally frozen, having only the traits required for cursory work and a perfunctory family life. They are in suspended animation.

Flexible people, those who choose value in work over the lure of material wealth, will continue to develop spiritually, test out strategies of change and then, most importantly, create change, taking active responsibility for their own self-development. Hopefully, they are paired with a company that allows contributions toward making "green decisions" that are environmentally sound and add to the community rather than detract. In this way, career adaptation and one's emotional values develop a view of normalcy and success that is a better fit.

Those of us who want to minimize risk by playing it safe, who desire comfort over contentment and material over spiritual rewards, will be mesmerized by a big paycheck, tidy insurance plan and a retirement package. We are shackled by "Golden Handcuffs." When these perks are viewed as the equivalent to integrity, ethics, and value, we might experience anxiety. When insanity has taken such a twist, we suffer not from the absence of reason but reason "gone amok."

Adapting to meaningless work offers a narrow version of reality, which perverts the heart. It allows work to dictate and enslave us but give us the illusion of freedom and independence. We must make our work stimulate our emotional aliveness in order to avoid "surface sanity," the feeling that you are normal on the outside but dying on the inside. We have to remember that our insides are attached to what happens to our outsides. Our very relationship with reality counts on just that attachment.

For our lives to be rich, we must acknowledge that narrowed versions of activity, only serves to narrow our sensory input which in turn narrows our version of bigger concepts like play, love, compassion and wisdom. Our body provides the link, it supplies the logic and it creates our image of the world. Without exploratory movement linked to activities that are meaningful to the body, and activities that provide information to the joints, senses and muscles, our body will feel like it is out of its mind.

Juhan notes, "Knowledge of our body is from our actions as we touch and move through the world." Authors George Lakoff and Mark Johnson go even further saying that there is a "strong dependence of concepts and reason upon the body" and that all of our projections about reality depend on the "inferential patterns used in sensorimotor processes that are directly tied to the body." The mind is so economical, it will borrow sensorimotor pathways and patterns to understand abstract concepts like love. The pathways evolved together. Therefore, we will understand a concept like love as a journey. When going well, we will say, "we are on track, the relationship is moving forward, or we have found our path together." When our relationships are difficult, we will say, "we are stuck in a rut, spinning our wheels, or there is no commitment to move forward together." We understand our environment, our abstract concepts and our very lives through movement.

Darwinian medicine tells us that the interaction between the human organism and the environment is absolutely essential to the understanding of health and disease. We need to apply evolutionary principles to our daily practice of living before the two are so separated by technology or by the unintended outcomes of inventions and by our lack of sensory experiences, that we lose the embodied reality wherein our body and mind are one.

There are signs and symptoms that warn us of a mismatch between body and mind. Some of our addictions can make surface sanity a less bumpy ride, literally medicating our disquiet. We should be weary of anything we have to consume to make our day go better at work, for work should be valuable in and of itself. We should be comfortable with the ebb and flow of energy throughout a day rather than "self medicate" in an effort to ignore or dishonor our natural rhythms. When we do self-medicate, we are merely attempting to make our insides match what our outsides are doing, rather than matching our outsides to what our insides are feeling. We might drink coffee when we feel tired and still have a lot of work to do. We might drink wine when we feel wired and want to wind down. When we imbibe in such things, we're craving the feeling of wholeness. We want our insides to match our outsides.

How many of us say we "cannot function" without a morning cup of coffee? Caffeine is the only drug written into labor law and is institutionalized as a right whenever we take "coffee break." In many workplaces, coffee is provided free of charge, a drink that contains the most neuroactive drug on the planet, influencing your brain quicker than marijuana, alcohol or nicotine. Caffeine signals the brain to be hyper-productive, fast thinking, and multi-tasking while denying the body the need for rest, siesta or "down-time." It is an employer's dream. And for those workers who feel anxiety and unease when faced with a body that doesn't want to get going on Monday morning or at three in the afternoon everyday, coffee is labeled as a solution. Coffee allows us to stuff any ideas we might have to seek rest even though our biological clocks signal respite. It offers hyper-productivity when we are feeling the need for serenity. And it makes the mind explode when the soul might require contemplation. After all, we have work to do.

Every culture known to history (excepting Eskimo) used and uses psychoactive plants to alter their consciousness. While hunter-gatherers used certain drugs for shammanistic rituals, they did not rely on them to cope with "dawn-to-dusk" manual labor. In the book, *Forces of Habit*, the author notes, "taking drugs to get through the daily grind…is peculiar to civilization." He outlines how civilized societies routinely stupefy their infants and children to free the adults for labor.

Before the twentieth century, opium, cannabis or alcohol was used to quiet young children in many developing regions. "Such practices," he notes, "are further clues, if any are needed, that our social circumstances are out of sync with our evolved natures." We would be hard pressed to discount the fact that in the twenty-first century, we substitute the quieting effects of opium with the sedative effects of television or the appeasing effects of sugar in our children. We do this to free us to work and do chores without their interruptions. Should our bodies, or those of our children express the need to move or play, and defy the eight-hour work/school day, we drug ourselves and stupefy or pacify the children with culturally accepted externals. We are teaching them that the only way to get calm is to medicate or entertain ourselves into a stupor.

Goleman, in his book *Emotional Intelligence,* states that the craving for calm and release from anxiety is the emotional marker for alcoholics. Alcohol increases the availability of GABA, an amino acid that induces calm states. In fact, GABA (gamma-aminobutyric acid) is the major inhibitory neurotransmitter in our body. Anti-anxiety drugs like benzodiazepines (such as Valium) target the GABA receptors in the brain, offering a sense of calm. Since anxiety shows a genetic susceptibility for decreased GABA levels, the solution of alcoholic drinks or "benzos" could be quite therapeutic for some people, offering a balance toward a calmer state of being.

Researchers at the Brookhaven National Lab in New York have found that obese people have fewer dopamine receptors and the disparity is increased with a higher body mass index. Drug addicts also show fewer receptors, thus reducing the availability of one of the brain chemicals that stimulate feelings of pleasure. They hypothesize that brains with fewer receptors are less sensitive to everyday joys, causing a person to turn to food or drugs to simulate pleasure. Eating causes the body to produce dopamine and so seems a likely solution to the chemical imbalance. So, too, does watching a sunset or playing with a baby or any other routine pleasure, but they might be too routine for someone without enough receptors. There is another answer of course, as the body is meant to move. Exercise not only increases the receptor sites for dopamine, it releases more dopamine into the system.

Anxiety implies disharmony, a lack of rhythm in the way we are experiencing our lives which skews our sense of time. Further complicating matters, heightened anxiety leaves us feeling in a greater hurry to get nowhere faster. Larry Dossey notes that most diseases are related to a skewed sense of timing. Heart problems are a timing problem; either too slow (bradycardia), too fast (tachycardia), or too many pauses between beats (arterial fibrillation). Hypothyroid is an underactive thyroid while hyperthyroid is overactive. Attention Deficit Disorder (ADD and ADHD) portends that attention is scattered with not enough time spent on only one thing. A component of ADHD is intrusiveness, not allowing others time to talk. Addicts spend too much time on immediate feedback, unable to evaluate the long-term consequences of their action. They give all their attention to "right now" rather than "later" and right now they want to have more drugs, more food, or more TV. It's interesting to note that some addicts have insufficient anxiety, as noted by Randolph Neese and George Williams, premier Darwinian medicine chroniclers, "either because of genetic tendencies or anti-anxiety drugs…the pathologically non-anxious may be found in emergency rooms, jails and unemployment lines." They fail to become anxious about the consequences of their actions or non-actions, never understanding they will one day "pay the price" for their behavior.

Lung disorders like COPD (chronic obstructive pulmonary disease), emphysema and asthma show a disproportionate amount of time taking air in with failure to spend enough time expelling air. Obsessive Compulsive Disorder (OCD) is an inordinate amount of time doing one task and repeating it over and over. OCDer's might wash their hands or check the stove dozens of times a day, paying too much attention to one stimulus, which severely impacts the amount of time spent in more meaningful pursuits. Parkinson's is the poor timing of mental and motor responses from low dopamine, while schizophrenia is accelerated motor and mental responses from too much dopamine. Heartburn is a failure of the stomach to empty on time, while malabsorption is the stomach emptying too quickly. Diarrhea is too fast; constipation too slow. Speech even has its timing demons with stuttering, cluttering and any number of language rhythm disorders that can severely hamper the comprehension and sociability of communication.

Rodolfo Llinas, a researcher from New York University Medical School, finds that neurological and psychiatric disorders like Parkinson's, OCD, tinnitus, and depression have similar underlying causes. He notes disruptions in the electrical rhythms between two brain regions: the thalamus and the cortex. He explains that, "What we call reality is produced by electrical oscillations between the thalamus and the cortex. If you destroy that, there is no consciousness." Everything that gets inside the brain passes through the thalamus which is linked to the cortex. If anything is damaged between them, altered vibrations occur which vibrates everything else. Problems arise when slow rhythms are produced (low-frequency oscillations) which in turn sets off a high level of activity in the surrounding areas. High activity is what triggers symptoms which vary depending on what part of the brain they occur. Since high activity is the same as consciousness, "you get a conscious event that isn't related to the external world." A person might then experience voices that aren't really there or be depressed about things that don't exist. They might worry about events that might not happen or wash their hands dozens of times when they aren't dirty. Many neurological diseases, he suggests, have the same mechanism of vibrations gone amok but occur in different parts of the brain.

The amount of time we spend doing an activity can have a great bearing on our health. While at work, we may repeat a limited number of movements, at the neglect of other movements. The body might accustom itself to this restricted use and as the skeletal structure adjusts to the restrictions, muscles shorten or lengthen as their attachment sites change. When we change the hip muscles during prolonged sitting, we change the way we breathe as most of the muscles of the respiratory system are connected to the lumbar vertebrae at the bottom and the cervical vertebrae at the top. Breathing then affects the position of the spine just as the position of the spine will affect the quality of breathing.

Our hip girdle is designed to rotate in the opposite direction of our shoulder girdle, as seen in the way we throw with one arm forward and the opposite leg forward. This is different than in our cousin the chimp, who has to throw underhand as they cannot use hip rotation to accelerate the torso during the arm swing. One way to determine if you are losing hip rotation is to test if you can throw overhand like any limber human being. If you are lacking a ball to throw at this very moment, see if you can reach back with your right hand and rest it on your right shoulder. Lacking external rotation of the shoulder? Then you are probably lacking hip rotation as well.

Our hip socket is designed to work in a large arc of motion, which can be experienced when we squat. Seated in a chair, we use the socket in a flexed position at a ninety-degree angle to our hip. Once we stand to walk, we again use the head of the femur in a forward and backward arc, never or rarely to the side. This allows a wearing down in a limited arc of movement, increasing the propensity for hip fracture. Other cultures that squat wear the hip down in a huge arc and as we have noted, rarely if ever require hip replacement. By using the hip more, one wears it out less. Self-supported sitting (squat, cross-legged, on a stool or simply at the edge of the chair) frees the body and the mind from even a subtle dependence on outside objects. The body can do something as simple as sitting on its own.

Hip fractures are epidemic in cultures that spend inordinate amounts of time sitting in chairs. Yet, to correct poor bone density we are instructed to "spend more time" drinking milk or take calcium pills. In a massive twelve-year study ending in 1997, The Harvard Nurses' Health Study followed 78,000 nurses and recorded their milk drinking habits and subsequent hip fracture rate. The nurses who drank the most milk, over two glasses a day, broke more bones than any other group with 1.05 times the risk of arm fractures, and 1.45 times the risk of hip fractures. China has one-fifth the hip fractures of Western nations and a lower rate of calcium consumption. So what is at work here?

The Physicians Committee for Responsible Medicine found that it is not that we consume too little calcium; it's that we consume too much protein. To metabolize excessive protein, the body takes calcium from the bones, and in that way, milk negates itself. It is calcium rich but even more protein rich. The Physicians Committee asked the Federal Trade Commission to investigate the ad campaign "Got Milk," contending that milk may contribute to osteoporosis.

What we eat and how we stand can alter the way calcium sets in the bones. By standing with our feet pointing out like a duck, rather than forward, the bracing power of the femoral head of the leg bone is lost. The weight is no longer directed through the strong portions of the ilia bone, which increases the spread at the iliac joints. The weight is uneven on the sacroiliac ligaments and the sacroiliac is displaced. There are thirty-six muscles that attach to our pelvis, all requiring the correct amount of force, slack and tension to maintain pain-free posture and provide normal feedback through the tension on the bone. Without the proper feedback, we will change our calcium absorption, our shape and our agility.

This area, then teaches the importance of understanding the body in space and time. Juhan notes that short-term emotional reactions or long-term habits change the degree of tension in muscles. He says "my perceptions of mass, weight, and effort can all be changed merely by increasing my resting tonus, without the slightest amount of actual 'work' being added to my burden." The amount of tension in our muscles will exactly mimic real work and change our notions of the amount of effort it takes to be alive. At our worst, no movement, no work and no effort "to do" is taking place, only the effort to exist is. Effort then becomes what we feel, not what we do.

It is the hips that will propel us forward, unhinging the legs to take their precarious steps into the future. Stability is the link to mobility. Being sure of what you stand for, finding the creativity to move forward, knowing your work has meaning and having a spiritual quest is something the body can "sink its teeth into." Once properly fueled, we will find our forward energy.

HOW TO EVOKE CREATIVITY

○ This area of the body is considered the second energy center, called Svadhisthana Chakra. Key words are creativity, mobility and fluidity. It houses the most creative powers in the body embodied by our sexual organs. It is here we are subject to Hatha energy where *ha*, the active solar force and *tha*, the inactive lunar force, are brought together. We realize the power to move around obstacles and leave addictions behind which is embodied here as the "out-breath." The quadratus lumborum, so important to the health of this area of the body, functions for forced exhalation and the release of what we no longer need. Our bowels and bladder eliminate what was not used. This area is symbolized by water, especially dark water where things lose their differentiation. It is defined by taste; what we can accept into our insides from the outside. And it is mindful of dreams and fantasies, which are indicative of a creative and flexible mind. It is a place where genius is born. If one is inactive in this energy center, one might be reclusive, never letting their dreams see the light of day. If energy is poor here, one might constantly weigh what is owed them and feel as if living takes too much effort. Life itself weighs too much. Restore energy here by allowing a prolonged exhale of breath. Let it go. Life's not so heavy that you can't let go of all that you hold inside you. Create, recycle and develop. Take your dreams out for a walk.

O   Our goal should be to connect our deepest aspirations with our personalities and with the performance of our bodies. Become a competent authority. Be able to make decisions with a reputation for doing the right thing at the right time. Taking risks defines our national character and choosing to live with authority is the biggest risk of all.

❖   If we fail to live according to our society's version of success, we are termed lazy, uneducated or under-motivated. If we are sick we are thought to have "bad genes" or "prone to viruses." In a way, thinking that the source of bodily discomforts lies in the make-up of the individual, benefits our society. People then lobby for safety, ergonomics, environmental clean-ups, improved nutritional guidelines or medical research. Groups make a call for action when an individual cannot. We seem to think that if we could fix all the dangers out there, we would be well. But waiting for a group to cure life's ills, takes an individual off the hook. Become your own authority and take stock of the bad memes in your life. What activities take too much of your time and don't give much back? "Score" an activity as meaningful, useful or restorative and if it is none of those, think about eliminating it.

❖   Time is the basic currency of life, not money or objects or job titles. If time feels like the enemy, we probably aren't making choices about how to spend it wisely. The way we spend our time should reflect our values. Our actions should reveal who we are. What is it you "pay" attention to? How do you "spend" your time? Remember, you can't put time and attention into a bank account to use later. Spend it wisely now. Workaholics might think they are going to buy their life back after retirement, but they are often wrong. Hospitals are full of people who waited to live and now will live with the effects of a stroke, heart attack or cancer. Can you "afford" to be wrong?

❖ Instead of shaping muscles with addiction to exercise in the gym, shape your opinions and your identity with your choices. Get off the treadmill and take a walk outside. Be someone who can choose to walk without it being a matter of plugging in a machine so you can distract yourself with television in order to exercise. We were built to walk. We are the only animals on earth to walk upright and we're the only animals on earth that built a machine to do it for us.

❖ Instead of blaming your genes, or germs, or parents, or your boss, take responsibility. Make choices when you can and do what needs to be done. Sit with your hips squarely on the ground, touching the earth and then sit with who you really are. Once you get up, act instead of blame.

❖ Do not practice prejudicial thought by taking only the familiar path. Cease to pre-judge the unfamiliar and those different than yourself. Become enamored with diversity. Try eating something from a different culture, or put your body in different positions and soon you will feel comfortable in different situations. Become one of the un-addicted.

❖ Heraclitus said, "Nature rests by changing." Nature is not addicted to one version of weather, one kind of tree, or one species of bird. Become variable; grow different feathers than the ones you wore last year, and sing a different song than the birds you usually hang around with.

☙ Practice Yogic breathing as it defeats all attempts to overdo. You cannot take in more air unless there is room for it. If our minds are crammed with thoughts, our behaviors predicted by habit, our organs clogged with toxins and our bodies stiffened from lack of use, there is just no room for anything else. Breathing symbolizes letting go of more than you take in.

☙ Practice the yoga ethic of non-stealing. Do not steal from choice by getting stuck in addictive, familiar behavior. Do not allow your attention to be stolen by the media or meaningless pursuits. Drained of your attention and concentration, the energy you need to reach your goals is stolen.

☙ Practice the yoga ethic of non-violence. We violate the laws of nature when we refuse to act. See yourself sitting on the couch as an act of violence that you do not approve of.

❖ Pavlov found that any novelty will distract an animal from its behavior since it instinctually turns toward interruption. We do this in case the interruption is life threatening, something we absolutely need to attend to. In Western culture, there are far too many interruptions, very few of which are truly worth our attention. This "orienting reflex" seeks novelty, increased complexity, change, and surprise. Once the reflex kicks in, the body prepares itself for emergency action. Choose what deserves your interrupted attention. Eliminate so called "urgent" false alarms like faxes, e-mails, pagers and phones for part or all of a day. See what your attention is truly pulled toward and go there.

- See both sides of the story. Read about yin and yang, polar opposites in Chinese medicine. See your yang body in its muscularity, its need for a stimulating environment, its immunity to harm and its ability to recover quickly as well as its capacity to take in lots of food and activity. Yang bodies are exalted in Western culture. Cultivate your yin body with its yearning for calmness and rest, thriftiness and reflection. If you are a collector and accumulator, or are over-indulgent and protective, you have lifeless yang energy and are focusing on your yin self too much. By accumulating (yin) but lacking any energy (yang), one is inert and frozen. If one is flexible between the two, a rhythmic timing is re-established and work equals the time one rests, and action equals the time spent in reflection.

- Take a sabbatical or alter your career path instead of looking for the next promotion. Read Douglas LaBier's book, *Modern Madness: The Emotional Fallout of Success*.

- Look closely at reward systems you use with your children or how you reward yourself for work. Research in the 1970's found those children who were rewarded with gold stars or candy painted lots of pictures. But the rewards had a curious effect. As soon as they were discontinued, the children painted fewer pictures than children never rewarded and many stopped painting altogether. Artificially reinforcing desired responses could backfire.

- Become fascinated with the evolutionary possibilities of your own body—allow it to evolve and grow. Transform the fear of falling into the joy of flying into the unknown. Sam Keen in *Learning to Fly*, a beautiful metaphoric account of trapeze flying and his journey through life, suggests, "Each day befriend a single fear and the miscellaneous terrors of being human will never join together to form such a morass of vague anxiety that it rules your life from the shadows of the unconscious. We learn to fly not by becoming fearless, but by the daily practice of courage."

- Increase the value you place in ordinary moments. Wonder. Become interested in risk. If you ever concern yourself with the idea of death, wondering if you have the courage to die with grace, wonder if you have the courage to live.

- Choose anew each day instead of falling into a trance or a rut. Goethe says, "To this opinion I am given wholly/And this is wisdom's final say:/Freedom and life belong to that man solely/Who must reconquer them each day."

- Be determined to rid yourself of "inattentional blindness." Be ready to pay attention to what your body is telling you. Listen to your feelings when something doesn't feel right to you. Don't distance yourself from critical thinking when it comes to technology by thinking it's an inevitable force of nature rather than something you've designed and chosen. Read *Information Ecologies: Using Technology with Heart* by Nardi Bonniet and Vicki O'day. Remember that unawareness is the thief of the mind.

❖ With many things, it is not the object itself that is useful, but the empty space it surrounds. A guitar will not make a sound without the hollow belly. A bowl cannot be filled with rice or room filled with people without the empty space. Heed this Rumi poem: Thirty spokes will converge/In the hub of the wheel/ But the use of the cart/Will depend on the part/ of the hub that is void/Cut out windows and doors/in the house as you build; but the use of the house will depend on the space/ in the wall that are void/A clay bowl is molded; but the use of the bowl will depend on the part this is void/Advantage is had from whatever is there; but the usefulness arises from whatever is not/We work with being/but non-being is what we use.

❍ Try Urdhra Bhujangasana: Raised Cobra pose. Once this posture is adopted, you gain a sense of '*atha*,' the auspicious moment of dynamic awareness. It is the energy inherent in the cobra as it decides where and if to strike. Prepare yourself to take action with this posture. You will either strike or move on, but, like a cobra, you will not slither away in fear. Sit in this pose when you need to make a big decision.

❍ Try Pranamasana: Pose of Greeting. This posture places you in the position of the first meeting of another person, thought or situation. Every time you walk in a room, greet it. When you meet another person, greet the spirit in them, acknowledging that the meeting will change you. Imagine you are meeting your new self. The potential for creative change is all contained in that one moment of greeting. This posture honors the creation in that pregnant moment.

❍ Try Maha Banda: Great Lock pose. Banda means binding and is the energy bound in the right pathway. This posture forces the energy to move between the second and third chakra and allows organization to turn to actualization. Sit in this pose when you have made a decision and need energy or reassurance.

❍ Virabhadra II pose connects us to an inner courage as we reach toward the divine. It allows time for reflection while remaining grounded; something we should all do after an accomplishment.

❍ Niralambana Paschemottanasana is the unsupported back pose. In this pose, all our weight flows to one focus just as water would flow down the path of least resistance. Journey down one sure path remembering that our journey is always first taken inward.

❧ Imagine the water in you as a river, coming upon a collection of large boulders. You cannot go around and you haven't the strength to go over them. Collect your attention and strength by becoming a deep pool; deep enough to harbor large fish and big ideas; deep enough to offer the reflection of the surrounding trees. Once you have gained reflective energy, you can go around or over the boulders with creative and graceful effort, sure that it is the right thing to do and grateful for the delay.

❧ Visualize the earth in you as narrow paths, just wide enough for one person to travel. Bless the animals that repetitively trod across the soil to make a pathway to guide you to a new landscape that will broaden your view.

❧ Become the air in you that offers a strong breeze to clear the daily fog of meaningless work from your life. With that breeze are inspirations and a community of ideas. Do not allow work to exhaust a narrow portion of yourself. Bring to all you do a broad spirit, and a full breath.

❧ Let the fire in you clear a space for new growth, eliminating frivolous objects and pursuits. Imagine the new landscape rich with nutrients and just warm enough to make something out of nothing.

❖ Our hips and pelvis are the bony structures that attach our vital organs to our legs. We don't leave parts of us behind when we walk, so be fully present in an activity. I once asked a very disabled patient of mine what got her through the day, a day of inexplicable pain and isolation. She said she relishes in getting her hair washed by a caregiver. The hot water, the scalp massage, and the smell of soap brought relief. From that day forward, my morning shower is a fully present activity. I don't think of making children's lunches, or what I'm going to wear, or what time I have to be somewhere. I take a shower.

❖ From early on, we are told which parts of us are allowed in a classroom and which parts are not. We are told not to express the parts of us that are messy or half-baked. It is as if only half of our ecology is welcomed. A farmer knows that planting a single crop is unecological, exposing the entire farm to a single pest, water or weather requirement. Like present-day high tech farmers, we plant one version of success and thus require ever increasingly potent poisons to keep it going. What poisons do you sell yourself to keep parts of you at bay? What would it take to make an equal place for ambition and soul in your workplace?

❖ One of the most powerful forms of labor strikes is called the "obedience strike" wherein workers can bring a factory or business to a near standstill by strictly conforming to all regulations, policies and procedures. The rules we have made for ourselves are undermining and do not represent the way we really work. There is a separation between what we do and what we should do. What rules have you made for yourself that you don't obey? Maybe you need to rewrite your policies.

❖ Join the "greening of religion" movement that is being taken up by many of the world's religious leaders, where saving the resources of the earth is seen as a moral issue. St. Thomas Aquinas, in his 13th century *Summa Theologica,* noted that a deadly sin is "deadly if its commission promotes further committing of the same sin by others." Refuse on moral grounds to be part of an armaments race, or to imbibe in food that is gained by the torturous processing of cattle, pigs, sheep and chickens. Refuse to stand separate from what is happening around you. If you believe that no god is separate from his creation, then believe that you are not separate from what you eat, not separate from how food is grown and not separate from the earth you live on. This is a world with a new order of disease—the dying off of the environment. It will probably take a soulful, religious revolution to cure it.

❖ Poet David Whyte says, "The point is to make an equal place in the psyche for both strategy and soul." Our stable hips connect to our movable legs and tell us to make an equal place in the body for stability and movement, and an equal place for our insides and our outsides. Whyte notes that a mid-life crisis might occur that will feel like the solid ground is giving way beneath our feet. The poet Rilke said it was "as if standing on fishes." Soul searching can bring the ground back under your feet. Search your soul for the place where your strategy for living is attuned to the rest of the earth's resources.

❖ Notice the "greenwashing" of advertisements by companies attempting to sell their products to a population who is longing for environmental responsibility. Greenwashing, like whitewashing, is deceptive. The choice is not going to be whether we buy a "low environmental impact jet ski" versus one that pollutes as much as 17 automobiles for every hour it is ridden. The choice needs to be that we do not buy any jet ski. The lakes can't afford it.

❖ Take responsibility for your injuries and cease to look for the guilty deep pocket. We have created a nation where pain is given monetary value. We have an entire population that finds it illegal and dangerous to be undefended by insurance and lawsuits that sell our self-responsibility to the highest bidder. Gregory Bateson suggests that being uninsured is our new version of being naked and unarmed. When we remove ourselves from responsibility by blaming a third party or buy false security for when we are hurt or injured, we are engaging only in an act of subtraction. We are removing half of the problem and giving it to someone else better equipped to deal with it. Western medicine often fixes half of the problem; the half that is easily explained. It leaves the other half of the problem; the half which is difficult to explain. While emotions, feelings and behaviors are left to the supernatural, the physical body is left to medicine. Imbibe in natural forms of preventative practices—your own version of insurance against illness. Try Yoga, a word that means, "to join" or "yoke together." It takes the fragmented self and makes it whole. It takes the physical and joins it with the spirit of the breath. To join something, the number one criterion involves moving two things closer together. To bring awareness to the body is to bring an energy that links our physical power with our spiritual awakening.

❖ The word "holistic" is listed in the Old English Dictionary as, "The tendency in nature to produce wholes from the ordered grouping of units." Jeffrey Bateson tells us that a holistic understanding of the universe will not be orthodox but a wide and compassionate recognition wherein we can build our nests and find spiritual rest at the same time. "We know enough that the new understanding will be unitary." He shuns the narrow focus on parts. Our genetic predispositions have to be aligned with what we know of culture. We have to look at both nature and nurture at the same time. Our genetic nature is that of hunter-gatherer and aggressive male-dominate societies. But with the unleashing of cultural adaptations, we cannot afford to be guided by our genes any longer. Our cultural memes have to take an about face or we will continue to commit "bad biology." Our genes may be telling us to have as many children as possible to spread our DNA, but now overpopulation is our number one environmental disaster. Our genes may be guiding us toward warfare but our cultural inventions now offer global nuclear annihilation. E. O. Wilson notes, "With primitive genes, our ultimate guides must be our deepest and at present, least understood feelings." He calls for an escape from the sovereignty of genes so that we would base our social organization entirely upon a new cultural ethics.

❖ Jeffrey Schwartz M.D. is a leading authority on Obsessive Compulsive Disorder (OCD) and brain plasticity, the brains ability for life-long learning and remodeling. He teaches OCD patients to remodel the message to relentlessly repeat an activity (such as hand washing, counting, or checking the stove). Depressives can use the same methods to re-route thoughts of hopelessness and Tourettes patients can use them to disconnect motor tics. It involves re-valuing the dysfunctional thought and reassigning a healthier motor response. Instead of responding to the thought to wash the hands, the OCD'er notes that the thought is merely a faulty brain connection. They then think, "Go to the garden" instead of "Wash your hands." If these healthy thoughts fire enough synapses regularly, those connections will take less effort in the future. Schwartz's strategy is born out on PET scans, diagnostic imaging systems that show where activity concentrates in the brain. Instead of firing the orbital frontal cortex and the caudate, the parts of your brain responsible for habitual behaviors, the prefrontal cortex now shows neuronal firing. The prefrontal cortex is where volitional, willful thought occurs. As mental function improves through practice, changes occur in the gating function of the caudate. As one circuit activates, the other unhealthy circuit atrophies with disuse. It is survival of the busiest neuron. Called Self-Directed Neuroplasticity, Schwartz's work shows that the most dysfunctional brain patterns can be altered. Imagine how mindful, thoughtful, and willful behaviors might change your life. The mind, he says, can reclaim the brain.

❖ Alter intrusive thoughts of pain in the same way Schwartz's OCD'ers do. By understanding that after six weeks of any tissue injury, healing is complete, you can re-value pain signals by telling yourself they are just faulty, habitual brain patterns. This could bring about systemic changes in the metabolic activity in the pain circuit. This is exactly what religious fanatics do in the face of ritualized crucifixions or floggings. They re-value the pain into religious ecstasy. Re-value your pain by reading David Butler's book, *Explain Pain.*

❖ Does your past dictate how you behave today? There is a Zen teaching that says, "No seed ever sees the flower." You can have beginnings that can be transformed into someone unrecognizable in the future. Choose to create a new self.

☯ In Buddhist psychology, volition and choice are given a central role in the workings of the cosmos. Until a choice is made, nothing definite happens. Think about where you place your attention. Is it healthy or unhealthy; wise or unwise?

❖ Thomas Merton wrote, "To allow oneself to be carried away by a multitude of conflicting concerns, to surrender to too many demands, to commit oneself to too many projects, to want to help everyone in everything, is to succumb to the violence of our times." If you watch television and complain about the violent programs, think of the war inside you. Fix that war first. Put a peace sign up where you can see it first thing in the morning.

❖ Metaphor is a mental phenomenon that is pivotal to all thought processes—we are always putting two and two together. We compare the difference between things just as metaphor itself takes two complex ideas and sets them side-by-side. They are then equated by juxtaposition. They are yoked together to gain a new understanding of both. Gregory Bateson offers us yet again another clue into understanding our complex world when he looks at language. He suggests that English depends largely on nouns while the biological world communicates around verb patterns and conjunctive relationships. A shark, he says, only knows to relate to the ocean rather than knowing about the ocean or that it is in an ocean. When we describe the hand, we might say it has four fingers and a thumb. Yet the hand is actually only useful when the relationship between the four fingers and the thumb is clearly understood. A rehab therapist might find it prudent to measure the grip and pinch of a hand, the range of motion available in each finger and the prehension patterns afforded after an injury. But if that rehab therapist is lacking the understanding of what it means to have a hand, what the hand has to do with the patient's relationship to their job or their wife or to their version of their future, then much will be missed. A great therapist will be sensitive to metaphor, and to the meanings and relationships behind the injury they treat. By thinking about relationships, we come closer to the way the rest of the biologic world does things.

❖ View other cultures' dances and try them out yourself. Try clogging or flamingo dancing, the hula or stick dancing. Break out of your cultural tendencies and experience new modes of movement.

❖ Remember to stay just as invested in the body when it is well as when it is sick. When your muscles are no longer strong, find strength in your experience or memory. When your memory is no longer dependable, find new experience in music or art. Figure out the lessons in aging, in sickness and in dying. The three heavenly messengers come to us in a sick person, an old man and a corpse.

❖ When faced with the feeling that you are "damned if you do and damned if you don't," always do.

❖ Even in the womb, the fetus practices moving. Embryonic activity keeps joints, tendons and muscles operative. Fetal activity can be seen as the inborn need to practice and emphasizes our capacity and desire to move at very early stages of development.

❖ The number one indicator of childhood obesity is a television set in a child's bedroom. It is as if it is a permission slip from the parents to be sedentary. The television excludes alternative activity regardless of the program. In *The Evolving Self*, the author notes, "The mere act of watching TV has different consequences for the mind from reading or listening to music, and very different from those that follow on more active forms of leisure." As our children get fatter from sedentary activities, their brains are getting sluggish too.

☯ For increased energy, awaken before dawn. Ayurveda theory notes that the first choice you make in the morning can build or break down your resistance to disease. Aligning with nature's rhythms occurs best about twenty minutes before dawn. Vata energy, symbolized by movement, is highest as the sun moves into our view. At that time, you are witness to a special energy. The first item you eat sets the mood for the day. It is your intention about how you will fuel yourself for all the activities you will choose to do. Warm water starts the movement of the GI tract and breakfast should be a gesture of health; light and nourishing. It's the first promise you will keep to your body each day.

❖ Buckminster Fuller said, "If success or failure of this planet and of human beings depended on how I am and what I do, how would I be? What would I do?" Act as if the world depended on you. At least, act as if your body depended on you because it most certainly does.

CHAKRA THREE—CHOICE

THORACIC SPINE, ABDOMEN

"We have more experience of movement and more capacity
for it than of feeling and thought…We know much more about movement than
we do about anger, love, envy or even thought. It is relatively easy to
learn to recognize the quality of movement than the quality
of other factors."—Moshe Feldenkrais

"Embodied courage chooses not to wait until illness
or notice of death demands attention."—Jack Kornfield

"What happens if I try to build a life dedicated to avoiding
all danger and all unnecessary risk?"—Sam Keen

"There is enough for everybody's need but not
for everybody's greed."—Gandhi

In the human body, the thoracic and upper lumbar spine, lying mid-back, function as a point of protection to allow vulnerability. It is where we make a choice—here we either open up, or keep ourselves closed off to new experiences. It is a subtle but important postural distinction. The thoracic spine is the part of the backbone with the most stability, heavily reinforced with overlapping musculature at the back. It protects and houses the sympathetic nervous system ganglia and gut ganglia in the front of the spine, which sends signals to our vulnerable organs. It is the nerve bundles in the upper back that control the stomach, intestines and diaphragm, all organs that lie quite exposed, lacking the protective nest of the ribs. It is also the area where the cosmetic of the body, our upright posture, is either displayed with integrity or deformity.

The thoracic curve is considered a primary curve, curving forward and maintained by the shape of the rib and sternum bones. The lumbar spine is a secondary curve, curving backwards and bolstered more by the balance of muscles and fascia for stability. The dorsal outline of our body is very much like a series of waves, curving forward and back, forward and back. If the t-spine is allowed to exaggerate its forward curvature, it will call on the secondary curve of the lumbar spine to do more work. Work that bones once performed is now offset to muscles and the wave is not only disrupted, it is agitated. As stiff lumbar muscles desperately try to mimic the density of bone, a therapist can labor hours on the low back without improvement when brief attention to the thoracic area would achieve remarkable improvement throughout the spine.

Spiritually, this area represents how we appear to other people and relates to self-respect, the courage to take risks, the ability to generate action and our strength of character. Although each vertebra in the thoracic spine turns and rotates, they do not move forward and back like our cervical or lumbar spine. They offer stability and strength; a jumping off point for the parts of the body that function as movers.

Were we to have wings, they would emerge at the t-spine, which begins at the large bump at the base of the neck. Sam Keen suggests that we all yearn to fly and in fact possess what he calls "the aerial instinct." What defines us as human beings, he says, is the drive to transcend our present condition. To express our aerial instincts, we need to feel strong enough to take a leap of faith, to fly in the face of the unknown, and to live free of the gravitational pull of tradition. At some time in our lives, we all need to choose our own way.

Just as a strong lumbar backbone allows stability for movement, a strong thoracic backbone allows us the personal power to make things happen. A weak t-spine directs our energy toward the ground, hindering our upright energy just as weakened personal energy directs decision-making to someone else. We may weaken our personal power in an effort to gain physical security by choosing poor fitting jobs for the money, while our spirit is crushed by monotony. We may have chosen to live in a frozen tribal phase, having never filled the gap between living with our parents and starting our own family. We might have avoided the move toward our individuality forfeiting relationships with friends, athletic teams, or group leisure activities. Perhaps we filled the gap with solitary activities like watching television or having computer "relationships." Again, the graceful developmental wave of living within total dependence, searching for your individuality, reattachment through mature relationships and finally combining with an idea bigger than yourself, is disrupted.

Psychologists suggest that if you have in fact missed this gap-filling phase, or filled it improperly with artificial relationships, you are ripe for experiencing a mid-life crisis in your forties or fifties. Rehab specialists suggest that if you have failed to find stability in the t-spine, you will loose the mobility of the lumbar spine, experiencing a health and activity crisis in your forties and fifties. If you feel you have chosen relationships or picked occupations that reinforce any of the above trade-offs, you might want to explore and understand this part of the anatomy.

In a body with good range of motion, where each vertebra can twist away from the vertebrae above and below it, the surrounding muscles are supple and moveable, massaging the internal organs with each twist. This is what rehabilitation therapists call, "transitional movement." With every step we take, the pelvis rotates and transitions away from the trunk, one arm and its opposite leg forward. It is the movement we use to transition from lying down to sitting, from sitting to stand, from standing to walking and in walking itself. Every step and every transition massages the internal organs and wrings out each spinal segment with nutritional fluids from the cerebrospinal, lymphatic and circulatory systems.

In a spine with poor range of motion, little lateral twist is available and the pivot is locked at one segment, usually in the t-spine near the area where a bra strap would lie. Once these locked segments become the fulcrum from which we bend, the bulk of our weight then hangs forward from the t-spine rather than from the waist. Should our upright posture be allowed to weaken, we will pivot forward even in standing, usually from this new, dysfunctional fulcrum at the t-spine. With the spine fulcrumed forward, the muscles are now called into action to do the stability job of the dysfunctionally mobile spine. The muscles will act like bones, a job they were never designed nor trained to do.

Stiffened muscles are unable to massage the organs housed in this area, and are no longer even wringing themselves out with movement, which further stiffens them. They are frozen into action, an oxymoron if ever there was one. Poor posture in walking, standing and sitting, if coupled with prolonged postures held for work tasks, can become ingrained in our bodies leading to habitual holding patterns and chronically toxic musculature. As muscles pull on bones, reshaping and shifting can occur, pulling vertebral discs from their center, tensioning nerves, tugging at attachment sites and distorting the bony integrity of our upright posture. Our poor posture can make for painful muscles due to poor circulation, which leads to stiffness, further distorting bony structure and signaling to the brain that the system is under stress.

Additionally, anything that depresses fibroblast activity, the healing mechanism that re-builds micro-traumas incurred during a day's work, interferes with the normal healing of wounds, bruises, infections and micro-tears. Cortisone is just such a depressant and is released along with adrenaline into the bloodstream by the adrenal gland during physical or emotional stress. Cortisone can serve a direct purpose in reducing swelling and removing some discomforting symptoms, but it does little to affect the course of an infection or tear. The side effect of high cortisone in the bloodstream is that it allows a weakening of the connective tissue. The length and pliability of the connective tissue is the decisive factor in creating all the possibilities of movement—those transitional motions that are so important in the twisting and wringing actions that determine health. Connective tissue is the "bed" or "nest" for nerves, lymph and blood vessels and supports them, offering enough room to keep them in their appropriate channels. Stiffen the connective tissue and we might pinch a nerve or reduce lymphatic flow thereby taxing our immune function. Is this the "nest" we want to offer our vital organs? Will they feel and act in a manner that allows us a vitality of life? It's doubtful.

At either end of our body are the neck and the pelvis that twist around and away from the trunk. Like a candy wrapper twisted on either end, our neck and pelvis muscles are allotted great flexibility while holding the trunk together in the middle. The neck muscles will be covered in another chapter and could be considered the most important muscles in the body as they bridge the gap between the head and the heart. The second most important and often dysfunctional muscles lie to the side of the abdomen. The quadratus lumborum are twisting muscles attaching the pelvis to the last rib. If stiff they pull our ribs down, tugging at the thoracic spine. By distorting the thoracic spine and ribs, our organs are further squished, the bones acting more like a prison than a protective nest.

You can feel the quadratus easily, in a posture that appears to be possible in order to allow us easy access to this profound muscle. By placing your hands on your hips, your thumbs will be palpating the quadratus. Press in slightly. There should be no discomfort. If you feel an ache when you push in, your quadratus may be too tight and has lost its hammock-like form. If pulled into a taut band rather than a flexible, slack sling, it pulls on the ribs, which distort the ribs on the opposite side, pulling the other quadratus. Well, now you've really done it! The pain from a tight quadratus shows up as two aching, fist-sized areas near the sacrum, which radiate pain into the buttocks. Your outsides hurt. When your outsides hurt, you might lean to the side or pitch forward with low back pain, leaving sparse and distorted room for the stomach and intestines. Your outsides have affected your insides.

Mid-trunk, another twisting action occurs on a much smaller scale. At the sixth thoracic vertebrae (about the area of the bra strap), the trapezius and latissimus overlap in one thin insertion of the sixth rib. Just under your armpit, these huge muscles balance each other in opposition in this area of common origin. The action of both is steadied in order that the movement of either muscle does not disturb the spine as it redirects weight from the thoracic to the lumbar regions. If either muscle stiffens and is not allowed to glide over the other muscle that shares this insertion, it will carry the other muscle with it, giving the body the look and feel of a robot. This increased tone gives the brain the impression that the body is doing more work, yet as anyone who has a robotic stiffness to them can tell you, you get little real work done. Your body feels like it's been invaded, and the invader is you.

The area in front of the thoracic spine is called the solar plexus, home of the adrenals, stomach, pancreas, intestines, gallbladder and liver, all organs that digest and filter. Their job is to utilize what is good and to rid our body of what is toxic or not needed. They are the decision makers. It is the area that symbolizes choice. When healthy, our solar plexus is our personal and physical power center, providing us with energy and stamina to make personal decisions. The muscles and bones which surround and house these organs, provide protection and space to function as decision makers. When our muscles are held in poor posture, the bones rest on the organs, trapping them and taking up their space. This disallows the flow of fluids and disrupts vital functions. The area can become stagnant, marinating in its own toxins, with organs now struggling for space and consuming vital energy for damage control. They couldn't make a decision unless their life depended on it. And perhaps it does.

Literally, this area is the "body of the body," the trunk from which our extremities exit like branches out into the world. The trunk is the part of the body that remains stable, allowing our legs and arms their greatest mobility. Movement then depends on stillness, mobility depending on stability. Should the thoracic area pivot forward, it is unstable and forces our extremities to work as stabilizers. Hands that should be productive and engaging are recruited to hold the head up while we sit. Arms that should swing with each step we take are held rigid against our sides or in our pockets; the humeral bones in our upper arms acting like second and third spines. Hips and knees that should be bent and mobile are locked, seemingly fearing that the body will topple off the face of the earth.

The "body of the body" dictates the health of the parts and their very availability to perform their own functions. An impaired trunk posture will monopolize the extremities in work they were never meant to perform. The extremities will "talk" to us, whispering their discomfort and then finally shouting for relief. If we could translate the pain signals from arms and legs into words, they would most often be screaming, "Make the trunk do its job. We're dying out here."

This conflict could be called "The Cinderella Syndrome," wherein the small, expressive "Cinderella" muscles of the arms and legs are called on to do all the work that needs to be done to keep a castle in shape. The large, undemonstrative muscles of the trunk, the stepsisters, are allowed to become lazier and lazier, always increasing the work of Cinderella. A therapist who thinks they are of the ilk of a Fairy Godmother or a Prince Charming might work on the Cinderella muscles, strengthening and "rescuing" the arms and legs. A more insightful therapist must step out of the fairy tale and engage the stepsisters in work. This returns vitality to the Cinderella muscles and doesn't rely on magic.

In martial arts, Tai Chi, Yoga, Qigong and other ancient practices, the trunk is where the practitioner centers the self so as not to be moved. The first stance one learns is the stance of stability as it is the place of strength and empowerment that begets all other movement. It is the spot where we decide what will finally move us. It is the place where we decide to respond with movement and action rather than letting our thoughts and emotions grow destructive inside us. It is a place where we have the "internal fortitude" to express moral outrage, the "guts" to be courageous in action, and the intuitive "gut feeling" to act even when reason tells us not to. In the Bible, Jesus is often described by the Greek word "*splanchri-zomai*" meaning, "his guts turned over," when he was so outraged by oppression that he was moved to generosity and compassion. His gut feelings were transformed into action.

The word "body" comes from the Anglo-Saxon word "*bodig*" meaning "a vessel." A "bodig" was a vessel used by alchemists for transmuting elements and gained its name from the body's capacity to change food into energy. Wishing to turn metal into gold, alchemists took stable elements and made them unstable, transforming them into something other than what they once were.

This area, like no other part of the body, is all about our transformative powers, turning food into nourishment and stillness into action. It is the home of our gut reactions, which, when listened to, are a gift telling us what was first in our attention. If energy is low here, we are without a stable sense of self and great peaks and valleys will occur in our energy levels. If energy is too high here, we cannot see ourselves in others and self-worth is too high. Our ego lives on blind ambition and power over others. Illnesses that are over-reactions are heartburn, muscle tension, allergy, obesity and diabetes.

Balanced energy here shows a person who is constantly transforming themselves. They also transform every person they meet and every situation they encounter. Everything is changed by their energy as the mundane is transformed into the extraordinary. This is the area where we can transform our lives. Overwhelming fear can be transformed into small acts of courage just as large bites of food are transformed into micronutrients. Alternately, belittling criticisms can be set aside just as bits of food are left unused, formed into waste products and eliminated. Accumulated bits of intuitive wisdom and gut feelings are the food that nourishes our choices, while sometimes the opinions of experts is left to starve. The Indian leader, Black Elk once said, "I have a good dog fighting a bad dog inside of me." A follower asked, "Which one wins?" Black Elk said, "The one I feed the most."

This is the area where some people "feed the bad dog" and experience anxiety and hypochondria. Hypochondriacs think everything is a threat, all their thoughts are real and every bodily sensation is an illness. Hypo means "under" and "*chondria*" means "ribs." Centuries ago the vague physical complaints were thought to be a disease of the spleen, a small organ below the ribs thought capable of a great variety of illness. But perhaps it is the solar plexus under the ribs where we make little problems bigger than they are, as this is the area of adrenal energy. If this area is always on alert, we are likely to suffer fatigue and burnout. Out of balance, we live on adrenaline allowing the body to become overburdened, literally eating itself up with stress. The adrenals are on overdrive since every stressor looks like an enemy, and these little organs that sit above the kidneys are required to constantly push adrenaline for even benign battles.

"Flight or fight" is a primitive defense mechanism wherein our body switches over to the sympathetic nervous system, the system that reacts to a sudden danger. Should an enemy cross our path, we might take flight and run away or stand our ground and fight it out. It can be an all or nothing response in some people. Instantly, every bodily system is either heightened or inhibited depending on its function. The blood pressure rises, allowing the brain to make lightning quick decisions and shoving blood into the large muscles and away from the hands and feet. Our feet, after all, might be needed to transport us out of harms way and should they get cut, we wouldn't want to bleed to death before we found a safe haven. The blood in our hands is shunted since they may be needed to protect our vulnerable neck, chest and head. At the same time, adrenaline floods into the leg muscles to make them unusually rigid and strong.

Other functions slow down. We certainly don't want to expend vital energy digesting food when our lives are in danger, so our stomach becomes lax, storing most food for later. (When we are calm, the parasympathetic nervous system is in charge and is referred to as "rest and digest" rather than flight and fight.) We might suddenly eliminate any additional weight that would slow us down and experience diarrhea. Our reproductive system may shut down when we are under such stress; our body knowing that it can ill afford procreation when it is faced with immediate extinction. However certain aspects of the fight or flight response were never supported by scientific evidence and sometimes overwhelming threats find us paralyzed with anxiety, resignation and fear. Perhaps a more apt name for the response is fight, flight, or freeze. In other chapters, we will discuss variations of the response with fight, flight, and bite and the research by Dr. Shelley Taylor, wherein she describes "tend and befriend," the stress response of women unable to flee fast enough, or fight well enough.

Unfortunately, our culture has a too rich assortment of so-called emergencies with little to discriminate between danger and no danger. The traffic jam is quickly superseded by the thought that we might be late for work, which is dwarfed by the thought that we just missed a meeting, which pales in comparison to our worries about violence in our children's school. High blood pressure, cold hands and feet, upset stomachs and diarrhea, or conversely in some, constipation and weight gain become the norm rather than a heightened state we use only in emergencies. We become our own worst enemy and may feel as if we are fighting and fleeing from ourselves.

This sympathetic nervous system is made up of nerves that travel to every inch of our body but originate in our thoracic spine. Complicating our already complicated and stressful lifestyles, if the thoracic spine is pivoted forward and held in poor posture, the sympathetic nerve bundles are at a constant stretch, telling them to "wake up." They are facilitated merely by the fact of our poor posture. The parasympathetic nerves, the ones responsible for calm states, good blood flow to our extremities, and proper motility in our stomach and intestines, originate on the stomach side of our lumbar spine. With poor posture, we bend forward, our ribs resting on our organs, which press into the nerve bundles, inhibiting them. It's a viscous cycle leading to a hyper-alert state, an all-systems-go type of living, yet a life, when reflected upon, where one gets very little done. As Mark Twain noted, he worried about hundreds of things in his life, a few of which happened.

Where might this excess energy go if it doesn't translate into function? Who are these worriers, these people who are tired and expending energy on the same thought over and over, living the same burdensome routine day in and day out? They are the opposite of the Type A personality. While a Type A personality happens to fit into our culture's version of success with their hyper-get-ahead activity, gladly overworked dispositions, and devil-may-care impact on others, there is a personality type that cares very much. Who are the uncomplaining, passively cooperative, slumped over ones trying desperately to stuff their emotions, feeling they aren't important enough to stand up for themselves? They are known as Type C personality.

Nicholas Cummings, former President of the American Psychological Association, says "Like energy in physics, the stress caused by emotional conflicts cannot be destroyed, but it can be transformed; and somatizisers translate it into physical symptoms that are easier for them to acknowledge than the psychological issues." Psychologists Lydia Tomoshok and Andrew Kneier at UCSF, coined the term "Type C personalities" and defined them as uncomplaining but resentful, cooperative but passive-aggressive, resistant to negative emotions on the outside but hateful on the inside. While the Type A's are at high risk for heart attack, Type C's are said to be prone to cancer. Their trapped emotions, feelings of unimportance and locked postures that serve to squish and distort their internal organs, leave no space for health. And cancer tumors are the ultimate robbers of space, invading the space held by organs and arteries, pressing on nerves, creating the worst known pain in medical history. Internal, visceral pain.

Might a tumor symbolize growth interrupted? Might Type C's be living lives with little reward, where internal pain symbolizes that their outsides are living a life incompatible with their insides? When we lose our vitality or when growth is misdirected, our cells lose their integrity just as our brain cells wonder at times, "Who am I?" "What is my true purpose?" When we ignore the laws of the universe, we engage in futile attempts to keep things from changing, and we try to "not grow." Cells may become confused, not knowing who they are.

Donald Ingber has theorized on the "rules of assembly" when it comes to nature's patterns. He is an associate professor of pathology at Harvard Medical School and has contributed greatly to the study of tumor angiogenesis, with degrees from Yale University including a B.A., M.A., M.Phil., M.D. and Ph.D. He writes on how mechanical forces are transmitted over specific molecular paths in living cells and how cells sense mechanical stimuli that then regulate tissue development. He notes that a phenomenon called "linear stiffening" results as an applied stress that increases, and then pulls on other parts of a cell. It is that same with a tendon, a crystal, a virus, a human body, it doesn't matter; they are all built with the same architectural feature called "tensegrity." Soon enough, all members of the unit come to lie in the same direction of the applied stress. So stress on the bones, stresses the muscles, which stress the organs, which pull on the tissue, which distort the cell. It is a "global increase in tension" and is balanced by an increase in compression within the structure.

Ingber notes, "changing cytoskeletal geometry and mechanics could affect biochemical reactions and even alter the genes that are activated and thus the proteins that are made." Investigators Rahul Singhvi, George M. Whitesides, and Christopher S. Chen at Harvard, forced cells to take on different shapes, either spherical or flattened and found that by changing their shape (with a tug and a pull), they could switch cells between different genetically driven programs. It is worth quoting Ingber at length:

> "Cells that spread flat became more likely to divide, whereas round cells that were prevented from spreading activated a death program known as apoptosis. When cells were neither too extended nor too retracted, they neither divided nor died. Instead they differentiated themselves in a tissue-specific manner: capillary cells formed hollow capillary tubes; liver cells secreted proteins that the liver normally supplies to the blood; and so on. Thus, mechanical restructuring of the cell and cytoskeleton apparently tells the cell what to do. Very flat cells, with their cytoskeletons stretched, sense that more cells are needed to cover the surrounding substrate—as in wound repair and that cell division is needed. Rounding indicates that too many cells are competing for space on the matrix and that cells are proliferating too much; some

must die to prevent tumor formation. In between these two extremes, normal tissue function is established and maintained."

These conformational changes alter the shape of adjacent proteins, which then trigger a cascade of molecular restructuring inside the cell. "Indeed," Ingber states, "this is how cells sense and respond to changes in their environment. Thus, from the molecules to the bones and muscles and tendons of the human body, tensegrity is clearly nature's preferred building system. Only tensegrity, for example, can explain how every time you move your arm, your skin stretches, your extracellular matrix extends, your cells distort, and the interconnected molecules that form the internal framework of the cell feel the pull all without any breakage or discontinuity."

Tensegrity is the most economical, ecological way to build, and structures with tensegrity were no doubt selected through evolution because of their efficiency in using a minimum of materials with the highest mechanical strength. Tensegrity allows everything to take on different shapes even though they are made the same. It is the very definition of bone, the strongest yet most economical structure on earth.

We've seen what happens when our physical shape gets distorted, but what happens when our sense of self is distorted? The taming of our real self can be likened to domestication. We train our emotions to be docile, thinking and acting like the rest of the herd. In dog breeding, domestication has taken the wolves' pointed ears and flopped them over to inhibit sharpness in hearing. It has taken clear eyes and covered them with a flop of hair. A full-grown Labrador's brain is one-fifth smaller than its wild wolf relative at three months old. To become domesticated is to shut off our senses. There are over fifty million dogs in the United States and less than 10,000 wolves remaining in the world. Freedom and the ability to fully sense our environment is dangerous. Just ask the wolf. Wendell Berry notes, "Cloning, besides being a new method of sheep stealing, is only a pathetic attempt to make sheep predictable."

In an effort to prove his evolutionary theories, Darwin researched dog breeding, finding that man's obsession with similarity led to highly inbred, and subsequently dysfunctional dogs. It is notable today that Chows are almost blind due to the turned in eyelids, Doberman Pinschers suffer narcolepsy due to inbreeding, and Dalmatians are excellent sources for researching epilepsy since it is rampant in their breed. In manipulating and rushing evolutionary change by breeding for certain characteristics, we have eliminated variation and often endorsed weakness in the breeds. Sunny Boy, a Dutch bull that died in 1977, sired two million calves and six other bulls sired another million calves, offering a very limited gene pool for Holland's herds. One finely selected bacterium could find the same host in a majority of the herd, with no one more immune than the next due to inbreeding. Once one gets sick, the others will follow. A wild animal such as a wolf is far less sensitive to genetic mutations than a dog and shows flexibility in gene expression under far greater environmental pressures.

In her article *"Eat Locally,"* Gretel H. Schueller tells us that in the year 2001, only ten to fifteen species of plants and livestock account for 90% of global food production. While there were fifteen breeds of swine in the United States just five years ago, eight are now extinct. Two kinds of peas make up 96% of the United States harvest. We are breeding similarity as fast as we can. As it turns out, not every animal or plant lends itself to domestication and their behavior determines which will be successfully raised and which will not.

In the book *Guns, Germs and Steel*, Jared Diamond offers that plants which evolved bitter seeds were favored in evolution selection as humans and animals ate the sweet fruit and spit out the nasty seed. Indeed, spittoons and compost heaps are thought to be the first agricultural sites as seeds sprouted and offered more fruit. So selection acts oppositely on seeds and fruits; one has the characteristics so it will not be eaten and one has the characteristics favoring that it will be eaten. Human behavior can then reverse such wisdom by breeding seedless grapes and oranges. A melon found in Africa would never lend itself to mass production despite human behavior, as it must pass through an aardwolf gut to germinate. It is immune to our behavior. The strawberry is an example of a fruit that had to wait until humans invented powerful pesticides to become successful as a mass-produced food source. But the benefit of huge, juicy strawberries comes at the cost of ingested poisons, as it is the most chemically treated fruit on earth.

Animals, Diamond notes, must pass the Anna Karenia principle, which requires the avoidance of many separate possible reasons for failure. The Anna Karenia principle says that for a marriage to succeed, it must succeed in many different respects such as physical attraction, agreement on money, child rearing practices and religion or ethics. A domesticated animal must also avoid separate reasons for failure. It must be relatively small. It must not be a carnivore. It must have a fast growth rate. It must breed in captivity. It cannot have a nasty disposition. It cannot have a tendency to panic or trample. And finally, it must have a specific social structure.

Domesticated animals can be insects (bees for honey, silkworms for fiber), but most are larger mammals either at or over one hundred pounds. Only fourteen big animals are domesticated and only five of those are seen throughout cultures around the world—the cow, sheep, goat, pig and horse. Tamed animals differ from domestic animals in that they are usually not bred in captivity and humans do not control the food supply. Cats are tamed but not really domesticated. We (the domesticators) favor size and animals with smaller brains and sense organs.

We do not breed wolves; we change wolves into more docile dogs. As Diamond says, "If a wild animal fails in one small particular, it is destined to wildness."

He notes that no mammalian carnivore has ever been domesticated for food as the conversion of biomass is inefficient and we could very well become its meal. An elephant does not lend itself for food production even though it has the most meat on it because it takes over fifteen years to reach maturity. A cheetah, although perhaps good eating, will not copulate without a long chase and many animals will not copulate in captivity. Zebras and hippos have an "incurably dangerous disposition" as do bears and tigers. Deer and gazelles occur in huge numbers but have the tendency to panic and jump fences so that they have never been domesticated for food in any culture. In short, we do not domesticate animals that move too much. We like slow moving cows, fat, short-legged pigs, and poultry that we can fatten after clipping their wings. In fact, an animal must have three social characteristics to be domesticated: it must herd, have a dominant hierarchy and it must occupy overlapping home ranges rather than exclusive territories. Herd animals, in other words, must tolerate each other to the point of being docile and must sit still. Might humans have all the above features as well?

Computer scientist, Hubert Simon, suggests that humans are socially docile. Human beings are receptive to social influence because it is "cheaper" to do what other people do than to figure it out for yourself. We are designed to watch each other's failures and successes and learn from their mistakes, leaving the risk taking to someone else. A scientist or artist might be a type of human being that is neither domesticated nor docile. A scientist or artist may be defined as someone who wants the accident to happen. They create favorable conditions for the unknown and the unusual to happen and then record it. Seymore Benzer, founder of the field of atomic biology wherein genes determine metabolism, which determines behavior, noted that the key trait to his success was his curiosity. Nobel Prize winners Feynman and Pauling also noted they thrived on curiosity and novelty. They moved toward the unknown.

Novelty seeking is possibly what determines who is happy and who is tamed. In 1996, an Israeli team of researchers noted that those who scored high in novelty seeking had more dopamine receptors. While amphetamines, cocaine, nicotine and alcohol change our mood by altering dopamine levels, those of us with more dopamine receptors don't need artificial additives to feel engaged. With adequate dopamine, the amount of effort required to move toward a goal is not overwhelming.

Aaron Antonovsky, a medical sociologist, studied why some Holocaust survivors did better in the face of severe adversity and he found that a "sense of coherence" was a key factor. Coherence is a fancy word that just means, "life makes sense." There is enough meaning to justify effort and the investment of energy is worth what the problem demands. In other words, they have energy even during severe hardship. Findings showed that people with auto-immune disorders such as rheumatoid arthritis (where the body floods the joints with enzymes usually used only to rid itself of foreign invaders), have a low score on a sense of coherence test, and indeed when the body has determined that it itself is the enemy, effort would not make much sense. Life becomes a burden and our body, a beast of burden.

What makes animals flock and herd? In 1987, computer scientist Craig Reynolds, devised an ingenious study he called "Boids," to figure out the flocking abilities of wild birds. He used a collection of "boids," computer renditions of birds on a screen full of walls and obstacles. Each boid followed three simple rules of behavior for flocking. First, they each maintained a minimum distance from objects, including other boids. Second, they matched their velocities with other boids around them and third, they moved toward the perceived center of the mass. The center then, keeps transforming, as each boid moves in and out and back in again. That is what moves a flock forward or to the side—an individual trying to get to the center. What is fascinating about Reynolds' finding is that none of the rules said, "form a flock." The rules were entirely local referring only to what each individual bird could do in its own vicinity. And they aren't flexible about this rule; they want that center spot and it requires a lot of other birds for there to be a center spot to get to. It is when native flocking is further narrowed by confinement that illness marks the center.

The rise of agriculture is the idea to grow plants in crops rather than seeking out individual plants from which to gather. The domestication of animals is the idea to benefit from herds and flocks. Both, of course, take advantage of the crowd and both triggered the evolution of "crowd diseases." Not only did farmers and ranchers lead a more sedentary lifestyle than a hunter or gatherer, they increased their exposure to diseases by creating towns and cities centered around the farms. The very animals that were easily domesticated harbored the viruses that would plague Europeans. Measles is an adaptation from the rinderpest virus found in cattle, as is tuberculosis and smallpox. The flu finds its way to us from domesticated pigs and ducks.

American Indians, Aztecs, and Inca did not infect European explorers with mass diseases because they did not harbor domestic animals; there were no crowd diseases to give. Instead, those societies died en masse from imported smallpox or tuberculosis. While Mexico had domesticated turkeys, the Andes cultures had llamas and the Indians had dogs, these animals did not carry the diseases of cows and pigs.

And it's not just a matter of genes and immune systems that are not equipped to fight such crowd exposures. Just as our behavior finds expression in raising domesticated animals, our behavior is responsible for the spread of disease from animals. Symptoms are a microbe's way to modify our body and our behavior so we will spread that microbe. We either eat the host (eat pork and spread trichinosis), are bit by the host (mosquitoes, fleas, lice, and flies as they spread malaria, plague, typhus, and sleeping sickness) or have lesions such as herpes or smallpox that infect those we touch. We might cough and sneeze spreading the cold, flu or pertussis, as well as tuberculosis. We might have diarrhea and spread cholera in the water supply. Our behavior spreads disease just as our behavior might ideally spread tolerance. American Indians did not have epidemics because they did not live lifestyles that promoted crowd diseases.

There is no flexibility within the species when our behavior and our habits are considered "less than" our genetic make-up. If anything, our behavior is most likely far more powerful than our genetic make-up. Scientists conduct studies in what is called "x-fostering," wherein a pup with the genetic risk factors for a disease is fostered out to an unrelated mother. When certain rearing behaviors are flexible, the genetic risk vanishes. This uptake in healthy behaviors would then be transmitted by the pup into the next generation, showing the plasticity or flexibility of genes in different environments. Called non-genomic intergenerational transfer of behavior, it simply means we can make each other healthier as a crowd or increase our risks, depending on who we hang around with.

There is a tendency to blame our genes when we get ill or when our body goes out of control. For instance, many of us are overweight, citing that our parents and their parents are overweight. Steve Jones in *Darwin's Ghost* says, "Fat parents have fat children, in the main, not because stoutness is in their genes, but because they feed their off-spring with a diet like their own. Fat people have fat cats, too, but nobody blames that on DNA." John Ratey notes that our interaction with our environment (our lifestyle habits) can influence the severity of a disease activated by our genetic makeup much like avoiding obesity can make diabetes less severe. He says in *A User's Guide to the Brain*, "Genes are over-ruled every time an angry man restrains his temper, a fat man diets, and an alcoholic refuses to take a drink."

Many studies actually show that genes urge us toward more socially harmonious actions rather than self-serving activities like over-eating. Thomas Eisner of Cornell and Edward O. Wilson, the leading authority on ants, used radioactively labeled sugar water to trace the distribution of liquified food through a colony of common black ants (*Formica subsericea*). They found that portions of food brought in by a single worker, reached every other worker in the colony through a regurgitation process within twenty-four hours during "prolonged bouts of reciprocal feeding." Within a week, all colony members were carrying the same amount of radioactive material. What a worker holds in her crop at any one time is the same as what the rest of the colony possesses. The researchers called this "the social stomach" in that when one worker is full or hungry, the colony as a whole is full or hungry and so each individual seeks food that ultimately, they will share. The majority of the 9,500 known species of ants evolved this distribution system.

With a million billion (ten to the fifteenth power) ants in the world, their biomass weighs four times as much as all birds, amphibians, reptiles and mammals *combined* making them the most successful social animals on earth. Social colonies like ants, termites, wasps, and bees make up 80% of the biomass, removing and recycling 90% of the corpses of small animals in the world. Their social organization gives them competitive superiority over solitary insects in a resource rich environment. Wilson notes that the elaborate food sharing in ants reveals no command center but "instead, the activity of an ant colony or beehive is the summation of a vast number of personal decisions by individual ants. When everyone has roughly the same stomach content, individual decisions become similar and a more harmonious form of mass action is possible." While humans are considered successful social animals, we certainly have not gotten close to distributing food in an ecological and fair manner.

Humans have skewed the amount of time and resources spent delivering large amounts and varieties of food to only a few people. It takes ten to fifteen calories of energy to deliver one calorie of food to a United States consumer, according to Gretel H. Schueller in *Eat Locally.* A head of lettuce represents 2,200 calories if it is grown in California but eaten in New York, which is the amount of calories for a full day's amount of food. Food consumed by each person in the United States takes the energy equivalent of 400 gallons of oil a year to produce, process, distribute, and prepare. That is 17% of the *global* energy supply. African and Asian nations use forty gallons per person for all activities (not just eating). "We use ten times the amount just for food" notes David Pimintel, Professor of Agricultural Sciences and Ecology at Cornell. Why do we use so much compared to other nations? We eat 3,800 calories a day—twice as much as the Chinese. And are we making our farmers rich? Not when sixty-five cents of every dollar goes to package, deliver and market food and another thirty cents goes to the fertilizer and pesticide company. The farmer is left with a nickel for every dollar spent on food. A nickel.

Obesity causes 300,000 U.S. deaths a year as noted in the article, "*Obesity Goes Global.*" According to the study, 1.1 billion people worldwide have a body mass greater than twenty-five, which classifies them as obese. Researchers at Worldwatch Institute in Washington D.C., blame the trend on the spread of the sedentary urban lifestyle. Our capacity to over-eat and avoid activity is spreading to other countries with the U.S. taking the lead with 61% obesity, Russia with 54%, UK 51%, Germany 50%, Columbia 41%, Brazil with 36% and China with 15%. To put it simply, we insist on moving food into our mouths as much as possible and we insist on moving our bodies as little as possible.

It is important to remember that for us to be healthy and to live on a healthy earth, we must pay close attention to the real benefits and the real costs of our actions. A California based think tank called Redefining Progress, suggests that governments utilize a GPI (Genuine Progress Indicator) versus GDP (Gross Domestic Product) to determine the true cost of making and moving products. We may gain twenty calories from a head of lettuce but it costs the earth 2200 calories. It doesn't add up and that's just one head of lettuce. It is no small matter when we fail to calculate the role of social inventions and instead focus on scientific breakthroughs. Better nourished people resist getting ill in the first place so the most important intervention for health lies in the success of a farmer, not a physician. Social change in sanitization, purification, and pasteurization lead Sobel and Ornstein to say in *The Healing Brain*, that a decrease in mass deaths was due to "social change led by food handlers and sewage engineers rather than the heroics of doctors." We pay our farmers a nickel for a head of lettuce and our doctors hundreds of dollars per hour to fix us when we are ill from eating fast food. We simply do not understand the cost and benefits of most that we do.

Many of us have come to view the benefit of health as something that happens to us between illnesses. It is unlikely, for instance, that we notice when we don't have a headache unless we experienced one just minutes before. Perhaps feeling well is our right, but certainly, feeling well has the right to be appreciated and is something we should acknowledge every day. In the same way, we shouldn't anesthetize our emotions and illnesses but rather feel them and understand their message. Instead of medicating a cold by drying up the mucous, spraying a sore throat and suppressing the cough and fever, let the symptoms exist. They are telling you to rest, stay home from work and to allow the mucous to carry the virus out of the system, the fever to burn the germs and the cough to clear the lungs. Medications are trapping the germs in and allowing you to go out, a perfect carrier to other people. It's supposed to be the other way around—the germs go out while you stay sequestered so as not to infect anyone else. We need to coordinate our medical therapies with our brain and body's efforts to heal itself.

When we have a narrow perception of difficult things, where even a minor sniffle is seen as so troublesome we should medicate it, we are out of practice when tragedy strikes. We haven't practiced on the little things and we've kept the clock running, meeting every demand without rest. In real tragedy, there is no time and the rhythm of life is stopped. If we aren't used to it and if we haven't practiced stopping and slowing down, we might succumb to the crisis at a time when there is no room for error.

Ray Rosenman and Meyer Friedman coined the term, Type A personality, in 1958 after noting a "coronary-prone behavior pattern." As reported in *The Healing Brain*, not only do Type A's display time urgency, an excessive devotion to work, but more importantly, and what separates them from time-urgent but calmer Type B's, they show a denial of fatigue. They don't rest. Type A's perform quadraphasic activity, doing four things at once and they must do so "against the opposing efforts of other people around them." Their "hurry sickness" does not show up just as aggressive or hostile, they must retain their aggression and hostility long after the event that first prompted the behavior. In other words, they keep in close contact with the situation, persevere longer than Type B's in the face of fatigue and they avoid cooperation or attempts to be calmed down by others. They are not just a busy person; they set themselves apart from their social framework.

Paul Ekman studied extraordinary people and found they excelled in a range of admirable qualities. Extraordinary people exist in every culture or religious tradition and share four attributes that offer a "palpable quality of being." They emanate a sense of goodness, where their personal and public life are transparent (unlike the charismatic who are wonderful publicly but deplorable in their personal life). They are selfless, unconcerned with ego, status or fame and unconcerned with whether their importance is recognized. Their presence is found nourishing and people want to be around them. Finally, they display an amazing power of attention and concentration. Clearly, our social commitment matters. If we show characteristics of domestication, we can succumb to illness startlingly quickly. If we choose to separate, we increase our risk of coronary disease. If we show positive social traits despite adversity, we thrive.

Steven Levine and Jack Kornfield write elegantly on what they call "healing meditation" wherein a deeper healing takes place in the face of illness or adversity. They suggest a folding in of the part of us that is sick, more like a hug than a pull or push away (remember what cells do when their shape is deformed). Instead of sending aversion signals to wounds and illnesses, such as visualizing soldiers attacking cancer cells or saying we hate the back pain, they suggest we bring loving kindness. They note that too often we meet our pain with hate, thereby hating that part of the body. If this injured part feels we hate it, might it be slow to heal? It is thought that cells respond and conform to messages they receive and in *The Healing Brain*, Robert Ornstein and David Sobel offer that words may be scalpels, capable of harming, or healing. Beliefs and resiliency, they cite, are shown to offer a kind of "psychosomatic plasticity" in cell healing. Thoughts can make cells more flexible to stressors.

Yogic viewpoint suggests a unity of polarities versus either/or thinking. When we choose one side of the polarity against the other, we dwell in constant light or constant darkness both of which are deadly. Pleasure vs. pain, gain vs. loss, love vs. hate, fear vs. wish, and dread vs. hope—none of these can be pursued without the other. It takes an enormous amount of energy to push away the denied parts of ourselves. It is thought that whatever aspect of reality we split off from awareness, it will be presented to us in life over and over again. The more energy we use to suppress it, the more powerful it will re-emerge in our lives. If you fear loss, it will happen to you time and time again until you can learn to live in tolerance of that denied part of existence. It takes a certain type of person to live with what they fear, to express emotions they used to stuff inside, or to act when they used to avoid. It also takes a certain type of brain activity.

There is a strong correlation between tolerance or ambiguity and theta wave activity. Theta "wavers" do not suffer from "psychosclerosis," a hardening of attitude. They thrive on the duality and complexity of thought, insolvability, and flexibility. They are the intuitives, the questioners, and the true seekers in the world. They ask "what if" and "I wonder if" and most importantly, they are not deterred when the answers come up other than they expected. They are undeterred by ambiguity and are dominated by theta waves when engaged in a life of creativity and flexibility in thinking. Brain function is essentially movement; neurons connecting and sending messages down pathways much like a walk in the park. Movement is the stuff thinking is made of. As John Ratey reminds us in his *User's Guide*, "only an organism that moves from place to place requires a brain."

Again Sobel and Ornstein orient us when they decipher the subtleties of the Type A personality. While a Type A person who has chronically high blood pressure is simply disconnected from social ties, the one who suffers a heart attack but survives is more hostile and self-involved. It is the Type A who shows an inability to tolerate ambiguity that dies of sudden heart failure. What happens on a physiological level in sudden death is that the sympathetic, flight or fight nervous system kicks in and elevates blood pressure. At nearly the same time, the parasympathetic nervous system turns on and decreases the ability of the heart to provide extra output. If the person remains erect, that is, if they fail to lie down, denying the need to rest, the blood flow to the "flight muscles" in the legs increases. Meanwhile, those same muscles are inhibited by the parasympathetic activity. They don't rest and they don't flee. When both the sympathetic and the parasympathetic nervous system become active, rapidly alternating in their signals, the ambiguity is simply not tolerated and the heart goes into a non-functional spasm or fibrillation. It is working hard but not pumping blood. In this case, even skillful CPR cannot save the patient. The patient is stuck, failing to decide to stay in sympathetic or parasympathetic drive and the result is death. Beta-blockers are offered these types of patients, a drug that works not on the heart but the brain. The frontal lobe and limbic system are responsible for some of the Type A behaviors such as pressured speech, chronic interruption of others, constant activity levels and denial that "anything is wrong." Beta-blockers work on the frontal lobe and limbic system to make them decide between the incompatible messages from the two nervous systems. Thus, the heart no longer receives a signal to speed up from the sympathetics and does not get the message from the parasympathetics to reduce its tone.

Flexibility is not only ideal when it comes to our thinking or our attitude to life's problems, but also in our ability to realize that many of life's problems derive from our inability to align with themes throughout nature. We aren't making good decisions. One of the critical problems the U.S. faces is our over-use and near monopoly on the earth's resources. The U.S. spends more money on trash bags than ninety of the world's two hundred ten countries spend on *everything*, according to the U.N. Environment Program. In his book titled *Affluenza: The All-Consuming Epidemic*, John de Graaf coins a new disease, affluenza, which is a "painful, contagious, socially transmitted condition of overload, debt, anxiety, and waste resulting from the dogged pursuit of more." He notes we live in a country where public storage facilities bring in $12 billion annually, more than the U.S. music industry. More people are declaring bankruptcy in the U.S. than are graduating from college each year. Automobiles kill more people than all the wars in U.S. history. Parents spend seven times the amount of time shopping as playing with their children. Clearly, we stand at a point where we should choose to reject a culture's demands for lifestyles that are so incomprehensibly skewed.

As we look next at wise ways to develop our personal power, we must be alert to avoiding what de Graaf calls, "The Willpower Deficiency Syndrome." We must find the will to behave in a powerful and meaningful manner. Hopefully, we can be more than we are today—taller, prouder, and our lives aligned with what we know to be right. Hopefully we can stand up straight; so straight we can see the forest for the trees.

HOW TO EVOKE CHOICE

❖ We learned that the first chakra is where we listen to the world's vibration with our feet and sacred bone. The second chakra is where we seek union with another to gain strength and the third is where we choose to move into the world. Instead of yielding your strength to others, come into your own, and understand your bigness. Become a spiritual warrior. Stand up for something. A true warrior never thinks there is no way out. A true warrior doesn't blame, or wait for others to act or waste the earth's resources because they are lacking internal fortitude. All the needed resources and power are within.

❖ A hero is not domesticated or docile. A hero is not afraid to take up the search for life's meaning, to listen and see the truth and to call on support when needed.

❖ Practice Tai Chi which locates our power in our center and extends it to our muscles and limbs and finally into our spiritual attitudes. Find the energy in the middle way and become grounded in the body, honoring its capacities to balance greater asymmetries.

❖ Shift away from stories that present a small sense of self. Eliminate the words "I need" or "I want." As Oprah says, "Wanting things just makes you good at wanting." Appreciating what you have shows the universe you understand its gifts.

❖ Discover the treasure in each difficulty. We are a species who can formulate values but then act in opposition to those values. Stick with your ethical self even when it is difficult.

❖ Jared Diamond cites fourteen factors proposed by historians of technology as to why some cultures have receptivity to invention and others do not. Some of them include: long life span so years to accumulate knowledge and individuals can wait for reward; labor scarcity prompts innovation; patent and property laws protect inventors; training or apprentice opportunities; investment opportunities; individual gets to keep rewards; risk taking behavior encouraged; and tolerance of diverse views. If you wish to foster an inventive personality in your children, delay gratification, let them keep rewards, give them credit for good ideas, and encourage them to live life in ways you did not.

❖ Bring an appropriate level of awareness to your activities. Shop only when you need something, and eat when you're hungry. Act like a person of thought and think like a person of action.

❖ Seek intellectual independence. Figure out what occurs to you to question. What facts do you challenge? Thoughts are the food of the brain. Eat well here and you might cease to over-feed the stomach.

❖ Expand your sense of self rather than expanding your girth. Carve out new territory by spreading your generosity, not your waistline. It is thought that once the world's population reaches 10 billion (we are over 6 billion as of October 1999), humans will outweigh the earth we live on. If the entire world consumed at the same rate as the population of the U.S., we would need four more earths to sustain us all. Don't take more than your fair share.

❖ Do you know that an entire ecosystem exists inside you? Andrew Beattie and Paul R. Ehrlich write in *Wild Solutions*, "Our small intestine holds about a million micro-organisms per gram, and our bowels about a billion per gram. In our bodies, therefore, the human cells are outnumbered about ten to one by the creatures that inhabit us." Be a good planet for those microorganisms to live on.

❖ Release past hurts. Holding on to events that happened years ago crowds the inner mind. If you keep bumping into the same old hurts, you create the event anew and soon there is less and less room to move around. Clean up your brain and create space for something new to take its place.

❖ Perhaps you can *feng shui* your insides. Do you have imperfections or habits of moving that require "cures" just like a room requires a mirror if the door enters at the wrong angle? Do you overuse one leg because the other one doesn't work right? Do you stiffen your lumbar spine because your thoracic spine is bending? Avoid the use of "cures" or quick remedies and design your life and body with wisdom and forethought.

❖ The more unnecessary energy we expend on stiff muscles, the more we deplete energy we could use in other activities. One can choose to be over-burdened or not; out of balance or not; every cell seeing life as a struggle or not. Choose wisely. Eliminate any source of irritation that is leading to a heightened muscle tone and perhaps you will eliminate heightened emotional tone.

❖ Explore the education system and balance it with home schooling. Although schools might teach our children to accept, compete, and conform, counterbalance that with questioning, collaboration and invention when they are home.

❖ Medical personnel have long known that a person is made of stories, not cells. That is why they take "your history" and listen to your version of your health story at every appointment. Discover your pattern according to how you tell your story. Are you the workhorse, the victim, the lost soul, the resentful caregiver, the helpless? Irini Rockwell in her book *The Five Wisdom Energies*, classifies stories this way: If you live in perpetual anger, frozen with so much self-hatred that you lash out at others, you live entirely in the *vajra* or hell realm. If you are needy and always expressing "poor me" with your behavior and your actions, you live in the hungry ghost realm or *ratna*. If you desire too much and manipulate others to always get what you want, you are in the human realm, called *padma*. If you are on edge, wary of anyone who might get the best of you, *karma* or the jealous god realm is where you live. If you only relate to what is under your nose, you are living in the animal realm, or *buddha*. If you live in blissful ignorance, you are in another *buddha* realm called god realm. Living a healthy existence finds a portion of each of these energies (*vajra, ratna, padma, karma and buddha*) balanced in one being.

❖ Remember the saying that God gives every bird all the food he'll ever need but he doesn't throw it in the nest. Don't wait for things to happen to you; go out and search for them. You're guaranteed to find all you'll ever need.

❖ Let your desire grow larger than your fear.

❖ Is what you call "thinking" merely a mish-mash of other people's ideas and values bouncing around in your head? Remember these postulates—You have the choice to operate mindfully or mindlessly; You have the choice to give away your personal power by blaming others for your circumstances; If you choose to hold yourself responsible for matters beyond your control, you will fail; If you choose to deny responsibility for matters in your control, you will fail.

❖ In an 1981 interview, Richard Feynman was asked what winning the Nobel Prize meant to him. He said, "I don't see that it makes any point that someone in the Swedish Academy decides that this work is noble enough to receive a prize. I've already got the prize. The prize is the pleasure of finding the thing out, the kick in the discovery." Discover things because you want to. Do work that you are surprised someone pays you to do. Have relationships despite what you might get in return. By not looking to win the Nobel Prize, scientists have.

❧ If you are having trouble appreciating opposites or opposition, visualize that you are in water that presses equally from all sides. Picture that you are a fish, being hugged by something on top, on bottom, on the left and on the right. You are being held by opposing forces and that is what gives you substance.

❖ When faced with problems, our physical body acts as if it owns the problem. It does not recognize that help may be available from our spiritual nature. If the body attempts to relieve the discomfort by itself, it may turn to self-destructive behaviors in the form of alcohol, drugs, or even neglect. There is an extra support system available in our spiritual being; gut instincts that offer solutions, dreams that can practice what is unsafe or unready while awake, and time freed up that was once used in judgmental and ill-formed emotional reactions. Healing can look like a burden when the body thinks it has to take it on by itself. Burdens are carried on our backs. Lift the weight from this area with a sound spiritual practice.

❖ If you are prone to depression, try thoracic breathing (from the chest area). Thoracic breathing slightly heightens anxiety, which can be interpreted by the brain as an excited, engaged, spirited energy. If you are prone to anxiety, try diaphragmatic breathing (from the belly). This heightens the sense of calm stillness, and reflection. Engaging in different types of breathing can be thought of as "facilitated tranquility" where you seek the opposite to gain balance and comfort.

❖ Find the artist in you. Artists are types with such high self-esteem they want to share their self-expression with the world. Phyllis Greenacre conducted studies on children and found that those destined to become artists were children without reliable caregivers. Lacking someone to rely on, they learned early to rely on themselves. Lacking the love of a caregiver, she found they substituted it with a "love affair with the world."

❍ The genius of Yoga is its recognition of the critical role of the body in the development and transformation of character. Get a yoga video from the library and use your body as a teacher for the spirit.

❍ Jathara Parivartanasana: Belly Twisting pose. This posture taps into the profound intelligence of the gut, combining our lower brain (gut) with our upper brain (mind).

❍ Try the Vajrasana yoga pose: the thunderbolt posture. This pose depicts us with a weapon to slay our most potent enemy, the one within. Internal judgments inhibit our potential and we need a mighty weapon to quiet them.

❍ The "hara" in Jathara pose means "belly," the center that is essential to a person's character. This pose offers us our physical center coupled with a balanced character.

❍ Try the Uttanasana pose: the standing forward bend. This posture builds digestive fire, rejuvenates the nervous system and massages the internal organs. "Ut" means 'intense deliberation' in Sanskrit, and this pose makes us confront ingrained resistance by forcing the mind into a very alert state. Gaps are filled in our attention, focusing us on the third chakra. By assuming this posture, one feels the full power of the situation and can overcome the struggle inherent in confrontation. The confrontation you are faced with is with yourself.

❍ Try the Paschimottanasana pose: Back Extension. This increases immune function, eliminates toxins and is a release posture that bathes the internal organs in blood. "Paschima" means "behind" in Sanskrit and in this posture, what is behind is the experience you have already undergone. It is then you can take responsibility for new experiences. It is important not to force yourself into this position like you are forced to conform to others thinking. Stretch slowly, giving yourself time to formulate the position for yourself.

❍ Try the Nataraj II pose. This is the perpetual dance of metabolism, building up and breaking down, making the large into the small and building the small into the large. It symbolizes digestion. Use this posture when you have made small problems appear large or have minimalized large problems to make them appear as if they are small.

○ Try Ardha Buddha Padmasana: the Half Lotus Stretch. Modern living can cause exhaustion and burn-out. If you have lost vitality, this posture will keep energy inside the body.

○ Try Janusirshasana: Head to Knee pose. When we react to everything with our gut, the pain can transfer to the thoracic or lumbar spine. This stretch releases reactions from this area.

○ Try Chakrasana which opens the front of the spine. This drives the fire within to connect to the outside world. The desire to connect awakens the spine by placing it in its opposite curves, showing your body opposite ways to deal with information, stress and old patterns.

○ Ardha Matsyendrasana pose, called Half Lord of the Fishes pose, activates the third chakra, the chakra symbolized by a polished gem. Its element is fire and it increases vitality, fans the flame of self-esteem and burns with the confidence to take risks. The pose itself helps us look in another direction as it twists and polishes the inner gem. Integrating the left and right sides of the body, elevating the right leg helps the colon, liver and gallbladder. With the left leg elevated, the spleen, pancreas and descending colon are invigorated.

❖ The Chinese word *Qigong* holds the seed word "qi" meaning life force. It is represented in the ideogram with three lines at the top meaning "steam or vapor." It is an energy produced when opposites are brought together: water and air, diet and breathing, earth and wind. It is also the character for "rice," the food that brings life force.

☙ Refuse to commit violence against yourself. Eliminate judgments about yourself such as "I'm fat, ugly, skinny, sick etc." We don't allow other people to talk to us like that. Quiet yourself and listen for self-appreciation.

☙ Refuse to steal from others. When you always seek others' counsel instead of your own, you are stealing their identity.

❖ Always leave a little space in your stomach for the movement of energy. If this area is stuffed, energy has no space to move.

❖ We spend 10-15% of our waking life eating or thinking about food. When we are rehabilitating people who have been very sick and sometimes have lost the ability to swallow safely, we use twenty minutes as the guide for functional eating. It takes twenty minutes for a newborn baby to eat a meal and twenty minutes for a 101 year old to eat a meal; it never changes. If we are of the habit to eat three meals a day that would add up to one hour a day.

Energy is wasted when we think about eating or spend more time eating than that hour. It is that simple.

❖ Remember that you can be a bigger version of yourself. Try this experiment to witness a primitive reflex. Dribble ice water down the back along the spine. You will facilitate a profound reflexive piloerection, or what is commonly called goosebumps. It is a now useless (perhaps) throwback reflex from when we were furry, the shivers serving to trap warm air in our fur near the skin, pumping us up to look bigger and more threatening or more capable. It also served to warm us up, allowing us to calm down after danger has passed.

❖ Our myofascial integrity defines our size and contour. It is what you look like to others. In the absence of fat, you see muscle shapes and fascial connections. Muscles and fascia, not bones, hold you together. The bones are held erect by flexible muscles, not the other way around. Don't mix things up. Don't use erect muscles to hold up floppy bones. Determine what shapes your life.

❖ Physical illness challenges the walls between you and your body. Addiction challenges the walls between you and your will. Relationships challenge the walls between you and your heart. These walls should be replaced with boundaries that protect without requiring walling off or withdrawal behind something. We should have the ability to create a distance in any relationship when we need it, but a distance that allows us a deep connection with our values. The distance should build up our resources and allow a graceful reconnection.

❖ Books are transformed into food for the mind and spirit so be careful what you read. Try eliminating the newspaper in the morning and reading something that will inspire you to action rather than drain or paralyze you.

❖ What you see is transformed into food for your inner vision so be careful what you watch. Try eliminating the television and fill your eyes with sights of nature that will inspire you to take care of Mother Earth.

❧ Imagine the water part of you has transformed into a new form called snow. Now cover your past mistakes with a blanket of snow knowing you have learned the lessons of what lies underneath.

❧ Envision the earth in you has erupted with energy and volcanic ash is adding new acreage for you to inhabit.

❧ Seek out the air in you that is loyally transforming oxygen into carbon dioxide, the life source for the trees and plants. In turn, bless the trees for transforming it back into oxygen.

❧ Feel the fire in you that is turning a dull clay pot into a beautifully glazed vessel that will hold nutritious food.

❖ Practice voluntary simplicity, buying carefully and consciously with full attention to the real benefits and the real costs of what you do.

❖ Realize how we have domesticated nature's energy. Scan your house. Reflect on the fact that sinks, toilets and fountains have confined water. See the earth as it is confined by fenced in gardens and potted plants. Notice the domesticated fire in the fireplace, heaters, and stove. Witness that fans, vents, and air conditioners manipulate the air. By domesticated energy, we change its reality by containing it. Bring mindfulness to your use of energy in your home. Realize you are unharnessing a life force when you open a tap for water and you will be unlikely to waste it. Live in the elements as they are rather than changing them. Put a sweater on instead of the heater. A Swiss physician in the time of the Renaissance, Paracelsus, taught that all things are composed of the four elements of air, earth, water and fire. The human soul on its journey through time must inhabit and bring into harmony all the elements of which the cosmos is constructed. Change the climate of your being if you want to change something. Possess energetic possibilities.

❖ Dogs are descendants of wolves. Each dog breed shows an arrested developmental stage of a wolf pup. Wolves play, stalk, chase, pounce, dig, grab, kill, dissect, carry food and practice each stage as it grows to adulthood. Dog breeds are frozen in one of these practice stages. Some breeds stalk or herd, some retrieve, others attack while some cuddle and play. What stage of human development are you frozen in? Dependency and fearfulness? Social and independent? Rebellious or wise? Jealous or compassionate?

❖ Move flexibly between the emotions. Identify emotions you don't use enough and strengthen those emotional muscles. If you are jealous, strengthen your grateful muscles. If selfish, exercise your generosity muscle. If irritable, strengthen the patience in you.

❖ Participate in a creative tension between your ideals and your current reality. Does your current way of life contribute towards your goals? Is there a gap between what you want and what you have? How can you creatively bridge that space between?

❖ When it comes to changing behavior to overcome a bad habit, remember your choices. You can do nothing or you can take control.

❖ Hiatal hernia, the condition that finds your stomach protruding up through the esophageal hiatus (sphincter), is very rare in Third World countries (as is colicky babies). Our over-full stomachs coupled with the way we seat ourselves on a toilet, increases the intra-abdominal pressure. Our diet also contributes to constipation and we strain while defecating. This also increases the pressure, which brings blood flow out of the legs and up to the abdomen resulting in varicose veins. Be aware that your lifestyle changes your body. This one seemingly minor disorder called hiatal hernia, changes your gut, your esophagus, and the veins in your legs. It is just like when we act out in anger: We change our family, the community and ourselves.

❖ When pregnant, many of us say we are "eating for two" and use this as permission to overeat and indulge in junk food. Perhaps we could think we are eating for two with regards to quality of food instead of quantity. Eat for the spiritual growth of two.

❖ Most of us cannot shepherd animals but we can shepherd good ideas. Keep them moving. Gather up your good habits and feed them the best food. Take them to the best watering holes so they grow stronger. Keep the wolves of bad ideas and bad habits at bay.

❖ Just as the first step is the most important of any action, the first bite is the most important of any meal. The first step releases forces that will not stop until you consciously end them. In Buddhist thought, the mouth is a spiritual laboratory where we express gratitude in tasting each morsel. It transforms matter into joy. Nutrition can birth energy, mood, and thoughts and can be used toward good or bad. It is your choice. "Yama" is moral restraint and one of those restraints is moderate eating. To overeat is considered a form of stealing the food that could have gone to someone who needed it.

❖ John Robbins, who wrote *Diet for a Small Planet*, says the fork is the most powerful tool ever placed in our hands. Use the tool wisely. It is one of only a very few tools we allow to touch the inside of our body.

❖ Every day you fail to work toward your dreams, is a day you've allowed fear to conquer you. Susan Everson published a four-year study of 942, middle-aged men in the *Journal of Arteriosclerosis, Thrombosis and Vascular Biology* in 1997. She found that hopelessness was a strong link to hardened arteries. In fact, it is as strong a link as smoking one pack of cigarettes a day. Feeling like a failure and feeling you have an uncertain future leads to a 20% faster progression of hardened arteries, according to the study. When your dreams stand still, so do your arteries.

❖ We fear our feelings because they have the potential to overwhelm us. Do you want to be overwhelmed, knowing you tried? Or would you settle, knowing you never attempted to live the life you wanted?

☯ Buddhism's main aim is to train our abilities to change directions. What if we thought of failure as our teacher? What if we thought of death as being born to a new situation? What if we began to move with integrity and began to think with integrity?

CHAKRA FOUR—LOYALTY

CHEST, DIAPHRAGM, SHOULDERS, HANDS

"The point is to make an equal place in the psyche
for both strategy and soul."—David Whyte

"You can't shake hands with a clenched fist."—Indira Gandhi

"Why do strong arms fatigue themselves with frivolous
dumbbells? To dig a vineyard is worthier exercise for
men."—Marcus Valerius Martialis (40 A.D.–102 A.D.)

Next to the heart muscle, the diaphragm is the most continuously active and thus loyal muscle in the body, moving 20,000 times a day. When healthy, neither the heart nor the diaphragm fatigues for they obey one simple physiologic rule; the rest periods are longer than the work periods. Expiration, or breathing out, is 1.3 to 1.4 times longer than the breathing in of inspiration. While inhalation is an active process requiring muscular effort, exhalation is a longer, passive process occurring when the lungs recoil and rest. Like the circulation of blood, breathing is more about letting go than holding in. It is about moving air, not trapping it. It is about making space and emptying rather than hoarding and stagnating.

Both the mobile pleura of the lung and the diaphragm use points of stability, one at either end of attachment. Imagine the domed shape of the diaphragm as attached from above through the fascial bands of the neck, and below by the pelvis so that they morph into one continuous band. The neck serves as the superior attachment, which can thicken, and fibrose from chronic breathing problems, especially anxiety driven hyperventilation syndromes. Muscles that support and anchor expiration, especially during high demand times such as running, singing, speaking, coughing or sneezing, might just as easily experience excessive torsion from poor breathing habits. The small quadratus lumborum fixes the last rib to the pelvis while pelvic floor muscles serve to attach the pelvis to the spine. Both are hammock or domed shape and anchor the diaphragm from below.

Stability of the breathing muscles allows for the stability of gaseous exchange. It is CO_2, a waste gas, which has the prime role in regulating breathing. One would think that breathing is regulated by a sensitivity in maintaining oxygen, but we have a huge reserve of oxygen in the bloodstream, and exhale 75% of the oxygen we've just inhaled with each breath. This is exactly why we can offer our exhaled breath as the inhaled breath during CPR. Breathing then is the regulator of CO_2, which creates a narrow zone of homeostasis. As Christopher Gilbert notes, the zone is so narrow, it is "bordered on both sides by physiological disaster." An attempt to avoid such disaster evolves into the "misguided regulation" of breathing patterns.

During a normal function such as walking, breathing is rhythmically coordinated with two steps of inhalation, two steps for expiration and two steps of breath holding or rest. In the absence of exertion, our breathing slows with walking using twice the air as sitting. However, if a mental stimulus persists, evidenced by anxiety or worry, excess breathing can also persist even in the absence of physical exertion. As strong emotions continue to cue the respiratory system, a new equilibrium occurs, the body thinking that over-breathing needs to continue. Gilbert suggests, "No action means no surge in CO_2 production, even though the breathing is expecting it." If the perception of activity continues, but inactivity dominates, physiological disruption occurs. The chemical cascade then adds to the feelings of hyper-vigilance as the mismatch between real, and merely anticipated metabolic needs, persists. Thus, increased anxiety would occur with rest, and even while asleep.

As the blood chemistry attempts to return to a rest state, but chronic mental anxiety and thus chronic hyperventilation patterns continue, breathlessness and disrupted thought processes can worsen while sitting, driving a car (which demands high cognitive but low muscular effort), and sleep. A change in breathing toward normal and away from hyperventilation may then "feel closer to suffocation than it would if the person possessed normal bicarbonate buffering capacity," according to Gilbert. With the system set to expect hyperventilation, it is caught by surprise by the more normal breathing. Thus, a person who lives in a high anxiety culture would have the distinct impression that sitting still, resting, enjoying a siesta, or even sleeping, is uncomfortable.

We do not have two breathing systems with one that handles anticipated threats and another that handles real threats. Our breathing system is primed for a motor response with every threat. It likes problems it can run from. But industrialized nations aren't threatened by tiger attacks. We are fearful of heart attacks, which is an internal beast that grabs us as we are running from task to task and problem to problem. There is a promise inherent in the breathing pattern—it will increase its pace when we increase our physical effort. Unfortunately, this can go awry when less and less of our daily existence calls for physical effort. We breach the promise when we demand that the breath keep up with mental effort, future worries, daily anxieties and even daydreams that are never acted on. Our breath is a constant reminder to move toward that which can make our life feel balanced.

Like the lungs, the physiology of the heart embodies so much fascinating and unusual anatomy that it begs to impart quality of life lessons to any who study it. The heart is the last muscle to cease to function, promising to partner with us briefly even after the last breath is taken. It also has an unusual embryologic make-up in that the cells of the heart muscle never participate in what is called apoptosis, or cell death. The cells you are born with are the cells you will die with. While the cells in the lining of the stomach die off and rebuild every few days, most of our body's cells show a slower rate of sloughing off and renewing. Regardless of the rate of change, we are assured that every cell will have experienced apoptosis in seven years; all except the cells of the heart. That is loyalty of a different order. The heart then, promises to stay with us from beginning to end. No other muscle or organ can say the same. It will stay with us even if we are brain dead, even with multi-organ failure, even if every other muscle is paralyzed from the neck down and even when the lovelorn of us say we have a broken heart. It promises to survive as long as we do. It embodies loyalty.

There is an economic feature to loyalty in that once we have made a promise, we have saved time in the future. One well-placed decision precludes the need for minor decisions farther down the road. A promise to lead our life according to a moral purpose can be the gauge we use to weigh all our activities and relationships. Like muscles exerting only a pull to move bones, our life's purpose pulls us forward despite set backs. While the heart promises to survive, living with purpose is our promise to the heart that we will thrive.

The heart and diaphragm honor cycles of rest and work. Cyclic opposites are what Gandhi called "blessed monotony." There is unchangeableness and a loyalty in this pattern. It is a promise that after work, there is rest. The law of opposites is a key feature for both the heart and diaphragm with their two cycles of work and rest, two functions of input and output, and the heart's two chambers along with the diaphragm's partners, the lungs, with its two lobes. While the two sides of the heart are opposite in function, they never work in opposition to each other. They embody yin and yang. Yin, the stable, regenerating, unmoving, and hidden aspect of life is opposed by yang, the changing, circulating, moving, and revealing aspect. Yet all is relative in the life of true opposites.

Just as the moon is yin compared to the sun, yet yang when compared to the earth, the heart is yin to the sternum as it lies hidden underneath, while at the same time, yang to the sternum because the substance of the heart is mobile. Opposites can co-exist in harmony. Yang is a filling quality, with air filling our lungs, food filling our stomachs, blood filling our heart, and thoughts filling our minds. Yin is an empty quality with exhales, digestion, circulation, and rest.

The heart is one of many hollow organs. The bladder, lungs, stomach, intestines, and colon are all hollow, but oftentimes empty. The stomach is empty throughout the night, the intestines always pushing and passing things through, and the bladder and colon have great emptying abilities. The heart, however, is hollow but never empty as if to tell us that it is the hollow spaces that make things the most useful. The hollow of a violin resonates with music; the hollow of a bowl is filled with soup; and the hollow of a room is where our families gather. If there were no hollow space, there would be no room for life to happen. The heart is again yin and yang. It is like other yin organs; hollow. But it is yang like other storage organs, such as the kidney and spleen. It has still moments and yet it squeezes at the next moment; it is yin within the yang and yang within the yin.

In science, fuzzy logic is the admission that all things cannot be divided into true or false. Bart Kosko, the leading "fuzzy philosopher-scientist," notes "fuzzy things have vague boundaries with their opposites, with non-things. The more it resembles its opposite, the more fuzzy it is. In the fuzziest case, the thing equals its opposite." Black and white thinking is called "bivalence" with gray or fuzzy thinking called "multivalent." Bivalence has two options, black or white, true or false. Multivalent has three or more options.

As an example, take the glass half-empty/half-full question. Both answers are true with neither one more true than the other, thus giving it a strange bivalence. But if we were to be measuring a realistic versus optimistic versus a pessimistic answer, the question takes on the flavor of multivalence. Or take the binary system of using 0 and 1 denoting no-object and one object (computers use this system). Kosko suggests that if we have an apple, and take a bite, the object is now different, yet we would still count it as one apple. If the object changed shape, dimension, size, and texture, how could it still keep its same denomination? What if we take ten bites out of it? Still one apple? Say we cut an apple in half. Now we have two halves but one apple. How can we have two and one at the same time? Scientists merely use 0 and 1 because it is easy to denote objects that way, but the system in no way represents the fuzziness of an apple in all its incantations. Kosko says, "Scientists climb the ladder of bivalence, apply true and false to everything and then forget they stand on it." Bivalence trades the accuracy in describing an object for the simplicity in describing it. However, some of the complexity of being an apple is lost.

Interestingly, the Japanese leapt onto the multivalent bandwagon and began making machines that were fuzzy. Fuzziness, it turns out, makes machines smarter. While a U.S. washing machine washed dirty clothes, the Japanese models could "decide" that a load was large or small, filthy or lightly soiled, whites or colors, and adjust the wash cycle accordingly. The Japanese scientists had increased the machine's IQ. By the time the U.S. had its first "Fuzzy Conference" in 1991, Japan had passed the one billion dollar mark in annual sales of fuzzy products. Fuzzy vacuum cleaners, fuzzy television sets and fuzzy cars take in data and fuzzy rules adjust the output. The Japanese patterned their fuzzy logic from the greatest fuzzy logic producer in the world—the human brain. They mimicked how a brain learns, how it recognizes patterns and how it generates a fuzzy rule. DIRO, or "data in, rules out," is how the neural system behaves. The brain doesn't get information in either/or scenarios. The world isn't black or white. It's fuzzy.

While the brain works by categorizing ideas, oftentimes the categories are fuzzy. Where does 'short' stop and 'tall' begin? Is blood pressure healthy at 179, but dangerous at 180? Many situations fall between opposing or fuzzy concepts so that they seem to resemble both sides and we can elevate or deflate a concept at will. Take the concept of mind/body, wherein we often favor the mind by linking it to reason and deflate the body by linking it to base passions. Conversely, we inflate the body by saying someone is on solid footing and deflate the mind by describing someone as having their head in the clouds.

By being aware that our brain uses fuzzy logic as a thought pattern, we can recognize obstacles in a different way. We don't think in linear patterns, but back and forth, or around in circles. The words "discourse" and "conversation" mean just that. Discourse means "to run back and forth" and conversation means "to turn around with." This implies a more cooperative view of reasoning where knowledge is cumulative rather than an exercise in total elimination of one way of thinking for another. Knowledge is not an argument with winners and losers, successes and failures.

There is a Buddhist phrase, "like a lotus amidst fire," which offers the idea that we can flower in different circumstances, even in a situation that seems opposite to our present reality. Existence then can be likened to a weaving with one set of threads running vertical and one running horizontal. It is said that life is "not the warp alone, you need threads going both ways." There is an immaturity, in Buddhist thought, in getting stuck in a single line of thinking. We become enriched and in turn enrich the universe when we understand the varied creativity and complexity of moving in new directions. Goals that are tested through challenges and interrupted with obstacles offer skillful change. To avoid unpleasantries, to stop and start, or to hesitate with every difficult step, is like trying to start a fire by striking two sticks together. Fire will only light when the sticks are rubbed together rhythmically; the rest and the work fluid, not forced.

Studies show that the body has a natural work/rest strategy for developing new motor skills. At Harvard University, researchers taught participants a new motor skill and then tested mastery of the skill 12 hours later. In those 12 hours, one group took no nap, one a 30-minute nap, and one group a 60-minute nap. The hour-long nappers showed a "significantly superior" performance in the motor skill upon re-testing. Researchers speculate that the brain reaches a "saturation point of neural connections," which adversely affects performance as the day unfolds. Naps provide opportunity for the brain to store newly learned information, especially naps taken at 2 p.m. to 3 p.m.—the traditional siesta time.

Sustained work or in the case of the arteries, sustained contraction, decreases function. By squeezing small arteries and capillaries, circulation is reduced and transports less oxygen and glucose. With less food to the muscles, they work harder resulting in tissue exhaustion. If a muscle is unable to shorten and lengthen, that is "work," it cannot assist the arteries in squeezing circulatory blood. This leads to ischemia, wherein the cells that need the most nutrition get the least amount of food. When the muscles are not getting the oxygen they need, they go into aerobic glycosis, using ATP (adenosine triphosphate) to extend their stamina beyond the oxygen delivery rate. It is a costly move that incurs rapid debts. Increased lactic acid and toxins are produced resulting in tender muscles. As the body goes into metabolic debt, the only option available is to decrease the use of those muscles. This results in reduced feedback and support to the vital organs and they fall into eventual disuse as well. Deane Juhan writes, "What we normally regard as our 'vital organs' are, from another point of view, really only visceral support systems for the growth, function, and maintenance of the muscles…The organs respond to the level of activity of the muscles and not usually the other way around." The link between using ATP and lessening function of muscles and organs cannot be underestimated. We have a name once the system has used up all its ATP. It's called "rigor mortis."

Monitoring our breathing can help us identify fixed, maladaptive muscular patterns. Thoracic breathing, breaths taken from the middle back, is a sign of fear and worry. In turn, thoracic breathing traps CO_2 in our lungs and creates toxicity, which signals the brain that there is something to fear. In this case, the side effect becomes the only real problem. When we breathe properly, from the abdomen, we experience calm. As emotions stimulate a change in breathing patterns, so might breathing patterns induce an emotional change. Back, throat, or chest breathing it is too shallow and we lock away part of ourselves, retaining a part of the air, a part of our emotions, and a part of creation. This holding in, instead of letting out, is the reverse of a sigh. When we are unable to utilize energy effectively, entropy occurs. Entropy is at work when we are paralyzed by fear, anger, depression, or simply a lack of motivation. The Chinese character for depression shows a heart trapped in a doorway. A refusal to move with boldness and clarity, to hesitate to go fully in or fully out, is to be paralyzed by life's paradoxes. Our shortness of breath may serve as a justification for inaction—the air is trapped and so are we.

The act of respiration is not designed to cool the body, as is sometimes thought. Rather, it is designed to warm it with oxygen, for respiration is combustion, albeit slowly controlled combustion. Fire, on the other hand, is uncontrolled combustion. As Lawrence Krauss notes, "That is why respiration is only for the experts." With combustion, we can convert oxygen into useable energy or we can waste heat. Even at rest, we generate 100 watts of heat on a continual basis according to Krauss in his book, *Atom: An Odyssey from the Big Bang to Life on Earth and Beyond.* The muscle in charge of that combustion is the diaphragm.

The diaphragm, as noted earlier, is a huge dome-shaped muscle that separates our chest cavity from our abdomen attaching at the sternum, high in our chest, to our ribs and then to our lumbar spine. It is penetrated by the aorta, vena cave and esophagus; all vital tubes that supply nutrition to the rest of the body.

In deep inspiration, all parts of the diaphragm move, aiding venous circulation. The increased action of all the basic muscles that help breathing, are aides to the heart. The quadratus lumborum and the iliopsoas, which lies deep in the groin and attach up to T_{12} just behind the diaphragm, are not often thought of as breathing muscles. But their action drains venous blood from fatigued muscles, removing toxins and enabling arterial blood to be easily distributed to the cells. With poor standing or sitting posture, these two muscles cannot work properly.

With a deep breath, the shoulders move back several inches while expiration allows them to move forward. If your shoulders are stiff, they retard the movement needed for breathing, making it more difficult on the lungs and heart. It is important to note that respiratory demand takes precedence over postural activity. Our postural muscles, the ones that hold us upright, will be recruited for breathing at the expense of their true jobs if our breathing muscles are unable to do their job properly. When that occurs, it is as if everyone is working out of their job description and the system becomes more and more inefficient.

Inhaling requires elevation of the sternum, which rotates the ribs around the spinal attachments, spreading the lower ribs. The ribs must be free to move away from the spine to allow the diaphragm to expand the abdomen and lower rib cage. Hyperinflation of the lungs puts the diaphragm at a huge disadvantage, causing it to pull the ribs rather than lifting them up and out. A key point for all body workers is where the trapezius, a large muscle complex and the latissimus, another large muscle that lays along the ribs to the underarm, overlap. At one thin originating site on the sixth rib, a tiny bit of these massive muscles meet and balance each other so that the action of both is steadied. This is the most important area of redirection of weight from the thoracic to lumbar regions. It is where our lower body shakes hands with our upper body. Should this area be stiff, with neither muscle able to slide and glide away from each other, they will pull. Not only does this pulling leave the spine vulnerable to pain from any rotating motions, but the ribs will also cease to rotate. And when the ribs are unable to help with postural control, they will be used for respiration. They have to make a choice. The tiny muscles that would normally rotate the spine are too stiff to do so, and the muscles between our ribs just refuse to do so; they've got to help with breathing. This makes for a tight, robotic posture and shallow breathing.

This area is the heart and soul of a manual therapist's work as they try to release energy bound in tight muscles and return each muscle to its proper function. Wilhelm Reich, a student of Freud, likened the binding to armor. He claimed that the physical expression of our muscles converted into psychic energy. Our failure to breathe properly, for instance, grew from resisting our instincts to live a full life. Diagnosis was made by examining a patient's talking patterns, gait, facial expressions, and even the way they smiled. Our facial muscles, after all, are the most adept muscles in expressing our emotions. You can't know that I'm happy or sad by looking at my knee, but you might be able to see it on my face. That is, unless I am restricting that expression because I don't wish to show anyone how I feel.

Another method employed by the body to shield itself is restricted breathing. For reasons it only knows, the body will not let enough air in or conversely, hold onto the air too long, failing to let enough out. It is much like the differences between three people who hear a joke: one will laugh appropriately, one not at all, and one too loud. And laughter could be just what the doctor ordered. Reich worked with deep sighs, laughter, sobs, and deep breaths, all in an attempt to release the armor. Alexander Lowen, a student of Reich's, proposed that the modern world betrayed the body and he developed a method of bodywork called "Bioenergetics." As its basis, bioenergetics touted freedom of respiration. He found that a high-pitched voice was used to block a deep sadness and occurred in people with asthma. A low-pitched voice was an effort to fend off a scream due to excessive fear. Breathing techniques were critical to his work in releasing these guarded emotions.

Leon Chaitow, in *Palpation Skills*, notes that pain syndromes often have a breathing disorder as a component and lists the connection between breathing and muscle pain. A person reacts to stress by breathing in shallow patterns using chest muscles. The habit carries to times even when not stressed and erodes into times of sleep. Headache and muscle pain occur due to interference with circulation as chest muscles are overworked, leading to pain. When excess CO_2 is exhaled, blood becomes too alkaline, leading to vasoconstriction, which causes a feeling of apprehension. The breathing pattern worsens and alkalization leads to increasingly sensitive nerve endings until pain can occur even during tasks, which were once pain free. Overused muscles (once postural but now used for breathing) retain acid wastes becoming stiff and fatigue easily as they are used for non-productive energy even during sleep. Spinal joints stiffen as they fail to move properly during breathing. The person seeks more rest and less movement. Normal breathing muscles stiffen due to under use, forcing even greater work by the accessory and postural muscles and daytime and nighttime comfort are severely and habitually compromised. Finally, sleep deprivation then brings about mood and cognitive changes. This quickly becomes a case of physiology overwhelming psychology. By the time shallow breathers are seen in clinics, it may appear that the psychology is overwhelming the physiology and such patients are labeled psychosomatic, a label that brings about such anger in patients, it no doubt triggers breathing problems of its own.

Fear and anger can produce a suffocating, paralyzing reaction in the lungs. As is sometimes said, fear is just excitement without the breath. With no oxygen, the circulatory system is stilled, waiting for nourishment. The heart becomes weakened from extra work. Each muscle hungers for warming blood and without it, knots form and blood is further prevented from flowing freely (ischemia). Imagine that knots in the muscles are areas where energy is stagnate, fearing to move, and waiting for something to lead the way. When a bodyworker releases taut muscles and tight bands that are ischemic, a great release of tension occurs. A bodyworker can release the knots, encouraging blood flow and directing energy much like a leader who gets fear out of the way so people can perform. Redirecting the hearts energy is likened to eliciting courage enough to act and in fact, the word courage means "big heart" in Latin.

It is interesting to note that when the body requires great feats of strength and stability, we stop breathing all together. Called the Valsalva maneuver, the diaphragm can be called upon to provide postural stability rather than respiratory flexibility. There is a loss of respiratory function as we neither inhale nor exhale and the abdominal muscles actually force air out of the cavity as the diaphragm supports the spine. The tennis player's grunt, the shout in judo and karate, the yell in weightlifting, and the yelp in ski jumping, all rid the abdominal cavity of the variable breath in exchange for postural stability. When we hold our breath out of habit, we recruit breathing muscles for postural jobs.

Misuse of this stabilizing feature occurs in one motor activity in particular—toe-walking. As we rise on our toes, the diaphragm contracts. Studies show that 75% of pre-school children with unexplained (idiopathic) toe walking have significant delays in their speech and language development. In this case, a motor dysfunction becomes a marker for cognitive problems. As the motor patterns of the feet influence the diaphragm, inhibiting breathing, they just might link to cognitive problems down the line. To make a play on the old anatomy nursery rhyme—our brain bone's connected to our toe bones.

Breathing is a complex physiological system affecting all physical and mental processes. It is one of the critical links between the mind and body. Studies show that dysregulated breathing plays a critical role in panic disorders, functional cardiac disorders, and chronic pain. Wilhelm, Gevirtz and Roth found that subtle breathing disturbances like shallow breaths and sighing, can contribute to chronic hypocapnia and hyperventilation, which in turn mediates symptoms of pain and feelings of panic. Additionally, some people might experience a heightened sensitivity to CO_2, feeling increased pain and panic as soon as breathing patterns are disrupted by outside stimuli.

Hyperventilation, which is essentially breathing in excess of the metabolic needs and eliminating more carbon dioxide than is produced, rapidly affects all bodily functions. By elevating blood pH and depleting CO_2, symptoms of pain in all smooth and skeletal muscles as well as neural structures are triggered by an increase in sympathetic tone. In other words, poor breathing habits trigger the "flight or fight" response and over-work the adrenal gland. Studies by Gilbert show pain, tension, disturbances in mental arousal, circulatory problems, and cardiovascular function all respond to alterations in breathing patterns.

The shape of our body will also display our altered breathing patterns. In men, a potbelly will emerge as the abdominal wall fails to contract during exhalation. Women will display increased neck and shoulder tension as they raise the entire chest cage, ventilating only the top of the lungs. Remember, inhaling never really contracts muscles but rather stretches them. It is about creating space. When the space cannot be gained from the inside, it will change the space you inhabit on the outside. The shape of your body will change.

Understanding the evolution of the thoracic spine can give us insight into this important area. Animals that do not have control over their breathing can only accentuate respiration to vocalize. They hiss, grunt, growl, purr, chirp, or bark, having inherited a mostly automatic motor system. These expressions or vocalization of their respiratory pattern, indicate their arousal state, whether they be calm and content or threatened and aggressive. Their breathing tells us so. The hiss warns us of how a snake feels. Therefore, vocalizations are one outward manifestation of the integration between emotional and motor arousal.

It has long been thought that humans are able to talk, and animals only able to expel air as a hiss or bark, because our necks are just the right length to allow a larynx. But other animals have such a larynx including some species of deer. Additionally, the ever-increasing theory that man was once aquatic, that is, hunted and gathered food in the water, invades the larynx theory. Those with longer necks survived because they were able to reach below water level with their hands but still able to "keep their head above water." The survival strategy wins out over the language need and a long larynx can be termed necessary but not essential for talking.

Language was then thought to occur due to our enlarged brain, which is able to store more information. Language was needed to tell others where the herds were, or which mushrooms were poisonous, and was a way to encode memories. But again, many animals have memories that surpass ours, with some songbirds able to recall the placement of 30,000 seeds they hid a year ago in 30,000 different hiding places. Most species remember water hole locations, some recall that they should avoid toxic plants, and some monkeys routinely remember where to find medicinal plants when they are ill.

Paleontologists Pat Shipman and Alan Walker from John Hopkins, add to evolutionary insights by suggesting that the size of the upper thoracic spine dates the onset of human language. With an enlarged t-spine, an increase in the number of motor neurons ascending into this area, and an increase in descending connections from the brain terminating here, allowed a shift to cortical control over breathing. In other words, when this segment of the spinal cord became larger, we could hold our breath. If we can hold our breath, we can articulate. And if we can hold our breath and move our legs, we can walk and talk at the same time. While birds and fish are far more efficient breathers than humans, exhaling and inhaling at the exact same time, they cannot hold their breath. Diving birds merely utilize a prolonged exhale.

Research in breathing control in rabbits and dogs (and in most mammals aside from humans), shows that their diaphragm is inextricably connected to their hind legs. When tested on a treadmill, each kick of the legs causes most mammals to take a breath. Not only are they unable to articulate a language, they cannot disconnect their legs from their breathing. Disarticulating one part of the body from another is essential in the health of the human. We need to slide and glide.

Through its entire length, the aorta lies directly on the rounded bodies of the spinal column's segments. A stiff spine would therefore fail to take advantage of the elastic, stretching capabilities of the aorta and it too would soon stiffen. Keeping the spine moving well gives this king of all arteries a good home. Any artery is a triple layered tube, one of the layers being smooth muscle controlled by the autonomic nervous system. It is the smooth muscle that contracts during habitual stress reactions and as such, can lead to chest muscle pain which might mimic or contribute to angina.

Angina is the condition of chest or heart pain that may precede a heart attack. Its signs are crushing chest pain, shortness of breath, and radiating pain to the jaw, upper back or left arm. Angina is a Latin word from "angh," meaning "to choke" and is where we get the words anxiety, angst, anger, ache, and anguish. Pain radiates to other parts of the body since nerves carrying sensation from the diaphragm originate in the same segments of the spinal cord as those of the tip of the left shoulder and jaw. Oftentimes, just prior to feeling chest pain and shortness of breath, our left shoulder hurts. Pain from the heart is referred to the left shoulder. Many believe referred pain is the first line of study in diagnosing. It can lead you back to the source of illness, and in this case, might lead you back to the heart and its oxygen supplier, the diaphragm.

The flexibility and health of the arterial system is in direct relationship to the health of our musculoskeletal system. The first layer of health is the skin, the second the muscles and bones, while the third is the circulatory system. One lies on top of the other. The carotids are the two arteries carrying blood to our brain with the word coming from the Greek "karotikos" literally meaning 'stupefying carotids' because of the state we are in when they are squeezed. When the head is held forward off our supportive spine, our neck muscles fatigue trying to do the work of the spine and we usually then tip our head back to shorten and relieve those tiny muscles, thus overstretching the carotids.

Carotid dissections occur far more frequently than most medical personnel realize. This is where one of the three layers of the artery splits from excessive pull, allowing blood to flow between the layers. To repair the artery, the blood quickly clots producing scabs which can themselves break away and travel to the brain, causing stroke. Increasingly, studies are showing the risk for such strokes a few days after visiting the hairdresser, who might lay the head back into a sink and slightly bounce it back and forth during hair washing. This is enough to dissect the artery in some people.

Postural dysfunction can lead to traction of our arteries, according to Chaitow, as he describes changes found in association with diaphragmatic inefficiency. As breathing restrictions develop, drag on the fascia supporting the heart displaces the organ and places traction on the aorta. Nerves to the heart are mechanically stressed and venous flow is reduced below the diaphragm, leading to varicose veins and hemorrhoids. As the stomach becomes depressed and tilted, the esophagus is stretched along with the coeliac artery, promoting hiatal hernia. This goes on and on, influencing the health and arterial flow to the pancreas, kidneys, liver and reproductive organs. Bodyworkers should note that by working on flexibility in muscle attachments and range of motion, they are influencing health on many levels.

Our muscles, like our organs, require their own space in order to perform in an optimal manner. When healthy, they glide across each other even though they might attach at different angles or on different bony structures than their neighbor. For instance, the pectoralis minor and pectoralis major enjoy the same home across our chest but attach at very different angles on the shoulder and sternum.

When they become stiff and shortened from repetitively forward posture, they fail to glide over each other. As they lose their elasticity and are deprived of blood, they experience a further loss of pliability. The pectoralis are the muscles that radiate pain from angina attacks and are the muscles that house and protect our heart, giving it enough room to bring in and pump massive volumes of blood every day. If the pecs are shortened and stiff, imagine the house you are leaving your heart. Additionally, the pecs pull against each other when stiff. When the pec minor is fired in order to do its primary job of moving the scapula, it might pull on the pec major, whose job is to move the arm or the clavicle. When the bones are all pulled and rotated at the same time, they are forced one upon the other, leaving little room for movement. Movement requires space. You can't move unless there is somewhere to go.

The trapezius, rhomboid and levator muscles all serve to keep our shoulders back, allowing our pecs to be long, space enhancing muscles. Should the traps, rhomboids and levators lose elasticity, the shoulder cannot rotate. This leaves the shoulder only one option, to shrug upwards and forwards. Ever wonder why your shoulders are up to your ears after a long, stressful day? Wonder why you can't take a deep breath? Your traps, rhomboids and levator might be too stiff and fatigued to continue to stabilize the scapula. Your arms cannot move freely and they fatigue which then recruits the pecs to stabilize and shorten. Concurrently, they are not allowing proper space for the heart and lungs. Our muscles are not occupying their given space, which compresses joint space and severely hampers the potential movement available to our arms. If our shoulder is not able to meet and move in its full potential, what does that say of the possibility of reaching our full potential in other aspects of our life?

Many of us are unwilling to occupy all of our potential space. We fail to use our full chest, the full potential of our rib cage or the great and incredibly unique range of our shoulder. We shorten the body, curve the spine and fold our arms in front of us. We cannot freely use the arms without opening the armpit, yet many emotional states use protective gestures of tightening the arms down to the ribs or across the chest. Emotions are further repressed or exaggerated by our physical guarding. The arm folding of disgust or boredom, and the passive and tired gesture of the hands in the pockets, serve to monopolize our arms into non-productive inactivity.

The word "emotion" has its root in the Latin "*motere*" meaning "to move" and the prefix "*e*" meaning "away". We must remember there is a tendency to act in every emotion. The ancients, thinking that blood followed or moved with the emotions, thought anger moved blood to the hands, allowing us to firmly grasp a weapon. If afraid, blood moved to our legs to allow us to run. Surprise brought increased energy and blood to the eyes, opening them to increase light to the retina, and lifting the eyebrow to see more, all in an effort to increase information coming in about the unexpected event that faced us. Sadness decreased the circulation throughout the body, keeping us inside, unable to move. This kept us from straying too far from home when vulnerable and while our immune system was unable to protect us from germs. These ancient thinkers were almost right on the mark in describing the work of our sympathetic nervous system during flight or fight reactions.

The shoulders are the area where we initiate contact with our environment, our emotions translating into action. We reach out for what we want, and push away what we don't want. We remove obstacles, carry objects for use to another place or another time, and make products that provide us nourishment and comfort. They are the part of us that hug, caress, fight, and feed. Drawn up, they hide and protect our head. Held back, we suppress striking out. Crossing our arms, our body narrows, and energy is depleted leaving no freedom to get things done. We are no longer in charge of reaching for our own destiny. Hanging limp, we wait for things to come to us. Slumped shoulders reduce our breathing as if we dare not live too much.

With each deep breath, we move the shoulders, elongate the spine, and massage the aorta while rocking the pelvis. If we are shallow breathers, the shoulders freeze, the head is locked as if we are deeply hurt or tired and in need of support. We lack a fluid, unburdened personality and have a personality that is symbolically saying it has no wings to fly. Our arms are where we are placed in shackles and our tight shoulders perhaps indicative of our failure to reach for what it rightfully ours; a full life. Comedian George Carlin, in a lengthy piece entitled *The Paradox of Modern Life*," says, "We know how to make a living, but we don't know how to make a life."

Since the shoulder is the most flexible joint in the body, it literally embodies movement. What then, is holding it together? The clavicle or collar bone, has a protective function, keeping the shoulder away from the chest so there is no interference with the respiratory, circulatory, or nervous systems in that area. The arm is removed from the spine with no less than five articulations: glenoid, acromium, clavicular sternal, first rib and sternum, and first rib and its vertebrae. The direction of the clavicle as it joins the sternum, transmits any shock that passes the first three barriers, and passes it to the length of the sternum where it can be shared by all ten pairs of ribs. This little thought of bone, the clavicle, is only brought to our attention under disagreeable circumstances, like most parts of our bodies. And like all other bones in our body, it is an important point of leverage where the skeleton is made to do things in a certain way.

The shoulder girdle is the most complex joint in the human body due to its near total reliance on muscles to hold the arm in its socket. Other joints, like the elbow and knee, are hinge joints and have bony protuberances that fit one into the other. The shoulder thrives on complexity because it moves in more planes than any other joint. It is not merely a hinge like the elbow or knee. It is not a saddle joint like the thumb. Most joints have two movements: flexion and extension; bent or straight. The shoulder flexes, extends, internally rotates, externally rotates, horizontally rotates, abducts, adducts, depresses, elevates, retracts, protracts, anteriorly deviates, posteriorly deviates and circumducts. It is capable of many, many relationships.

The shoulder shares the look of its musculature with one other part of the body. It is neither the hip nor the hand. It is the eye. If you were to take a picture of the muscles surrounding and attaching to the head of the humerus and take a blown up picture of the muscles surrounding the ball of the eye so that they appeared as the same size, many medical professionals would be hard pressed to tell which is which. Thus, we have hand/eye coordination where the shoulder can place the hand anywhere the eyes see. The shoulder and the eye share a relationship like no other paired muscles in the entire body.

Nearly every bone in the trunk and head from the pelvis up to the occiput and jaw furnish surfaces for attachments of muscle, which are also attached to some portion of the shoulder apparatus. It is as if we are bony in order to make our arms move. If we are not occupying our hands with meaningful work or opening our hands with compassion, none of our bones will know what to do with themselves.

One of the keys to understanding this part of the body is in fully appreciating the link between the heart and the hands. Carolyn Myss, Ph.D. suggests that this area is where we find a steady and compassionate emotional climate from which to create. Our hands, in other words, are meant to do our heart's work.

The modern-day challenge is to use our hands and arms in compassionate work and avoid the pain and discomfort from prolonged postures required in much of our over-productive business practices. The shoulder girdle should adjust itself to every movement of the arms. Never, in motion or in rest, should it be allowed to sink its weight upon the rib cage. The first and fourth ribs should be easily moveable, the shoulders themselves moving back and forth with every breath we take as our belly expands. But with our reliance on work that involves the manipulation of machines, often while we sit for hours and hours in chairs, our trunk and shoulders are placed in a situation that is in opposition to the health of the body. While a chair may seem comfortable while we are seated in it, after an accumulated forty or so years of sitting, pain will make itself known in our hips, knees, neck, or hands. When we take a chair and place wheels on it, calling it a car, we've usurped walking time, time that could have been spent counteracting the time we sat at work in chairs.

Just as e-mail allows us to act out of accordance with simple manners due to its lack of face-to-face contact with people, computers limit our ability to have a relationship with our own body. Likewise, a car serves as a shield from face-to-face contact and such cocoons promote road rage and behavior one would never display to a person met while walking on the street. Armored away from people, we have only gross social cues to guide our actions and we miss the subtleties of body language, expressions of the face, movement of the body, and conversation to lead us toward understanding each other.

Sitting in a car is the most commonly shared position people in industrial nations place themselves in, yet bears the largest assault on proper body mechanics. In the name of comfort and ease, we sit in a contraption that moves us through space at 50 miles per hour or more, our legs stretched out in front of us, feet pressing on levers for hours at a time, exposed to vibrations and sensory overloads to our ears and eyes that amounts to a type of physical torture for our body. Every time we stoop to enter or exit a car, slosh around in our "bucket" seats and drive when we could have walked, we are not only fouling the air with exhaust, and driving on roads that are eyesores on the face of the earth, but we are dishonoring every rule of proper body mechanics and adversely affecting the way our body performs. Driving defies the one and only job our human body was designed to do; walk. In rehab, patients will tell us they cannot wash the dishes, and cannot work or clean the house due to pain. But just mention the fact that they should quit driving and they will blurt out, "I can't give up driving." They refuse to give up their freedom but are happy to let someone else do work that makes them feel trapped.

We should refuse to let our computer and car be weapons against our own body. We would be in error if we think that we would change our sitting habits "if only we had known." If we find ourselves saying, "But no one ever told me driving or computer work was so bad on my body," remember that our body is constantly telling us this in its own language—pain. Driving and computer work both encourage a posture that our body will silently allow for half an hour before it "starts complaining." When it does complain with discomfort or pain, we usually shift positions a little, seek shoulder rests or foot rests, padded keyboards, a more expensive chair, or other ergonomic solutions. What we should do is listen to our body and stand up, stretch, look across the landscape to ease our eyes, and get off the computer. Our body is right—we shouldn't be sitting longer than thirty minutes without a stretch, never mind hours on end. Our nerves and muscles will pay the price if we don't listen. Carpal Tunnel, Thoracic Outlet Syndrome, neck and shoulder pain, headaches, and backaches aren't cured by surgery, medication, ergonomic interventions, or substantial Worker's Compensation claims. They are cured with movement. Motion is the medicine, or as we say in rehab, "motion is lotion."

Recall the metaphor from the previous chapters of the "Cinderella Syndrome." This is where small, beautifully crafted muscles in the neck, arms and hands are made to do all the work of the large, but out of shape back and shoulder muscles. Cinderella is made to do the work of the lazy, out of shape stepsisters. Eventually, the smaller muscles ask to be rescued, not by a prince like Cinderella, but by illness and total fatigue. If the only way to get off the computer is to become ill, the structures will do just that. If the only way to keep us from getting in and out of a car is to have our "back go out," or our neck get so stiff we can't see behind us to turn, then that's just what will happen. But remember, we've ignored many signs and symptoms before that. We've ignored little twinges of discomfort. We've ignored fidgeting and irritability. We've sat around waiting for a fairy godmother's magic wand instead of getting out of our chair or car and helping ourselves. What we have done is coped and what we should get good at is what can be called "un-coping." We don't need more will power in this instance. We should listen to our bodies because, sometimes, what we need is won't power.

It should be brought to mind that the shoulders are where we carry our burdens. We carry all the worries of what we should do or feel we must persist at, to survive in a complex world. Herculean efforts are brought to work sites everyday as we struggle against awakening too early after staying up too late, and as we try to find meaning in work that is often mundane and has a mask of artificial productivity. We are not blind, many of us, to the fact that we are working hard and getting little done. We find ourselves doing work because we should, not because we are making our lives or the world a better place for all our efforts. When our hands are not doing our heart's work, it's our shoulders that are in the middle of it. It's our shoulders that have to hold it all up and it's the shoulders that will feel the weight of pain. It is also brought to mind that the word "should" is in the word "shoulder."

Remember the shoulders, once tight and held in forward posture, inhibit our breathing. Our shoulders can take our breath away. Diseases often have an emotional component where stress can trigger an exacerbation or attack, and this is especially true when it comes to breathing disorders. Asthma is an illness that is often thought of as an expression of pain from a person being stifled, always told what they should do, and what they could do better. Whether or not this is true, asthma is simply the inability to breathe on your own. If attacks occur when one is in the situation of trying to act independently or when made to march to someone else's drum, or even carry someone else's burdens, a correlation might be made. If such a correlation exists, then therapies can be aligned with the causative factors. While conventional medicine always medicates away from the pain, traditional medicines attempt to treat the source of the pain or impairment. As an adjunct to medication, people with breathing problems might use imagery to open up the muscles of the shoulder, letting loose of all the "shoulds." This gives the lungs a large home to live in and the muscular support they need to take and release deep breaths. Once the shoulders have learned how to stand up for themselves, maybe we could learn to do the same.

What if we were to imagine going into the feared event instead of away from it? What if we were to throw away the thoughts of what we should do and reach down to our depths to listen to what we want to do? A popular visualization for breathing disorders is to imagine descending to the bottom of a lake and picture yourself lying there, unable to take a breath. Feel yourself safe at the bottom, far from panic and then slowly float to the top. Once you have broken through the surface of the water, take a deep breath, as deep as you deserve from having stayed on the bottom for so long. When you try it again, imagine you are diving deep into your heart to discover what it is you want to do, not what you should do.

Yoga positions that stretch the shoulder are, of course, releasing tensions held in the upper back, shoulders, and neck while ensuring full use and range of motion. Normally, we should be able to reach one arm behind our back to touch the bottom tip of our scapula and reach over our shoulder with our other hand touching the top of the scapula. Better yet, our hands should be able to meet in "prayer" behind our back. When you assume these postures, imagine you are stretching the part of your body where wings would grow. As you become more flexible, possibly able to touch your hands together behind your back, imagine you are untying your wings, freeing your shoulders for the next big leap in your life. Allowing our shoulders to hunch forward is a sign of despair and grief, our wings folded in front of us, forgetting how to fly. Yoga postures used with visualizations can teach our body what it feels like to be freed up. Once your shoulders are freed up, your hands are free to do your life's work.

Each hand, when closed into a fist, is nearly the same size as our heart. This is no accident, nor is it a coincidence. As we open and close our hands, they pump blood back to the heart and are two little helpers out on the end of those long arms. Our ankles too have "heart helpers" in a series of valves and muscles that are termed "ankle pumps." As we walk or rock in a rocking chair, these ankle pumps are activated, helping the heart pump blood from the end of our long legs. For each stiff hand or swollen ankle, the heart has one less helper. And it's not just blood that needs pumping. For a person weighing 150 lb., twenty-two pounds of that weight is interstitial lymphatic fluid. When the hand or ankle can't pump, swelling occurs because this fluid gets stuck, the heart unable to do all the work alone. As your hands work or cook or even scratch an itch, remember that your hand is helping your heart pump fluid, offering assistance and rest to the entire circulatory system. When our circulation goes awry, or our hand/ankle functions go awry, both ends of the system suffer.

For instance, once the sympathetic nervous system is activated by something that stresses us, we run on adrenaline. Our blood is shunted to big muscles and to our heart, away from our feet and hands. After all, the body's primitive response is retained in modern biology. Our modern stressors don't require this shunting of blood, but occurs nonetheless and this sustained contracture and vasoconstriction gives us cold hands and feet, and even headaches. If your hands and feet are often cold, or your head aching, you may be in a prolonged stress response. In fact, cold hands might be the first sign your "headed" toward a headache as the system is preparing for battle by vasoconstricting.

Additionally, adrenaline triggers the movement of fat from the body's fat stores into the bloodstream. This increases the blood level of cholesterol which, if unused in fleeing or fighting, may accumulate in plaques. Studies show that coronary prone behaviors display this adrenaline response only when awake which tells us that high cholesterol levels are event dependent. Change your reaction to events and you change your physiology.

Women show a variation of the fight or flight mechanism, as they are neither good fighters nor fast fleers. Shelley Taylor found that women released the hormone oxytocin, which signaled the stress reaction "tend and befriend" rather than releasing adrenaline for fight or flight. When in danger, a woman's strength lies in befriending other women and together, tending to the children. These "gathering together" qualities rely heavily on loyalty, no one fleeing or leaving another behind and this loyalty releases more oxytocin so that behavior and gene expression provide a circular feedback loop. It is not difficult to envision that tending, carrying, huddling, and stroking to calm troubled children holds as a main feature, the function of warm hands and strong, limber shoulders.

One of the ways to allow good circulation to our hands is through posture in the shoulder girdle. Stand up and relax your arms to your sides. Note the position of your thumbs. If your thumbs are touching your hips, your arms are hung improperly from your shoulders and internally rotated, impairing nerve conduction and blood flow to your hands. If your thumbs are pointing forward with your palms touching your hips, your shoulders are properly retracted and open. The palmar side of our hands should remain protected against the body, not exposed to the elements. The knuckle side of our hands is supposed to be exposed, having more ability to register variations in temperature and literally being our messenger to get out of extreme heat or cold.

Our palms and tips of the fingers have more brain representation and sensitivity than our lips, the lips more than our face, and the face more than, a leg. It is the fingers that feel more exquisitely and it is our hands that rub an injured and painful site on our body. By pressing or rubbing a painful area, the brain must pay attention to both inputs at the same time, thus diluting the sensation of both as the second sensation leads to the reduction in perceived severity of the first one. Bodyworkers use this physiological response when pressing on the body as muscle tension yields to finger pressure, the fibers elongating and blood flow becoming unimpeded. Acupressure points, of which there are 365 sites on the body, are given poetic names like Hidden Clarity, Sea of Vitality and Three Mile Point, a spot that if given pressure allows an extra three miles of energy. Rubbing, like massage, releases morphine-like opiates, painkillers made by the body. Rubbing also stimulates the vagus nerve which initiates the release of food-absorption hormones such as insulin and glucagon, giving the body additional energy to escape the pain-causing stimulus if need be.

Pain is only relevant when the body can do something about it, which is why our brain and many of our organs feel little to no pain. We can move a limb away from a painful stimulus and we can rest when our heart hurts but we can't do anything about cancer in the liver or a stroke in the brain. That is why we can have advance disease in many organs, yet never feel a thing. There's nothing we could do about it anyway unless we have invented advanced surgical techniques.

So pain is a gift. If we didn't feel surface pain, our hands wouldn't swat the mosquito away; we wouldn't be annoyed and we wouldn't itch. Without itching, there is no signal to draw white blood cells to kill toxins, and we'd be left subject to infection. We wouldn't remove thorns from our feet, rub a sore muscle to move lactic acid, pick the dirt from our eyes, nose and teeth, or dress ourselves, wipe ourselves, or groom ourselves. If we didn't feel pain, we wouldn't need hands. It is said, "If an oyster had hands, there would be no pearls." When we do use our hands to care for our body, we use them both, as they button, tie, wash, pick, and clean. When we work away from our body, handedness comes into play with one hand dominating over the other.

To allow dexterity, the fingers must remain slim despite a lifetime of movement. Therefore, our fingers have no muscles. Long tendons travel up the arm to muscles located in the forearm, just below the elbow and it is notable that no fewer than 70 muscles contribute to hand movement, whether it be for stability to allow movement, or mobility in and of itself. Whatever we grasp with our hands gives us a smaller world to control, something we can hold onto, and something we can cope with.

Lucy, the most famous primitive human skeleton found, had full brachiation (able to turn her hand palm up and down), a three jaw chuck grasp with the fingers, and full axis of the pelvis and body which indicated that she was the first species found that could pick an object up and throw it. This anatomy allowed the hand to be in new positions, which in turn places an increased burden on the brain to monitor and spatially organize what the hand can do. And the most important function to monitor timing is the quick hold and release of objects.

The new, useful design feature of Lucy, or the species *A. afarensis,* is in the hand. She showed changes in the size and location of joint surfaces especially of the wrist bones closest to the thumb, index, and middle fingers. Great functional advantages exist with a three chuck grasp as it allows us to pick up irregularly shaped objects, manipulate them within our hand, and pound them. This new structure is able to absorb and spread the shock of repeated hard strikes, with the ligaments giving the hand the capacity to survive unharmed during prolonged percussion.

But like most great advantages in human design and function, vulnerability and overuse comes along with the package. The ability to pound and use our fingers in a repetitive manner, coupled with a brain that can decide when and how long to use those fingers, allows for our own will to override physical messages like pain and discomfort. So with the capability of grasping and using objects as tools, is the responsibility to let go. Unfortunately, cultural drivers can confound this "letting go."

We are all familiar with the overuse syndromes inherent in typing for hours on end. With the advent of computers, we can "word process" as fast as we can think. Manual typewriters offered an internal stopgap that prohibited us from typing too fast and from using our hands and arms in one position for any longer than it took to type one line. With a manual machine, a line is typed, slowly so as not to tangle the hammer-like keys and the arm is lifted to do a carriage return. Once we were at the end of the paper, we changed our posture to get another piece, insert it, roll the rollers, and resume typing. Mistakes also allowed rest time while we erased the error. Computer typing offers no in-built rest periods. We're working longer—far longer—than we are resting.

Carpal tunnel syndrome is a condition of repetitive work that doesn't exist in jobs that might even require more force, more vibration, and more hand use. It is the static and repetitive posture without altering hand and arm position that causes symptoms, not the hand use itself. We are meant to move and we can do great amounts of physical work especially in the squatting position. While in a squat, our arms rest on our knees, just above our elbows and our shoulders are relaxed. Working at a desk, our wrists are anchored on the table, leaving our shoulder muscles performing a constant, static strength maneuver. We are more suited to chopping wood or grinding grain for a two-hour stretch than to word process for two hours. It is the rest periods found in reaching for another log, stopping to sharpen the ax, lifting and stacking the wood, wiping a brow, and sipping water that allow injury-free yet forceful and repetitive chopping. The design of a computer keyboard is an example of how technology and productivity has become the centerpiece for our survival strategy in a cultural sense, but a tool gone awry in the biological sense.

The training of professional musicians and athletes are a powerful example of how culture can create and alter biology much the way genes evolve a species. Culture, though, can radically out distance genetic evolution, creating pressures to evolve or improve skills within a lifetime, whereas genes require millions of years to express a biologic change.

Hand surgeon, Dr. Frank R. Wilson notes in his book *The Hand,* that much of his work involves helping injured musicians. A hand used to play the guitar, for instance, utilizes a pick unless one wants to play jazz or classical which then requires playing with the fingernails. Switching to lute playing requires that you play with the fingers without using the nails and involves getting physically closer to the strings. Wilson discusses a lute player who developed tendonitis in his ring finger—what lute players call the "A" finger. To recover, he had to learn to play by avoiding unnecessary distal flexion in the fingers, a costly habit for a driven musician. Wilson notes that such injuries require a "letting go of a certain kind of goal orientation which has always told them to grip and grab everything as hard as they can, to get ahead in their career. It is as if a misguided life metaphor is visited on them in their hand…they have to learn to completely relax between notes, which of course they may never have done before in their lives. Perhaps they have never done that with *any* part of their personality, in anything they do. They move as fast as they can, play as fast as they can, and turn the metronome up a notch arbitrarily, once every day, force-feeding themselves the instrument." This hints also at what slowly escalating productivity standards do in the world of business. Clocks turn everything up a notch.

Wilson notes that a musician might recover when and if they have acquired a particular combination of insights wherein they forsake the goal of winning, of being better than the next fellow, or of making more money, and switch to changing lifelong techniques, habits, and patterns of living and performing. These would serve as good models for Western business as well.

Wilson further explores the culture of musicianship by noting that musical talent is invented and fostered in the brain if the culture offers enough reward and opportunity. A "cultural offering" exists once a piano has been invented. We would not be aware of a "natural ability" or genetic inclination to play a piano if we did not have one. One would not become a virtuoso if the culture did not reward it, if special environments were not created to foster them, and competitions were not developed to raise the bar on performance skills. Without such a culture memeplex for piano playing, perhaps the individual would find genius in another forum so that we might never know if their musical genius existed.

Whatever the cultural demands, the hand has its own wisdom and dictates how music sounds. Interestingly, musical instruments have what is termed "upper-limb requirements." That is, to be played, they depend on arms, hands and fingers that possess a certain range of motion, repetition rate, and force variation to make music at all. Wilson notes "how wide can you make the neck of a guitar? How far apart should the keys be on a piano? Where should the keys be placed on a flute?" The answer is, only as wide as the fingers can encircle the neck and only as far apart as the fingers can spread open.

The nervous system must also reduce the complexity required in the seemingly impossible task of organizing the thirty-nine muscles that exist in one forearm and hand as they play an instrument with the utmost precision and stability. It is thought that the nervous system uses common patterns of movement and that musical compositions are designed to take advantage of postural and cognitive "resting places" for the hand, allowing rest even while the hand is in motion. Grasping synergies exist in our primitive brain, that when called upon use very little cortical organization. Small deviations away from these patterns could account for skilled instrumental play. With the fingers physiologically designed for rapid contraction and relaxation, and ill-equipped for sustained contraction, the design itself offers notation, pauses between notes, and the rhythm that is in and of itself, music.

If the hand can span nearly twelve inches, a composer is unwise to require a chord whose top and bottom notes are further than that in distance. Clarinet music cannot ask the musician to reach the thumb over the third and fifth fingers to depress a key. Wilson notes, "Even if the idea is musically appropriate, the physical limitations of human musicians supervene." The beauty of music then lies in the anatomy of the hand. In other words, our body is the music.

Fascinating brain research shows that our brains think by using music. Neuroscientist Francisco Varela says, "The neurons in the brain oscillate all over the place. Each goes *whoomph* and then *ffhhh*, falling in deflation. The *whoomph* is when different phases in the brain oscillate, and these become harmonized. The phase of these oscillations becomes harmonized in what we call phase-lock. The waves oscillate together in synchrony. You create music. Many patterns of oscillations in the brain spontaneously select each other to create the melody, that is, the moment of experience." Be loyal to the idea of good and meaningful movement, for it is then that we can create good music.

HOW TO EVOKE LOYALTY

○ This area is called the Anhata Chakra and is symbolized by air. Here, our potential moves to the actual. By living up to our potential, we move everything we touch and allow the world to touch us at all times, just as air does. This area unites the inner with the outer, symbolized by breathing air from the outside to the inside. We connect our insides to the outside through the use of our hands with low energy here defined as "having lost touch with reality." Good energy here is a person who finds security, delighting in equal pressure from all sides. Security allows us to stand up to opposing forces, bridging them with actions.

❖   Many religious pictures show saints, gods, and religious leaders with out-stretched hands—the universal sign of compassion. Reach your hands out to help. Be loyal to the promise that our hands should always do our heart's work.

❖   Betrayal is felt in this area of the body. Betrayal creates high energy in this area and implies that someone has broken your heart. It happens to the front of you, right to your face, and right at your heart. It takes your breath away, leaving you speechless. It turns the misdirection of love into destruction. It is a broken heart. But don't be too concerned with people betraying you, for we betray ourselves all the time. Think of ways you betray yourself and feel compassion for yourself. Then translate that to compassion for those who betray you.

○   The Heart Chakra provides a liberating energy with forgiveness the ultimate liberation. It is not a forgetting but a letting go, allowing yourself to be hurt only once. Harboring bitterness against someone is like eating poison and expecting the other person to die. It is only yourself you are hurting as you allow the event or person to hurt you in your mind over and over again. Liberate vast amounts of energy by letting go.

❖   The Heart Sutra tells us that form is exactly emptiness and emptiness is exactly form. Coaches use imagery to get better motor performance during the execution of a sport. Visualization of a motor movement rearranges the circuitry of the brain and there is an underlying, lasting neural change. The motor image becomes reality at the level of the brain, at the ready when the motor performance is required. While an athlete might visualize jumping or swimming, might we visualize emotions as well? You can visualize hatred, compassion, success or failure. What do you think about? How are you rear-ranging yourself?

☕   Buddhist psychology uses the metaphor of a cloth soaked in oil to visualize the link between the mind and the body. You can't separate the two.

❖   Forgiveness is a pledge to not carry past hurts into the future, freeing oneself of burdensome repetition. Symbolically, our shoulders are where we carry our troubles, where we would be yoked if we were beasts of burden. Stooped over with extra weight, our heart is sheltered, not allowing anyone else to enter. Do not hold another person out away from your heart. Take them into your heart and take a load off your shoulders. Heed the words of Frances Burnett; "At first people refuse to believe that a strange new thing can be done, then they begin to hope it can be done, then they see it can be done, then it is done and all the world wonders why it was not done centuries ago." Forgive; go lighter into the future and you will see that you should have done it "centuries ago."

❖ When you keep the shining parts of yourself in view and hold only the dark parts of others in view, you are practicing intellectual cowardice. Investigate your dark and shadow sides, the parts of you that you think are ugly. Let them see the light of day, and in that way you unleash the energy they monopolized in trying to stay hidden. And let the light side of others shine through instead of always looking at what is wrong with people. Let them light up a room. Be brave enough to view other postures in "critical space." Douglas Porpora in *Landscapes of the Soul,* talks of the possible postures in critical space. The Intellectual Hero dares to accept painful or unpopular truths. The Intellectual Coward shuts their mind when the truth is insufferable. The Intellectual Sojourner realizes they are still on the road toward truth and the Intellectual Dogmatist is sure they have the truth at hand and quits investigating. Take up a posture you can be proud of. He notes, "We are distinguished by where we stand in critical space."

☯ The Tibetan word "lelo" is translated as "laziness" but it is a laziness of a certain type. It would denote someone with a Type A personality who works 12 hour days but has no concern for virtue. They are lazy with regard to the cultivation of ethics. They commit the Buddhist notion of "spiritual sloth."

❖ A common circulation condition happens to diabetics called "neuropathy," literally "nerve pain." Injury occurs to the small nerves supplying the skin in the lower extremities. The damage stems from microscopic vascular disease that deprives the nerves of oxygen and they suffocate or starve to death. Numbness results, which leaves the body without its usual messenger of injury, pain. Without pain, a small innocuous blister from a wrinkle in a sock can grow to be a wound, requiring medical care. Since the circulation is already impaired to the area, the wound heals slowly if at all, sometimes leading to amputations. The circulation disorder is called "shunting" and the blood to the skin surface is shunted or routed away into deeper tissues. We would all be wise to notice what we are shunting away; what we are not allowing to come to the surface. Listen to all the parts of you that want expression. By expressing even the shadow or dark parts of ourselves, the shadows might not gather so much energy and would then be less destructive. Let all the energies flow to the surface and allow wounds to heal.

❖ Synchronized brain waves pace our motor behaviors. This is seen in repetitive behaviors in animals such as feeding and hunting strategies along with mating rituals. It is easier seen in humans through music and dance, singing or sports. Rowing, running, walking, yoga, tai chi, and martial arts can synchronize brain waves when we feel "out of sorts." Breathing meditations, along with singing or chanting can be powerful transformers, able to give a rhythm to the way we move through our day.

❖ When you are confronted with a problem, ask, "How would my heart respond?" Go that way.

❖ Practice skillful change. If you are dieting, do so mindfully. Mindful goals would include dieting for good health or ease of movement. Dieting for vanity, or the desire for social acceptance, is an "unwholesome motive" and may increase the likelihood of failure. Whole ideas do not grasp after goals that are merely a substitute of one unhealthy thing for another. Such grasping throws you off balance. Balance a bad habit with a good goal.

❖ Jack Kornfield writes that we should "bless our wounds." He suggests that our dark times are just the kind of pain that is right for us at the time. The pain is from experiences we have honestly earned. Fold them in and give them some space. That way, they won't throw a tantrum trying to get your attention.

❖ Help those around you who are showing evidence of trapped energy (anger, fear, depression, low motivation) by offering energy from outside. Encourage them, support them, teach them, and mentor them.

❖ Fear inherently draws us away from the perceived threat, toward our center. Rather than being a source of stability, the contraction inward is too strong and unbalanced. A chronically caved-in chest cannot inhale. You are physically depressed, closed in, and caved in on yourself. You are placing pressure on your heart, making it smaller and the arteries narrower. The German word "angst" means "twisting and narrowing" and is the root for the word anxiety and angina. Qigong and yoga postures overcome and correct such reactions by emphasizing open and elongated patterns.

☖ Imagine the fire in yourself melting anger and bitterness. Transform it by cooking your hurts into ash. Ash nourishes and prepares the forest floor for new growth.

☖ Visualize the air in you becoming a swift but gentle breeze, gathering the dust and ash that is left from a fire. Let it go. Scatter anger and change its shape. It will never to be as powerful as it once was.

ℰ Become the earth in you with great valleys of scars and wounds. Cherish them by allowing rivers and streams to follow the scar, bathing it with forgiveness and lessons. Let the rivers grow into your greatness.

ℰ Picture yourself a great rolling wave. When grief arises in waves and cycles, give it its own time like the ebb and flow of a tide. The worst of it will be over when we have so deeply accepted it that it doesn't matter if it arises again or not; we have learned to float with it.

❖ Practice a simple gesture. Place your hands on your knees, palms up. This is a position of receptivity stating you are open to the energy of the heavens. Now place your hands on your knees, palms down. This is an act of self-containment where we are not looking for anything more, we are simply digesting what is.

❖ Which have been the most valuable lessons; comfortable times or difficult times? In illness and pain we abandon certainty and comfort and can be transformed toward the body's longing for what is truly meaningful. The poet Rilke noted, "Winning does not tempt this man. This is how he grows: by being defeated, decisively by constantly greater beings." Introduce yourself to the difficult.

❖ Let your heart be inspired to go on—breathe. Inspirate, expirate. Inspiration, expiration.

ℰ Delight in the three basic postures. Do a sitting meditation visualizing yourself as a mountain shrouded in fog. You are still there even if unseen. Do a standing meditation visualizing yourself as a tree, rooted firmly in the ground with your arms reaching for the heavens. Do a lying meditation visualizing yourself as a lake with immense stillness below even if the surface is rough.

☣ Understand the opposite energies in you. The lower part of the body is rooted and expresses the yin energy. The upper body moves freely and is yang. The front of the body contracts and is yin; the back opens and is yang. Your skin is exposed and is yang; the organs are hidden and yin. Blood itself is yin but its activity is yang. Mucous is yin but its excretion is yang. Any lack of activity blocks yang. If the blood does not circulate, yang cannot express itself and it burns out yin. The life force inherent in the cooperation of opposites is lost and vitality is extinguished.

○ Try Urdhva Bhujangasana: the Cobra Pose, a heart opener that can also increase kidney function. In this posture, the rib cage is opened up, allowing deeper breathing. Taking in all that the world offers brings greater joy into the body. This pose strengthens the serratus muscle, giving the shoulders a stable ground to work from.

○ Try the Seated Twist. This posture teaches you to relax when you find your-self in a tight spot. It can reduce anxiety as it frees open each level of the spine and wrings out our internal organs. It is an exaggeration of the movements required for a proper gait. When we walk, our left arm is forward while our right leg is forward, placing our trunk in a twisted position. This wrings out and massages our internal organs with each step. If we walk stilted, limping, or stiff with even the slightest lack of arm swing, we eliminate the twist. Our organs miss their massage and must work harder under duress.

○ Try the Crocodile Pose. The heart chakra is opened here but protected as you are lying on your chest. Although the arms are up, lifting the rib cage, anxiety is held at bay as the pose does not expose your vulnerable parts. A crocodile is comfortable on both land and in water. Lie in crocodile until you are ready to come out of the marsh and into the open.

○ Try Ushtrasana: Camel Pose. The position allows air to break free of restric-tions we've placed on it. We are free to no longer guard disappointments or shattered dreams. It challenges our defensiveness and like the camel, shows us how to persevere during our long search for an oasis.

○ Try Cow Face Pose, which connects the hands near the heart. It symbolizes that whatever connects the hands, engages the heart. Tension in the shoulder disconnects the two.

☙ Try Ayurvedic "bathing," techniques to nurture the body inside and out by balancing within ourselves the forces of water, fire, earth, air, and space. Take an Air Bath. Breathe in clean air to wash away anything that has become stagnate. Breathe out to release what you no longer need. This is a bath for your lungs. Try a Space Bath using deep meditation to create space between yourself and the world. Take a Fire Bath by consuming spicy, hot food to stimulate the digestive system and increase circulation. Or take a Water Bath by drinking water and weak green tea to detoxify the body. Enjoy an Earth Bath but using mud to draw out the toxins through the skin.

❖ Jon Kabat-Zin tells us that it is the whole body that breathes. Feel it and remember it is who you are. You are not just a resident of your head. Feel the rest of your body move as you take a breath.

❖ Become efficient with every part of your body. Free the soft tissues so the body can move freely. Allow the muscles to move and glide through all planes: up, down, vertical, and horizontal. Cease to squander your energy by working against yourself. Love yourself enough to move through your whole potential.

☙ Practice letting go of the ego. In Tibetan, ego is called *dak dzin*, which means, "grasping to a self," and is considered the absence of true knowledge of who we really are. We are doomed when we clutch and grasp to a makeshift version of ourselves. The fact that we need to hold on so tight shows that in the depths of our being, we know that such a version of ourselves does not really exist. If it were real, we would not have to hold on so tight. How can we know ourselves yet not hold on so tight? Try this—take a coin in your hand and hold on to it with your palm toward the ground. Let go. It falls away without your constant grasping. Now pick up a coin and hold it in your fist with your palm facing the sky. Let go. It stays on your hand. It's only the grasping that has changed.

❖ In order to play beautiful music, a violin string must be just the right tension, neither too taut nor too slack. That is exactly the same with your mind. Alert yet relaxed.

❖ Allow whatever comes your way to be a teacher. Remember this Buddhist concept—practice means that someday you will make the mistakes of a master and not the mistakes of a beginner. Make mistakes. Setbacks are an integral part of any significant change process. Perhaps we falter to slow the process down. Were we to be immediately successful in everything we did, we might find ourselves being successful at the wrong things.

❖ The pulse in Western medicine is taken at the ulnar portion of the wrist. Plain and simple. Count the number of beats, record the number in a minute and you have a dim picture of the health of the heart. In Eastern medicine, the pulse is many shaped, with sounds and feelings indicating the health of the liver, kidneys, and intestines, as well as the heart. Some of the descriptors of the pulse are: sharp bird beak, fine hair, dead rock, flowing stream, indented middles, hook on the end, floating feathers, elastic pole, taut bow, rooster lifting foot, strike of stone, edge of knife, string of instrument, multiple seeds, visiting stranger, mud ball, sparse earth, sword lying ready to be used, and smooth pill. These poetic descriptors make our western descriptor, "sixty beats a minute," pale in comparison. Envision your heart sounds as a metaphor. What sound do you want to make?

❖ Breath is a "silent thread" that we fluidly hold and release. Picture the different cords in your body: the threads of nerves and capillaries, the stout twine of tendon and muscle, the links of thoughts that make an idea. Prana, our life energy, is symbolized as a rope with the principle of life in the strand, pulled by the in-breath and released with the out-breath. By completing a full in and out breath, we overcome the short tugs of war between mind and body. Like our breath, out thoughts will be shallow if we seldom pull deeply.

❖   Navaho recognize the healing energy of the wind. As winds swirled through human beings, they left their mark as the lines on our hands. Think of these lines as evidence that you heal quickly and thoroughly.

❖   The respiratory center is located in the part of our primitive, reflexive brain called the reptilian brain, or brain stem. If we've had a stroke and one arm is hopelessly paralyzed, a yawn can make the flaccid arm move. It is not a sign of recovery, merely an ancient motor pathway closely linked to the respiratory center. There are parts of us deemed too important to leave to the conscious mind. A yawn reminds us of those areas where there are no mistakes to be made.

❖   If you want to see your heart enlarge without exercise, be generous. The word generous is from the Latin "to bring to life" and is related to magnanimous (*magna* meaning large, and *anima* meaning soul). See how much you can give away. Give away your gifts; the accomplishments of your hands, the ideas in your head, and generosity in your heart. Be aware that whenever you follow your heart, you will be offered enormous temptation to return to the common path.

❖   The wedding ring, a symbol of loyalty, is worn on the left ring finger in order to have direct access to the heart. The ulnar nerve runs from the ring finger to the shoulder and converges at T_{5-6}, directly behind the heart. The left ulnar nerve would lie closer to the heart than the right. This is also the reason why we have left arm pain with cardiac disease.

❖   The question never is, "What are my choices?" The question is, "Which choices am I prepared to act on from my heart?" If you act only when you are guaranteed success, or act on the condition that you be rewarded, or act because you don't want to look stupid, you are being guided by intellect alone. You are only using the cerebral part of you. Add passion and see what you act on. See what moves you.

CHAKRA FIVE—FAITH

THROAT, NECK, MOUTH

"The daydreamer must visualize the dream so vividly and insistently that it becomes, in effect, an actuality."—James Thurber

"If we fail to imagine our lives, we will become the victim of someone else's imagination."—Dawna Markova

"There is no reality except the one contained within us; that is why so many people live such an unreal life. They take the images outside them for reality and never allow the world within to assert itself."—Herman Hesse

The fifth area of the body is home to some of the most unusual anatomy in the body. It is an anatomy that defies the logic of biomechanics, suggesting we need faith to even begin to understand it. It is here where we must admit that things can be understandable, but sometimes not fully understood. This area has the strongest muscle, yet a muscle that spends most of its time moving invisible things. It has a bone in charge of our survival, yet is free floating and made to do its important job alone. It has the strongest joint in the body, but it's a joint that never bears weight, and it has the most coordinated muscle in the body, yet a muscle that never uses a tool. All of this is packed into an area about six inches long and yet, the area is entirely empty.

This area of the body is, simply put, where things go in. Air and food are the fuel for survival, with the mouth being the largest opening in our body. It is, literally, a big hole in our head. But more than just a hole, it is an area of extraordinary anatomy. The tongue is the strongest muscle in the body in that it has no bony support. It must move and manipulate food and words with neither end of the muscle attached to bone, leaving it without a solid point of stability. The tongue is also the most finely motored muscle in the body, with more dexterity required in speech than our fingers would ever use to write or manipulate objects. It is a master at moving the invisible.

The bone that moves enough to allow a swallow and maintain jaw angle for breathing is the hyoid, one of the most remarkable bones in the body, in that it is entirely free floating. Having no other bone it touches or attaches to, it hangs at the top of our throat by the narrow digastric muscles, which pierce through it like thread through the eye of a needle. The hyoid also defines the angle between the chin and the esophagus and is the keystone in the bridge between the sternum and the angle of the jaw. Allowed to slacken, we get a dreaded double chin, a build up of tissue from habitual tension and over-stretching of the platysmus and digastric muscles around the hyoid area. Tuck the chin slightly in, and the hyoid and its muscles tuck into the throat instead of stretching out and away from it. The area is probably the most posture, and movement dependent musculature in the body.

Swallowing demands a particular posture from the body as a whole. We are only neurologically prepared to swallow when every joint in the body is flexed. Our ankles, knees, hips, every vertebra in our spine, our shoulders, elbows, wrists, and fingers, are all bent toward the one goal—that of getting food into the system. The phrase, "eating a square meal," is a reference to the position of our body, not the meal itself. Square meals are a feature at West Point Military Academy, wherein a cadet must sit squarely; their hips and knees forming right angles and their hand moving straight up to the level of the mouth and over into the mouth at a right angle. Preparation for proper digestion begins with viewing food with the eyes, smelling food with the nose, and moving the hand slowly to the mouth. This allows the brain time to anticipate, salivate, and prepare for a safe swallow.

Efficient stomach emptying is also posture dependent. Remaining seated or standing one hour after eating is the most efficient use of gravity while awake. While asleep, lying on the right side allows for the most efficient emptying of the stomach. Even though anatomically, the left side lies lower to the jejunum, left side lying allows the usually stretched Western stomach to collapse in all but small children, thus pushing food up the esophagus, promoting reflux of stomach contents.

Efficient chewing relies on proper upright posture. The jaw is the most forceful joint in our body, capable of biting off a finger even without the help of teeth. Try putting your finger in the angle of your knee joint—your finger won't even suffer a bruise when the knee closes down on it. The jaw can take the finger off. The jaw is a sliding and hinge joint, meant to move up and down and glide when we chew food that requires a rotary action, like meat and leafy greens. If this area is tight, we can loose the sliding/gliding ability. If it is tilted from poor posture, the entire joint is held at an angle, wearing it down and adversely affecting its efficiency. If the muscles tire too quickly from being held at the wrong angle and if our teeth and tempomandibular joint (TMJ) are sore from muscle tension, we will fail to chew properly.

It is crucial that this area elicit the correct tone, for we have no room to spare when it comes to energy expenditure here. The fact is, we already swallow at the expense of breathing. Unlike animals, our swallow takes neurological precedence over breathing as is seen in studies of infants who will swallow ten times more frequently when experiencing apnea. In fact, dry swallowing can save us from drowning by inhibiting the urge to breathe if under water. The diving reflex, as it is called, suggests to some evolutionists that we evolved from the Aquatic Ape, an upright gatherer whose hunting grounds were shallow waters.

To test the Diving Reflex, take your pulse for fifteen seconds and multiply that number by four, which is the equivalent of heartbeats per minute. Inhale and plunge your face into a bowl of ice water for thirty seconds with both your nose and eyes immersed. Measure the heart rate again and it will have dropped 10-25% as we have less oxygen demand under water. Some primitive traits, like the diving reflex, have been retained and are the neurological equivalents of tails or gill pouches we had as embryos, which were reabsorbed during fetal development. In our fetal stage, we invest a majority of our developmental effort into building the throat as it monopolizes half of the entire embryo.

In a twisted version of logic, this swallowing predominance over breathing does not mean that swallowing is under our control. It is not. If it were, we would no doubt make a mistake and choke to death. Breathing, however, is under our control.

During difficult activities such as running, lifting, even laughing, the lower brain stem takes over breathing, evidenced by the animal-like sounds elicited when we grunt and guffaw as we redirect needed oxygen to big muscles. But both vocalization and swallowing will create a special relationship that is interactive with the respiratory tract and they will "steal" air to direct either words out, or food in. Our oxygen needs then dictate and adjust the rate of breathing, so it is best to walk slowly while talking and sit still when eating.

Between five and thirty percent of digestion occurs in our mouth, as we chew foods to a puree texture allowing time to mix with just the right amount of saliva. In effect, every bite of food we swallow is the consistency of baby food if properly chewed. The parotid or saliva gland is activated when it is massaged by the buccinator muscle, the muscle used for chewing. Amylase-rich saliva breaks down carbohydrates, with thorough chewing opening up more surface areas for these enzymes to get to the more difficult to digest proteins and lipids. Since digestion only occurs on the surfaces of foods, the mouth is in charge of creating as many of those surfaces as possible.

If we chew inefficiently and swallow before that 30% of digestion is accomplished, large food particles enter the stomach. The stomach is not equipped with teeth to break down food; only stomach acid and it will increase its acid output if the teeth and jaw haven't done their job properly. Increased stomach acid means heartburn, which is alleviated with more frequent eating, perpetuating the cycle.

The stress response known as flight or fight can also be termed flight, fight or bite, as the bite response is a primitive component of fighting. Animals would not be dangerous to us if they did not bite. We have phrases that reflect this bite response when we say, "I fought tooth and nail," or "He was armed to the teeth," and many of us display the motor response of clenching our teeth when under stress. The bite response may be especially prevalent in women, as they are unable to fight or flee from most predators.

Flight, fight or freeze is yet another version of the stress response, with victims frozen in fear or feigning death in response to attack. When a body is under stress, it increases its secretion of corticosteroids from the adrenal cortex, which increases the synthesis of fats or lipids. This may be a way the body replenishes the fat utilized for energy during fleeing or fighting. However, our modern day stressors rarely offer us an opportunity to flee (impossible in traffic or standing in lines), or fight (inhibited by manners and laws), and we fail to utilize fat for increased activity. In fact, we often display a marked decrease in our activity level when we are stressed (waiting, sitting, sublimating, inhibiting) and this may account for an increase in body weight from chronic corticosteroid stimulation.

Additionally, when the jaw is under tension, the tongue becomes too tight, distorting the back of the throat, the angle of the hyoid bone, and the esophagus and trachea, often leading to the feeling of having a lump in your throat, which is again relieved by eating. Animals vocalize to express any aroused state and each arousal state has what is called a "signature activity." Fear, sex, hunger, and anger each code to the animals' midbrain that specifies which vocal pattern to run. In this way, each vocalization is considered a "symptom" of the specific arousal state. A cat might run a "hiss" when fearful, a "purr" when pleased, and a "meow" when hungry.

Deacon writes in *The Symbolic Species*, that the larynx is controlled by the visceral motor system (animals and humans) and is stereotypic, while the tongue is an intermediate system between the visceral and skeletal motor system (humans). Thus, the tongue has both stereotypic and deliberate control and can modify the gated or programmed sound from the larynx to create intonated language. It is our vocal cords that convey arousal and so can vary our rhythm or amplitude of speech but cannot be used as a major conveyor of speech. That is up to our tongue. Interestingly, singing is an even higher brain function, involving totally independent mechanisms from regular speech.

Speech finds us rapidly inhaling between phrases in order to move words out with each exhalation. Deacon notes that this practice shifts the focus of information transmission from breath units to articulatory units and overrides respiratory drive. In the interest of speech, the usually inflexible link between the larynx and its breathing duties is broken for skilled articulation. Speech, he reminds us, is a "top down" controlled mechanism, coming from the higher brain to the more primitive brain. So the skeletal muscle system that drives the tongue, dictates and overrules the breathing pattern. This predominance of the cortical control over the visceral system (speech/tongue over breathing/lungs and larynx), is yet another example of our brain influencing our motor functions and motor functions dictating brain function.

Again, we will attempt to save energy for the huge expenditure the tongue and mouth require. We will store phrases in memory to use over and over again, rather than recreate new word combinations every time we talk and we will gesture and use body language to eliminate the need for more words. We will exaggerate the tone to convey more of what we mean by just words alone and we will make rules, grammatical markers, and word order constraints to make our language more predictable.

The acquisition of speech in babies is also highly predictable and again motor movement is the pacemaker for articulation. In fact, the first part of an infant to become touch sensitive is the mouth and when a baby wants to be fed, the entire body will move. As a baby begins to crawl, so they begin to babble. Even as adults, when we switch from the higher control centers that are linked with motor control (talking), to lower control centers (laughing and crying), we move to the non-motor linked brain. When a baby or an adult cries, they stop moving. When we have a hearty laugh, we stop walking until we can resume again. Motor control is the very stuff emotions are made of.

Paul Ekman of UCSF, studies how emotions leave their culturally universal signature on the face. Every culture expresses sadness, anger, surprise, and happiness with the same facial expressions. Since the face can so universally transcend speech, he proposes that children be taught "emotional schooling," wherein they learn to read their own and each other's faces, postures, and body language. Thus, less miscommunication might take place. He likens this emotional health schooling to the Greek schools called "eudaimonias," where the mindfulness of bodily sensations and body awareness was taught.

There is evidence that failure to move and failure to express our emotions in social situations has prognostic value in determining who will have heart attacks. More importantly, in those that have heart attacks, it may determine who will die. The personality known as Type D, or the distressed personality, has a mental state characterized by unusual fatigue, the feeling of being dejected or defeated, increased irritability, and demoralization. These personalities show a pronounced reluctance to move and their type of fatigue is termed Vital Exhaustion (VE). Increased VE among Type D patients has dire clinical implications. They have a marked increased risk of ischemic heart disease, and it is the leading predictor of first myocardial infarction (MI or heart attack). Studies by Appels, Hoppener, and Mulder, looked at nearly four thousand men and after four years of follow-up, found that fifty-nine of them had MIs. While control groups of the same age, matching high blood pressure, comparable elevated cholesterol, and identical smoking habits had far fewer MI's, the study group with VE, coupled with Type D personality, shows independent prognostic value. That is, their personality type was as high a risk factor as smoking or high cholesterol.

Other studies show that neither impaired cardiac pump function nor the extent of cardiac disease was predictive for first MI—only vital exhaustion. One of the major authors of Type D studies, J. Denollet notes, "There is an urgent need to adopt a personality approach in identification of the patient at risk for cardiac events." It is interesting to note that while Type A's (pressured, sensation seeking behavior, angry) show a correlation to risk of a second cardiac event, it is the Type B's and Type D's that show an inferior survival rate from their second event.

Expressing our emotions can keep us vital and keep us from suffering a broken or diseased heart. It is our emotions, in fact, that can keep us from acting out in socially unacceptable ways. They will express themselves when we chance to violate, or secure social living contracts. We will rage against those who transgress against the social contract and we will feel guilt when we are the cheats. We will be envious when someone has more than their share and will feel shame when it is we who do. Love is more durable than lust and therefore seals relationships with others, while forgiveness is a guarantee that the seal is unbreakable.

As the brain benefits from social living, it will always look for ways that other brains might be cheating. It will identify those that anger too quickly, and it will shun those who fail to interact in a pleasant manner. The brain's interior calculations and the body's outer behavior are mediated by emotions. Emotions are how one brain reads another brain.

We should be reminded of the game theory studies by Trivers and his Tit For Tat computer program that always searched for other cooperators. Dishonesty, he notes, is so physiological that even a machine can detect it. Lie detectors can easily sort out interior calculations from outer physiologic responses just by measuring sweating. So can our brains. We notice the fake smile, the limp handshake, the shift of an eye, the twitch of the mouth, the beads of sweat, and the blush on the cheek. The lesson is this—if you are distressed, not only will you know it in your heart, other people will know of it in their brain.

In *The Consolations of Philosophy*, Alain de Botton suggests that being distressed is to accept life's difficulties as always and only debilitating. Those who live longer, according to longevity studies, are those who show resilience during life's difficult moments. He notes, "We should not feel embarrassed by our difficulties, only by our failure to grow anything beautiful from them." It is Zorba the Greek's plea—be present for the whole catastrophe. De Botton uses the metaphor of a plant, that at its roots can be odd and unpleasant, but will bear beautiful flowers and fruit. "Just as in life, at root level, there may be difficult emotions and situations which can nevertheless result, through careful cultivation, in the greatest achievements and joys." He quotes Stendhal who, in 1822 said, "If you refuse to let your own suffering be upon you even for an hour and if you constantly try to prevent and forestall all possible distress way ahead of time; if you experience suffering and displeasure as evil, hateful, worthy of annihilation, and as a defect of existence, then it is clear that you harbor in your heart the religion of comfortableness. How little you know of human happiness. You comfortable people, for happiness and unhappiness are sisters and even twins that either grow up together or, as in your case, remain small together."

This "religion on comfortableness" suggests that state of grasping at "feel good" emotions and constantly trying to avoid unpleasantries. As Nietzsche notes, "To regard states of distress…as an objection, as something that must be abolished…is almost as stupid as the will to abolish bad weather." Some of us may avoid difficult emotions because we are unpracticed at pleasant emotions. How many of us are content, relaxed and calm? How many of us are just trying to get through a day in a state of numbness, unable to experience any real emotion, never mind whether it is unpleasant or pleasant? How many of us wouldn't even know where to begin if we were to have a day to relax? Relaxation can start with learning how to relax the largest opening in our body, the place practiced at letting in food and air—the mouth.

A simple way to ensure the mouth is relaxed is to place the tip of your tongue on the roof of your mouth while your teeth remain slightly apart. Many of us hold the mid-tongue against the roof of our mouth or against our teeth, causing us to set our jaw, which only promotes throat breathing. Rehearsing conversations in our mind can also lead to increased tension. Jaw tension is noted on biofeedback monitors even when we think about talking. As we internally "talk" to ourselves, the mind elicits a motor response. Constant internal talking leads to the anticipation that you will say something; yet nothing ever comes of it.

Throat breathing (versus abdominal breathing) strains the muscles at the clavicle, scapula, and top ribs, interfering with circulatory and lymphatic structures at the top of the heart. As breathing becomes more active, other accessory groups are called in, one after the other. First the psoas muscle is recruited, then transversalis, and finally quadratus lumborum, all of them located in the lower back and hip area. Accelerated breathing then involves the trunk on down to the levator ani and coccygeus, muscles used in defecation. The body will recruit a head turning and swallowing muscle, the sternocleidomastoid and in extreme activity, even the muscles of the legs, arms, and jaw may be included. Interestingly, the upper accessory muscles are the last to be called on. If the lower accessory muscles cannot move freely, they will recruit the muscles of the neck and head, muscles that have important work to do and should not be used for respiratory work.

The sternocleidomastoid muscle (SCM) is considered by Janet Travell, MD, as the most important muscle in the body. Dr. Travell, physician to Presidents John F. Kennedy and Lyndon B. Johnson, was the mastermind behind the bodywork techniques known as Trigger Point Therapy. Her studies of referred pain patterns led to the discovery of left-sided arm and face pain in association with heart attacks. She published landmark texts on other referred pain patterns, adaptations, and substitutions. Pain in the outer ear, for example, can be referred from any one of the "Ten T's": teeth, tongue, tonsils, thyroid, tempanic membrane, tempomandibular joint, trapezius, temporalis, pterygoid, or sternocleidomastoid.

The SCM is important as it attaches to the clavicle and sternum, passing over the front of the throat to attach behind the ear at the mastoid. It literally holds our head on our shoulders and is the key muscle sending information from our trunk to the head, and vice versa. It tells us which direction we are going in life. By attaching to the mastoid at the back of the ear, any tightness of the SCM can pull on the skull, sending faulty information regarding up and down, side to side, and forward and back. It can make us dizzy, confused, and can alter the sensation of weight held in the hands. A quick test for SCM dysfunction calls for the patient to hold a one pound weight in each hand. If one feels heavier than the other, the SCM is too tight on that side.

Referred pain patterns from a tight SCM, show up in the face as shared nerves flare-up the outer ear, the skin above the eyebrow, through the sinuses, along the top molars, and the back of the ear on the skull. The SCM rarely, if ever hurts. It is just the messenger, sending pain to the face and it can be excruciating. This complex muscle can also cause one eye to tear or twitch, as it puts an untoward stretch on the orbicalis ocularis muscle. It can cause ear pressure, ear ringing, and acute dizziness. The SCM becomes tight because the large trapezius muscle attached to the back of the head, shortens, pulling the head back. The SCM, fearing the head may be falling off, pulls forward. The war is on.

To bring peace, the trapezius must regain its length and the chin can then retain its slightly tucked posture, allowing the SCM to relax. The neck should never be overstretched to the point where you can see a pronounced trachea. After all, the neck is the only area on the body where pressure from someone else's hands can kill us. We should be reluctant to show such vulnerability as to bare our neck. It is also where obstructions in the trachea can take your life in minutes.

The Adam's apple, the lump at the front of your throat, is named from the Biblical story of Adam eating and choking on the apple from the Garden of Eden. The first bite of food "went down the wrong pipe." The word 'throat" is from the Old English '*prote,*' meaning "a swelling," a reference to the Adam's apple according to the Old English Dictionary. Aspiration pneumonia, once called "The old man's friend" due to its role in the early death of ill patients, can occur from aspirating food we are too weak to safely swallow.

Studies show that it's not the amount of food or even the type of food aspirated that is cause for concern but rather the health of the mouth. The mouth is a host to harmful bacterial if dental cavities, decay, and gum disease are present. With each aspirated swallow, the bacterium tags a ride into the lungs. When we swallow accurately down our esophagus, stomach acid serves to kill the bacteria, but our lungs have no such chemical antidote. Our lungs are not bathed by a constant flow of saliva, a basic chemical capable of neutralizing acid refluxed into the esophagus. The larynx is bathed only with air, thus the hoarse vocal quality that ensues when any other substance touches the vocal cords besides air. A clean mouth, with its quart a day of saliva bathing capabilities, is the key organizing feature to the health of our lungs if we aspirate, and to the health of our esophagus and stomach if we don't.

As it turns out, our mouth has a key organizing feature in our emotional health. During times of high emotion, our hands usually seek out our mouth in an effort to organize us. With surprise, we cover our mouth, with anger we bring a fist near our chin, and with indecision, we suck on or tap our teeth with a finger. We chew our hair, our nails, or an object when we are under stress. Studies show that third grade is the most pencil bitten grade in school, most notably when a student is stressed to learn cursive handwriting and multiplication tables. When we are nervous, we go to our mouths. We smoke, overeat, over drink, over verbalize, sigh, grind our teeth, clear our throats, and swallow more often. While babies cannot talk (the word infant means "non-speaking"), they will still use their mouths to communicate. Babies initiate a hunger signal by rubbing near their mouth with their hands often nearly a half an hour before they will begin crying out of hunger. Fed during this time, instead of waiting until they cry and suck air into their tummies, can avoid colic, a condition rarely if ever experienced in non-industrialized nations, nations that feed their babies before they cry. Not only is feeding time more successful if fed at the first sign of hunger, imagine the impression one could give a baby about the world in which it has been born. Feeding them before they cry tells them their signs are meaningful, they don't have to yell to get their message across, the world is safe not painful, and the one job they do as babies (to eat) is successful, not stressful.

The mouth and throat carry another important function besides allowing fuel into the body. They let words out. A Greek word meaning "door," the thyroid is a gland seated in front of the throat, allowing hormones to go in and out. Our mouth does the same with other invisible tools; words. The mouth of the river is called "delta," another Greek word meaning "door." And while the life can be squeezed out of us by holding the mouth and nose closed, the life can be felt to squeeze out of us when we fail to speak our truth. The word "prophet," a speaker of truth, means "to speak out" from the Greek "*prophetein.*" The mouth is where our will is given voice, where we choose our words wisely, and where we speak our own mind. When we swallow the false promises of advertisements and consume more of the world's resources than most all other countries put together, we use our mouth in an act of gluttony, a Greek word meaning "throat." It is important to remember that the mouth and throat are not a one-way entry for consumption but are also an exit where words and visions can be born. But speaking your truth is no easy matter.

Bird lovers know that mimicry in songbirds, where a bird sings the songs of other species, gives the illusion that the habitat is saturated. It is a vocal "no vacancy" sign. Those of us who are non-stop talkers, often do the same thing—monopolizing every conversation as if our reality was the only one worth mentioning. Many religious practices involve a history of verbal mystification. Sufi stories, Zen koans, the Oracle at Delphi, and Biblical allegories, all serve to jog our comfort level with language. Riddles and word puzzles challenge our version of reality. It is playing with words in order to confuse what is real and what is not. Scientific and medical jargon serves to alienate the uninitiated as well.

Daniel Palmer, Father of Chiropractics, Andrew Still, Father of Osteopathy, and Sylvester Graham, the health movement founder who invented the Graham Cracker to offer whole grains in the American diet, all agreed with the premise of John Gunn. He noted that the Latin names for medicines and diseases were "originally made use of to astonish the people." Palmer, Still, and Graham worked to demystify health and disease, and eliminate the "profit from alienation" they saw between the worker and his body, the patient and the doctor, and the person and their body. By changing the language of medicine, they sought to eliminate its mystical quality.

The ancient Egyptians thought language confusing as well, and the illiterate would use beer to wash the letters off printed paper and drink the ink in order to make them as smart as people who could read. Language might not be that tricky, but it is tricky enough—it allows us to say the unseeable as in the statement, "the red barn is yellow." We can say it, but it can't be true. Language allows us to lie. And, it allows us to live a lie.

Phonophobics are people who deny themselves the right to speak out. Continually silencing themselves, they are strangled by thoughts they dare not vocalize. Between their ideas and their words, falls a shadow and they are stricken by a mental judge that has decreed, thou shalt not speak. They lack confidence. The word confidence means, "to confide," and confide means, "to have faith." To speak out means that we value our message and have faith in ourselves.

Meditation practice holds one truth above all others, being truthful to yourself. As you sit in meditation, the drifting mind must be redirected. If left to wander, no one would ever know except you. Mindful meditation is a practice in taking responsibility for your truth, since it only has to do with you and your own integrity. It is practicing being truthful with yourself and thus, master of your own life. After all, no one would ever know whether you are drifting and giving time to a worry, idea, or incident and thus, "not meditating." John Daido Loori in his book, *The Heart of Being,* notes, "body posture alone creates a particular activity in the mind. Sitting like the Buddha is creating a Buddha. What we do with our bodies is who we are." What we tell ourselves with our inner voice is also who we are and we should choose our words wisely.

Socrates thought that wisdom in talking could only come while walking and as Dr. Ratey notes in *Users Guide to the Brain,* "Motor function is crucial to all the other brain functions…Movement provides the physiological release that we need to bring our bodies back into balance." When we walk and talk at the same time, both hemispheres of the brain are working together. This allows creative problem solving to occur, as all available resources and skills are joined together. Using only the left brain fosters obsessional intellectual activity and using only the right brain encourages day dreaming and fantastic ideas.

Thus is the beauty inherent in math and music, activities that use both sides of the brain. If you have little talent in those activities, certain movements utilize both hemispheres and inspire creative thinking. Crawling, walking or climbing stairs; all of these activities use one arm forward with the opposite leg forward. Cerebral imbalance occurs when we use either arms or legs at the same time. If you are prone to over-intellectualizing, avoid weight lifting or rowing. Instead opt for alternating forces of the arms and legs which is required by kayaking, cycling, dancing, swimming, and walking. When both hemispheres are utilized, we experience comfort as well as an increase in serotonin, the mood regulating neurotransmitter. Dopamine, the key neurotransmitter involved in the feelings of reward, motivation, attention, and initiation, also shows increased levels with reciprocal movement. A good walk, along with a good talk, might just be what the doctor ordered for they can literally make sense out of our lives by making sense of brain function. The brain is "listening" to every move we make.

The human voice is so soothing to us that we appreciate musical instruments which come closest in sound to the human voice. After all, the voice is both a string and wind instrument in its own right. The saxophone is most like the voice, followed closely by the cello in human tonality, both having a deep, somber quality to them. Vocal coaches note that there are three cavities in which the voice can be placed, and in doing so, the voice can be imagined as different musical instruments. The sounds from the sinuses in the head resemble that of the violin. The viola sounds like a voice spoken from the chest or upper back and the cello is from the stomach and abdomen. It is thought that the cello is the sound of the womb. In fact, wind instruments are played from the parts with which they share a tone. The flute is a mouth/upper chest instrument, the clarinet a lower chest instrument, and the saxophone is played from the abdomen.

Voice clinicians note that people who have a breathy quality to their voice, push more air through the glottis than necessary and they call this "free air," or, "will air." They cannot sustain phonation very long and are essentially using their voice as a prolonged sigh. This affectation, coupled with a high-pitched voice, can signal asthma or the habit of letting their free air and will power escape through their voices, rather than used to fuel the body. A tight throat may be indicative of a stifled scream, while a normally toned throat is one filled with potential to act.

There is some indication that language is merely movement inside the brain. Profession Patricia Greenfield of the department of psychology at UCLA, writes in a paper titled, *Language, Tools and the Brain,* that the human brain organizes object use exactly the same way it organizes the production of speech. She reports that the brain applies the same logical rules to both and uses the same anatomic structures to manipulate objects as it uses to manipulate symbols into language. In other words, how we talk will predict how we use objects and how we behave will predict how we talk. Her work, discussed in *The Hand,* by Frank R. Wilson M.D., argues that, "evolution has created in the human brain an organ powerfully predisposed to generate rules that treat nouns as if they were stones and verbs as if they were levers or pulleys." It is an example of the brains tendency to borrow motor patterns to construct abstract thought.

In the 1980's, archeologists Iegor Reznikoff and Michel Dauvois studied the Cro-Magnon caves in southwestern France and found that the caves with the most paintings, served as an ancient version of multi-media rooms. The caves with the most pictures were the caves that resonated song best as if vocalizations and tool use went hand-in-hand. Or is that hand-in-mouth?

The attainment of language milestones in children always takes place in the company of very specific motor milestones. Called the "motor blueprint," motor milestones can be tracked even in the womb, as in the case of reciprocal kicking and thumb-sucking. As we watch a child gain more and more motor skills, language follows but initially, motor and language are linked in what we call "body language." Wiggle your fingers at a newborn and they will stick out their tongue.

When a child says "mama," linguists note that the word does not just mean "mother"—it is more "mama come get me," or, "mama pick me up." When listening to the whole child, it's obvious that the word "mama" means "mama pick me up," as the baby reaches for his mother, stands on tip toes, gazes up, and actually initiates the motor behavior of being picked up. Language then becomes the bond that exists between objects. As the logical connection between things, a word becomes an object and a tool itself. The body transforms language and language then transforms the body as it changes our social behavior.

Secondary heuristic skills, that is, those behaviors that are a product of a heritable trait (a meme as a product of a gene), also have the capacity to express survival strategies. Once this body language is linked to vocal language, an individual will develop behavioral specializations that will act with the same stability as an inherited characteristic. Our habits can imprint and carry over to our children as if genetic. Learning to talk is genetically programmed. Learning how we say things is memetically programmed.

B. F. Skinner, a behavioral theorist, suggested that speech is only effective when the voice indicates the emotional tone of the message to the listener. In other words, we are ineffective in our social behavior when our voice and our speech carry conflicting information or simply put, when our body is saying one thing and our words another. This might occur when we say, "I'm fine" when asked how we are, when in fact, we are sad. The voice or tone with which we speak, thus reveals the truth about the personality more than language. Incongruencies in speech and voice allow us to set up double binds, where our actions and our thoughts are contradictory and where the rhythm of what is said is sarcastic or bitter but the words themselves are not. Imagine the different tones that could be used to utter, "You are always right, aren't you?" Six words that could be said in a positive, negative, disgusted, empowered, or bewildered way. We use the rhythm and spacing of words more than we use the content or meaning of words and we do it all the time. When you find yourself talking to a dog or even an infant, neither of which can understand words or language, you are relying solely on inflection and rhythm to get meaning across. What we must remember is that this is true even when we are not talking to dogs or infants.

Vocal flexibility is imperative to interpreting thoughts and if it becomes stuck, our voices will be saturated and represented in a single or limited emotional tone. If our voice is calm or child-like, it might be very difficult to express and communicate anger. Quivering tones suggest a lack of confidence. If our voice is flexible in its rhythm, showing a certain coordination and variation in its movements and thus its moods, we can communicate anger when we are mad, maturity when we are confident, and playfulness when we feel childlike. Utilizing all aspects of vocal tonality affects the health and tone of the structures used to speak and swallow.

Surgeon William Faulkner discovered that even imaginary situations of a pleasant or unpleasant nature affected the activity of the esophagus. In 1942, he carried out experiments that stand today, whereby unpleasant suggestions caused esophageal tightening. Pleasant suggestions elicited relaxation and relief from spasm. He also studied the diaphragm and found it altered with the mere suggestion of situations that aroused strong emotions. Pleasant emotions increased the amplitude of diaphragmatic movement and unpleasant ones restricted it.

One of the premier movement therapies, gaining renewed popularity today, is the Alexander Technique, which is derived from an actor named Frederick Matthias Alexander. He found himself in the unpleasant situation of losing his voice halfway through a recital and searching for answers that no doctor was able to provide at the time, set up mirrors and watched himself recite his lines. He noticed he pulled his head downward and backward whenever he spoke. Realizing that this pulling of the head had to adversely affect all other muscles in his neck, he developed a technique of resisting habitual movements and relearning a natural use of the musculature. Practicing what he preached, changing his movement changed the way he talked.

Voice therapists use such motor responses in the body in an educational method known as ideokinesis, wherein images of the body in motion (kinesthetic imagery) stimulate specific muscular responses. We use ideokinesis when we tell a child to "pretend you are a bird" and we see them flap their arms. We alter motor behavior with the suggestion of an image. When we tell children, "sit down like a good boy," we change motor behavior and the child's image of themselves for better or worse. We're telling them they are good if they sit down and bad if they do not. Ideokinesis then, translates complex or unusual movements (since in the case of flapping your wings, you neither have any nor can you, in fact, fly), into pictures and thus your body becomes the picture.

This psychophysical process, in which imagery and body sense stimulate body change, was used by dance pioneer and author of the book, *The Intelligent Body*, Mabel Todd in the 1930's. She taught that concentration upon a picture involving movement resulted in neuromusculature responses necessary to carry out complex dance patterns with the least amount of effort and with less repetition. Thinking about dancing, made you a better dancer.

In the early 1970's, Mary Fulkerson of Dartington College of Arts, found ideokinesis central to movement and body-release work required for voice therapy. A common visual device in voice therapy is to evoke the image of a ping-pong ball coated with honey, which is supported by a jet of water. Her studies showed that such pictures in the mind led to the least hampered quality in a singing voice.

Motor success is gained through expert imagery. Could that be true in the reverse? Feldenkrais noted that the neck and jaw were prime locations for "parasitic contractions," a tightening in one part that is feeding off the whole of the body. Note how often your neck is held in tension or your jaw locked tight and teeth clenched. What is it you are bracing for? What are you afraid you might say? Right now, relax your jaw and the inside of your mouth. Release the energy you hold in the back of your throat. Now act and talk as if you don't have to hold back. Let the world know who you are. Thomas Moore suggested that we "creatively deal with limitations as resources for a vital life. Arrive not at shadow self-acceptance but at a profound love of the soul." We will never profoundly love the soul if we are afraid to say or do something wrong.

In Trigger Point Therapy, ticklish spots are seen as diagnostic in that they advertise, "don't touch" and often harbor deep trigger points and excessive tightness. Our neck is certainly a ticklish spot on many of us. Just like we have a spot that is most ticklish (usually our too tender feet and our vulnerable neck), we store tension in a "favorite" spot. The most likely place is the neck and jaw. Remember muscles have only one expression—to contract in order to move bones. Otherwise, they are at rest. If we store tension in our muscles, they become fixed in a motor state that produces no movement. Perhaps we resort to tension in order to feel secure or to make the world stop spinning so quickly. By storing a motor response in our muscles, we physically store a mental problem. Man is the only animal that can be afraid all the time by prolonging conflict rather than reacting and moving on. This places our muscles in the unhealthy position of frozen conflict, paralyzing us with fear and tension. Our emotions then, have us by the throat. When Wilhelm Reich told a patient she was "wearing a mask in order not to feel," she told him, "But Dr. Reich you have a mask too." He answered her, "Yes, that's true, but the mask hasn't me."

Even laughter is seen as an evolutionary strategy to ease tension and save energy. When one laughs, they signal to another person that all is well, especially if one laughs from a surprise. The laugh can signal "false alarm" or "nothing to waste energy on," and show others that the surprise is not a threat, as it interprets and re-values events. Laughter itself is contagious and it is this contagious quality that brain researcher Ramachandran finds fascinating. He suggests that laughter is the antidote to conservative thinking and is a signal to spread the "OK" sign to others. By laughing, we are saying that things are other than they appear. Laughter, like metaphor and creativity itself, is a survival mechanism that playfully links seemingly unrelated ideas and makes new sense out of them. And that is exactly what is needed when thinking about the area of the body where laughter resides.

One of the key concepts in thinking about the neck is that inside is an empty tube—the throat. What gives it form is nothing. The high concept of Zen is in contemplating emptiness as an image to become full or fully human. Even an empty feeling such as depression can be humanizing if we imagine it as a part of the whole of the human experience. Our hollow, empty feelings help us observe the hollowness of life, the meaningless parts of our culture, and the regrets in what we haven't done. Embraced as part of the big picture, we are gratified with feelings of fullness and balance as we understand that empty space allows us to fill it.

Feel the throat as empty and then bathe it with life-giving air. Resist the urge to stuff it with food when you are not hungry. The throat is meant to be hollow and empty most of the day and all of the night. From the holes in our head—our eyes, ears, nose and mouth—we bring in information for the rest of the body to act on. Emptiness is one of the heaviest ideas in anatomy, religion, philosophy, and physics.

From nothing is created everything. This is why this area embodies faith. We have to believe without facts staring us in the face. Scientist Peter Medawar notes that some scientific explanations can be "analgesics that dull the ache of incomprehension without removing the cause." But some people live by the phrase "*credo consoluas*: I believe because it is consoling." Sometimes you have to cozy up to emptiness and sometimes you have to try to make sense of it.

Einstein called the expanding universe the "cosmological constant" or "cc" which is the opposite force of gravity. While gravity pulls matter, the "cc" repels it. This constant is thought to come from empty space and has been given names like "smooth stuff," "x-matter," "quintessence," NACHOS (not astrophysical compact helo objects), "roll-ons" and just plain "funny energy." It doesn't push on matter nor really pull it, but stretches the space between bits of matter, adding more nothing. Physicist Edward Tryon states, "Everything in the universe adds up to nothing." Physicists know that the net electrical charge of nearly everything is close to zero. An animal or a human being can have untold trillions of positively and negatively charged particles but they cancel each other out so the sum is zero. The universe as a whole appears then to add up to nothing, electric-charge-wise. And nothing is what creativity stems from.

In playwriting, there is something known as the "Pinter Pause," long stretches of silence that carry more meaning than the dialogue. In handwriting, it is the spaces between the words that account for the legibility and the beauty of the letter depends on the shape enclosed by the letter. K. C. Cole states, "Never underestimate the power of space. When you run from danger it is the space that is your shield."

Being empty can be good for your health. Studies show that frequent sneezers are sick less often as they expel germs into space at nearly 100 miles per hour, thrusting viruses and bacteria between two to six feet away. The ancients thought the sneeze cleaned out the brain. In medicine today, it is known to clean out the throat and lungs. Medicating ourselves in an effort to dry up our mucous membranes during a cold, not only keeps the virus inside us, it leaves us out of practice for big pathogens. "Our data suggests that the price of hygiene is allergy" notes Paolo Matricardi, immunologist for the Italian Air Force. He exposed two hundred and forty cadets to food borne pathogens and found poor immune response in those that had used over-the-counter medications. He showed the immune cells in the gut are primed to respond when they first encounter invading bacteria or viruses. Without such training on minor illnesses, the cells instead multiply in response to the enemy and essentially eat the body. Allergies are annoying because we are eating our mucous membranes. We are attacking ourselves, seeing our own bodies as the enemy instead of the germs.

Danger signals are a recurring theme in nature with plants able to utilize chemical signaling to ward off insect attacks and alert predator insects to eat the attackers. Dr. Marcel Dicke of the Netherlands states that, "Today, the scientific community agrees that plants talking to their bodyguards is likely to be characteristic of most, if not all, plant species." When a caterpillar bites into a leaf, the plant recognizes a compound in the insect's saliva and initiates a chemical defense. The plant might produce a toxin to kill the insect or a compound to slow down or stop the insect's ability to digest more of the plant. A second line of defense occurs when the plant releases a blend of airborne chemical repellants to attract predators of that insect, which can limit the attack by 90%. The plant can even send chemicals that "jump-start" the defenses of undamaged neighboring plants. Heavy pesticide use, however, dampens if not totally silences these alarms and quiets the calls for help. Like a plant's alarm system, biologist E. O. Wilson suggests that environmental groups, protestors, tree-sitters and picketers are much like an immune system for the earth, signaling danger and warning of attack.

Dr. Polly Matzinger's theories are revolutionizing cancer research at the National Institute of Allergy and Infectious Diseases in Bethesda, Maryland. Her Danger Model postulates that the immune system responds only when it receives signals from injured cells. For decades, researchers thought the immune system reacted to foreign cells entering the body. Instead, the body is alerted by damage-induced alarm signals, not foreign cells. Her theory explains why the immune system doesn't respond to the presence of a fetus or to the good bacteria that aid digestion. What this means is that a healthy body has good alarm signals, not buffered ones, not medicated ones, not silenced ones, but alert ones and ones that can speak and be heard. A healthy body talks to itself.

Stephen Hawking notes in, *The Universe in a Nutshell,* that "about six or eight thousand years ago, a major new development occurred. We developed written language. This meant that information could be passed from one generation to the next without having to wait for the very slow process of random mutations and natural selection to code into the DNA sequence…A single paperback…could hold as much information as the difference in DNA between apes and humans, and a thirty volume encyclopedia could describe the entire sequence of human DNA." He suggests that the current rate at which human DNA is being coded by evolution is about "one bit a year." But there are two hundred thousand new books published each year, a new information rate of over "a million bits a second. One hundred thousand times faster than biological evolution."

There are many theories touting how or why language developed, most giving a nod to the pressures of hunting and gathering, which ensured that only those hunters and gatherers who could pass on the best information, mated, ensuring their genes survived. This theory, however, quickly loses ground when put to the evolutionary theorem test. A trait has to be unique to that species to stand out as the driving force. Clearly, there are better hunters on the planet, found in bird brains like eagles and hawks who can pluck a meal from water or land, lazy brains like tigers and lions that spend most of a month sleeping with only the occasional "kill," and virtual no-brainers like starfish and trees, who seem to find food just fine. Other animals are expert gatherers, storing tens of thousands of seeds a year and recalling their location between their migrations from Mexico to Alaska. We have trouble remembering where the tulip bulbs are stored.

Marc Hauser of Harvard suggests that language developed to ensure fair trade. He notes that only humans have the power of recursion, the combining of words and numbers to create an infinite number of expressions. Language, then, allowed us to be better bookkeepers. Language theorists seem to like recursion, for they combine innumerable causes that may have affected the capacity for human speech. Fair trade, more successful hunting and gathering, density, sociability, larynx location, brain size, and even hand coordination as it coincides with the acquisition for language, are all supported in varying theories. Richard Dawkins reasons that throwing was the forerunner of foresight and language development. He says, "When we throw our mind forward in imagination, are we doing something almost literal as well as metaphorical? When the first word was uttered, somewhere in Africa, did the speaker imagine himself throwing a missile from his mouth to his intended hearer?" Although this theory is attractive in that it proposes that abstract thought is immediately derived from a motor movement, plenty of animals have unique motor patterns that have not evolved into language. Why would throwing so greatly change the brain, and diving through the air into water to snag a submerged salmon not change an osprey's brain? Humans are not the only unique species. In fact, all species are unique, most with stupendous motor feats that secure their survival.

Large brain size, and hence the capacity for language, is not accounted for by our increased sociability. Clearly, those with large brains like scientists, mathematicians and even artists are not known for their adept social skills. And talking is a huge energy drain, evidenced by the fact that when we are very ill, we cannot talk. Talking lacks credibility as a survival mechanism at all. Plenty of species thrive and cannot talk. So what is it, all this talking? It's about imitation and it caused what is called the "Runaway Brain," a spiraling in brain growth and skill acquisition. Imitation, or meme spreading, is social learning and requires three skills: the first is making decisions about what to imitate, the second is to engage in complex transformations from one point of view to another, and the third is the production of matching bodily actions whether it be hand gestures, motor patterning, mirroring or language. Since many animals imitate each other and many gesture or call to each other, something had to happen to humans to declare that they alone mastered skill number two.

Personally, my favorite theory reveals the pervasive catalytic event that forced the evolution of language. It is also the indicator that transforms cultural givens, provides breaks in mental habits, and is the one thing present in the creation of several of the world's religions—psychoactive drugs. Behavior, specifically, the ingestion of potent plants or fungi, spawned an increase in brain function. Research into the history of "transformed imagination" finds that drug use was crucial to nourishing and expanding human sensibility. David Lenson found that big leaps in artistic givens included the consumption of drugs and he cites the onset of romanticism in poetry, jazz, cubism, surrealism, modernism, rock and roll, and Blues as evidence. It is well known that Plato, Socrates, Artistotle, Aeschylus, and Euripides all participated in the Mysteries of Eleusis, a fancy name for the consumption of a powerful hallucinogenic potion called ergot, made from fungus-infected grains.

One of the world's earliest known religions, Soma, hails from the Indo-European area of Central Asia. Its sacred text is preserved in *Rig Veda* and the religion worshiped a drug called Soma, a powerful intoxicant. Only a few modern variations of religious orders are drug free but most religions pick and choose their drug of choice. While Catholics promote wine as a religious sacrament, Islam frowns on alcohol in favor of opium. Islamic and Hindu cultures used cannabis to ward off boredom and fatigue, increasing their concentration on prayer, while Sufis used it for mystical purposes. Between the use of peyote cactus, mushrooms, ergot, fermented grape, and cannabis, psychoactive plants and fungi were used worldwide in every culture except Eskimo. Ethnobotanists call these plants "entheogens," meaning, "the God within."

Remembering that any plant substance that alters cognitive function is considered a psychoactive or neuroactive drug, coffee, nicotine and even chocolate, then rank among the world's fastest acting neuro-substances. There are few among us that could admit to never ingesting a psychoactive compound. It is culturally accepted drug use in action when we start our morning with the lament, "I can't wake up without my first cup of coffee." We admit our brains won't work as well, and we can't start a day's work without a drug. Psychoactive drugs are themselves, runaway memes. Once used to encourage leaps of imagination and the birth of innovation, they were quickly usurped and abused by those in power. By ingesting them in larger quantities and for prolonged periods, innovation morphed into stupification, and independence blurs into dependency.

In fact, the history of drug use has been linked with the history of hard labor. From pyramid building, to the Great Wall of China, to cotton fields and coal mines, not to mention the Martini Lunch business deals, drugs have been used to sustain prolonged work days while allowing the worker to consume little in the way of food. The "boss as drug source" serves to imprison workers into servitude and domestication through addiction. This concept is retained in present day language as we refer to our bosses as managers. The word is derived from the French "*manige*" meaning, "the training and riding of a horse." The image then is of our boss getting on our back, kicking with their heels, and steering us in the direction they want us to go. It is an image of domination and taming.

We are easily addicted to psychoactive drugs because we happen to have a natural version waiting to be kicked into high gear. In 1988, a neuroscientist named Allyn Howlett from St. Louis University Medical School found a receptor for THC, the active ingredient in marijuana, in vast numbers in the brain. While they occur nearly everywhere in the body, even the uterus, they are clustered in the central cortex, hippocampus, basal ganglia, and amygdala. They do not occur in the brain stem, which is why one cannot over-dose on marijuana: it cannot adversely affect your breathing, heart rate and other involuntary functions. The Israeli neuroscientist, Raphael Mechovlam identified THC in the 60's and in 1992, he found the endogenous cannabinoid in the body and named it "anandimide," a Sanskrit word meaning "inner bliss." In other words, we make our own version of marijuana in our body everyday, albeit in very small doses.

A runaway or unintentional meme is very well responsible for the increasingly potent marijuana on the streets today. Due to the spread of specific penalties and strict laws for growers, plants came indoors. Once growing conditions were compacted, growers were successful only if they expanded and expounded on natural growing conditions. Thus, when they needed a source of light, they didn't have the sun, or the constrictions of the sun as it shines only certain hours and certain seasons of the year. Artificial light could be stronger and yearlong. Plants couldn't be allowed to reach their natural heights of ten and twelve feet, so growers bred for shorter plants, little realizing that the most potent buds grow on the lateral, stocky branches. The most potent plants were hybridized and cloned, with most of today's plants coming from one super-potent Eureka, California plant—*Cannabis sativa x indica*—which gained near perfection in the early 1980's. Laws prohibiting marijuana farms inadvertently prompted better growing conditions, allowing for knee-high plants with fist-sized flower buds. The manipulation of the genetic make-up of the plant increased potency from 2% to a whopping 15%.

While marijuana use is well known for its side effects, including short-term memory loss, mild sedation, and mild cognitive changes, it is touted for its ability to alter pain sensation and is becoming commonplace treatment for the side effects of chemotherapy and AIDS treatments. But many researchers are questioning the above "unwanted" side effects and suggesting that we might just "want" them. They propose that memory loss is desirable and far from being a breakdown of mental operations, it is a highly functional survival strategy. Forgetting is as important as remembering. It appears our brain functions best when it can bring sensory information down to a manageable trickle and sort the meaningful from the useless.

THC bathes ordinary thought with the "aura of profundity" and leads to insights found in everyday phenomenon. By imbibing and thereby enhancing the already naturally occurring THC, one might notice the sublime or just as easily the terrifying, perhaps "tripping out" that oil-saturated cars are like cells pulsing along the hardened arteries of Mother Earth, roads so clogged it is as if we ourselves are a macro-version of cholesterol. Or not.

What we do know from studies, is that time slows or even seems to stop after using THC and although sensory data has not changed, noticing the sensory data does. Objects are viewed as if for the first time, and what is forgotten is the familiarity. As author Pollan noted after smoking marijuana, "Something as ordinary as ice cream became *ICE CREAM!*" Of course, living like this all the time would be exhausting but it can serve to explain the on-going preoccupation required in establishing a religion or the mental leaps in developing language to convey abstract thought. In fact, our survival may depend on mental leaps of faith as George Bernard Shaw reminds us, "The reasonable man adapts himself to the world; the unreasonable one persists in trying to adapt the world to himself. Therefore all progress depends on the unreasonable man." Hopefully, we can all become unreasonable without ingesting drugs, perhaps finding the sublime within ourselves.

The trend toward "cosmetic psychopharmacology," wherein we use drugs to fine-tune mood and improve performance, merely masks uncomfortable emotions. However, that discomfort might be signaling a need for change whether it is a change in lifestyle or values. Psychiatrist and psychoanalyst Elio Frattaroli, in *Healing the Soul in the Age of the Brain: Becoming Conscious in an Unconscious World,* argues that drugs like Prozac enable patients to avoid the very thing that promises true healing—full consciousness. Anxiety is a useful human condition wherein the anxious question the fast pace of modern life. But, he warns, materialistic cultures fear self-exploration, the questioning of authority, or attempts to question reality itself.

Drugs that protect materialistic values, like caffeine and nicotine (stimulants) and alcohol (which is a mind numbing drug), along with the mood stabilizers, are legalized. Drugs that promote the questioning of values and alternate versions of reality, along with a sedative, calming, quality are targets of anti-drug programs. The three anti-drug themes are loss of control, loss of mind and loss of life. Little is said about a drugged out or drunk society, albeit legally drugged out, that subverts any real emotions (anti-depressants), kills more people than all genetic diseases put together (nicotine and alcohol), or prompts the working class to stimulate themselves (caffeine) until they can retire and buy their life back. It's as if the soul is being held ransom.

But perhaps, we don't need drugs at all to change our consciousness. After all, movement has a great capacity for changing brain function, even if that movement is in the form of kneeling in prayer or sitting in meditation.

Bill Moyer, journalist extraordinaire, delves into prayer, faith, alternative medicine, meditation, and belief. He calls religion "the Great Perhaps," as it calls for faith in the midst of ambiguity. It is faith that something exists despite the absence of fact. There is no evidence that God exists just as surely as there is no evidence that God does not exist. It is a self-consistent system of argument. While not a valuable trait in a theory, as it could just as well be stated irrefutably that an ant created Earth, self-consistent systems are attractive because they cannot be proven or disproved. It requires faith as a starting point.

This belief in the invisible is crucial in thinking about our very real bodies. Theologians suggest that Jesus taught that we couldn't love an invisible God, while at the same time, hate a visible neighbor. If we can understand and love the invisible, we can love the visible parts of us. Surely it is not too big a leap to find wisdom in our body, considering the leaps we are willing to make in believing the invisible; be it God, germs, gravity, or words.

We must first make ourselves sacramental, remembering from the first chapter that sacrum, our sitting bone, rests in the word sacrament. Sacrament is a name given to anything that has the power to evoke meaning that is already implicitly present. As W. Paul Jones states in, *A Table in the Desert: Making Space Holy,* "sacraments are hinge points of our journey when there is a promise to act in certain ways." Sometimes called "fulcrum moment," there will be times when we experience something we didn't choose; a lesson no one studies willingly. Grief, illness, pain, and loss will cause shifts to occur that might change our lives. They will be events that question what our life hinges on. Resilience in a personality is that ability to master such change. It all hinges on what we are made of.

Our jaw is that hinge point where our words are sacred. Our neck is the hinge point lying between the faith we have in our heart and the knowledge we have in our brain. This area, finally, is where we make promises to act in certain ways. It is where we can choose to be led by creativity and wisdom, instead of pain and suffering. It is the empty anatomy that is filled with the faith that we can be otherwise.

HOW TO EVOKE FAITH

○ This area is the Vishuddha Chakra and it is symbolized by space. It is here we live up to and approach our obligations. The detail of ritual in sounds and gestures grows from here. We act on whispered wisdom and we do so with integrity and attention. If we fail to bridge this open gap between how we act toward the earth and our responsibility to the earth, we will hear only its cries for help. The whispers will be gone. Weak energy here finds us silent and unable to speak our truth. Chaotic energy here finds us hyper-verbal, trying to "explain away" everything. Those of us who use logic to solve every problem will be at a loss when we experience the death of a loved one, chronic pain, or trauma. It is not easy to live in the empty space required by faith. With practice, we can feel full there.

❖ Many letters were developed according to the shape of a body. The letter "a," meaning "leader" in Greek, is thought to be the first sound made by man. It is made with the widest opening of our jaw, pharynx and lips, as if we came in yelling. The letter "b" means "mouth" in Greek (beta) and resembles the lips when the capital B is turned over on its flat side. "C" is thought to be the hollow of the throat, and "d" is from delta, meaning "door or opening" and also refers to the mouth. "E" is window, which is literally translated into the word "wind's eye," another opening. "L" is thought to be the body as it looks at its shadow and "I" is the pointed finger. "K" is the palm of the hand, "kapa." In a strange tale, it is said the name of man is written on his face (much like cartoonist, Matt Groenig writes his initials on Homer Simpson's head. He draws the hair as "M" above Homer's "G" shaped ear). The Latin word for man is "omo" and if you envision connected eyebrows as the "m" with two "o's" for eyes, you see the word as clear as day. It is good to remember that one of our most potent tools, language, is born from the body.

❖   To keep the GI tract healthy, eat plenty of vegetables. The increase in fiber requires more chewing which stimulates the gingiva and the periodontal ligaments. Slower chewing reduces oral intake. The fiber also holds more water, slowing gastric emptying, and giving the feeling of fullness earlier.

❖   Cursive writing is particularly stressful to both the anatomy and to the analogous brain due to its purely artificial nature. A child who has been taught to print, finds the printed word the only available writing to read in books, on signs, and on computer screens. Suddenly, in third grade, the child finds the rules have arbitrarily changed and they must link letters. Although they learn to write cursive, they will rarely if ever read it. When handwriting was taught at a blackboard, hand coordination found needed stability in the strength of the shoulder. When learning to write at a desk, shoulder strength is forfeited and handwriting suffers. Not only are desk-taught children less legible, they make more grammatical errors. Look at the handwriting of our grandparents, both male and female and notice the legibility that was gleaned from their use of benches versus chairs, and blackboards versus desks. Sitting at a desk removes another key feature in language acquisition—immediate feedback. Blackboard writing is a communal event and carries with it cause and effect, where you are immediately made aware of your errors. Handing in paper homework, a child will only be made aware of their mistakes when it is handed back to them the next day; a day late for the effect to be matched with its cause. The anatomy of the hand suffers too with cursive writing, as we see children's fingers moving as they connect letters to each other. Oftentimes, the fingers are blanched white, a bloodletting discoloration at the fingertips as they attempt a death-grip on the pencil. Chalk would break if we were to hold it improperly or with too much force. We are also forcing our children to color in the lines and write way too early. Fifteen years ago, a child had to be able to write their name to graduate from kindergarten. Now, they must be able to write sentences. Did our hands and brains evolve in the last fifteen years or did our work ethic just demand that children act like adults when they are five years old?

❖   Ask yourself if you are filling emptiness with talk, food, work, entertainment, and errands because it is too terrifying to do nothing and just be with yourself. If so, you are acting as if you are allergic to yourself or are your own worst nightmare. Don't die as your own enemy. Befriend yourself.

❖   There are more and more of us crippled by transportation, trading sleep for schedules, and silenced by engine noise. We are increasingly sickened by the food that should nourish us. The leading causes of death (cancer, heart disease, AIDS and accidental injury) all depend to some extent on our behavior.

Instead of treating the negatives of disease, we need to request action toward the positives of health. Walk, rest, and look into subsistence work, convivial tools, and inventive activity. Learn to play a guitar instead of listening to recordings. Garden instead of shop. Be who you wanted to be when you grew up. If you aren't who you wanted to be when you grew up, you didn't listen to yourself when you talked.

- Practice the Tibetan meditation practice of *tonglen* wherein you inhale suffering and exhale peace.

- Imagine the earth in you as a mountain range that surrounds a village, a village that experiences a cool breeze every afternoon. You are the mountain, faithfully taking its one breath each morning and gently exhaling each afternoon.

- Become fascinated by the water in you that offers a faithful ebb and flow of its tides. The tides rise and fall in our bodies twice each day just like the planet we live on.

- Let the air in you be the wind that whispers knowledge to those who will listen. Speak your truth, gently; but speak it. As the wind increases, help the trees shed what is no longer necessary and blow the leaves off the branches and into pillowy piles for children to jump in.

- Allow the fire in you to warm the snow, showing it how to be water. Heat the water, teaching it how to be steam. Change forms; make new choices. Water teaches us that things can take on many forms.

- Learn about Ganesha, a God in the Indian pantheon who is the remover and creator of obstacles. Accept paradox without attempting to solve it. Accept the presence of obstacles as much as you enjoy the removal of them.

- Try Pavighasana: Gate Pose. Place your body in *parigha* or "a bar" which is used in shutting a gate. As we stretch through the ribs, the body is the crossbeam that, when open, allows access for breathing the life force. A gate helps us to recognize what is beneficial and decline what isn't, rather than leave ourselves open to any and all forms of input. Don't let everything into your garden.

- Try Sirshasana: Headstand. In this posture, energy is prevented from leaving the throat and head. Sometimes it is called Supported Head pose, offering a landing for a part of us that rarely touches the ground.

- Try Simhasana: Lion's pose. This posture allows us to roar away all our irritations and frustrations rather than swallow them. It keeps us from having an outburst in our stomach. It tells us we are King of Our Jungle and that our instinct to feel rage is not frightening but part of the human experience. It expels toxic rage with a simple roar. Nietzsche used two poetic images to describe the spiritual journey. The camel represented dedication, the willingness to kneel, the ability to carry burdens honorably, repetition, real labor, and a trust in the earth; all aspects of the fourth chakra. The Lion, a symbol of the fifth chakra, is seen as the roar of freedom, the voice of truth, liberation, certainty, and grace.

❍ Try Hari Hara Asana. Hara is a goddess whose symbol is the broom as she sweeps away all things destructive. Hari is the preserver of all things that deserve to stay. Each ideal is in half of this posture. We destroy what is no longer necessary by sweeping our regrets away and we have room for what is of value in our lives. Practice standing like the broom in this pose. Decide what stays in a room and what needs to go. What is necessary in your life and what violates feeling at home on the planet? Be sure you are not making your home comfortable at the expense of ruining the homes of other creatures. The broom is not destructive.

❍ Try Dhanurasana: Archer's Bow. This posture stretches the psoas muscle deep in the groin, which is the muscle that initiates each step in walking. Keeping this muscle free of tension, we are able to see our way ahead and walk our particular path. Imagine yourself aimed as surely as you would aim an arrow at a target. Go there.

❍ Try Nataraj I: Dance of Shiva. In this posture, everything is falling apart and changing. It is an asymmetrical posture with the weight of one leg and both arms to one side as if you are being pulled in a direction you had no intention of going. It is war, an Old English word meaning "confusion." While in this unlikely position, imagine that you are being pulled in confusing directions with only a slim hope of finding peace again. The one leg you balance on is this slim hope. Say to yourself, "although I am being pulled into war (confusion), I remain balanced on a slim hope."

❍ Try Virabhadra I: Shiva Warrior. Done immediately after Nataraj I, these postures can be very powerful in transforming your courage. Warrior is someone who goes through war (confusion). This posture requires that you first focus your eyes on the point where you will place your foot to the side. Imagine you are confused and are searching the ground for a path to take. Now advance your foot to the path you have chosen. Bring your arm to shoulder height, committing to the path.

❍ Try the Camel Pose. The camel is an animal that offers support and has a determined faith that it will find water again. As you sit in this pose, your pelvis, from the Latin word for basin, is level. It will hold the precious liquid we don't want to spill, as nothing can be wasted in the desert.

❖ Don't wait for a more heroic version of yourself. Be a hero now. Practice the yoga ethic of truthfulness; keep your word to yourself. And practice the ethic of non-stealing; don't do something because someone else wants you to—it is stealing from your choice. Also, avoid keeping secrets as you are stealing knowledge from the person who may need to know. Ask yourself, what is the greatest lie I tell myself? Now ask, what secret am I keeping from myself?

❖ Express yourself with your body and your voice. Feel free to move. Avoid constrictive clothing. Open up your house by clearing clutter. The constriction of your living space can be seen as your compulsion to dictate movement patterns. Create space to gratify your strong motor needs. As a child expresses their needs with their body, dance with joy and play hard to give an outlet to anger or frustration. Remember that motor expression begets emotional expression, which begets intellectual expression. Give yourself room to move through life.

❖ Prem Prakash of the Sunnyasin order tells a story for all young men and women. In the story he holds a bell. He turns the bell upside down, holding it now like a cup. He tells youngsters, "You were meant to be a bell." He says to be wary of people who tell you, "But you are a beautiful container. You should be a cup." If you let people fill you up, if you take your parents values because that's what you were taught, if you only inherit ideas without thinking for yourself, you might never have the sound you were meant to have. On Prakash's tombstone is written: "Let it never be said that he never rang."

❖ Childhood is the most active stage in our life. Children who develop sedentary habits not only become increasingly overweight, they can develop enlarged tonsils. Weak tissues are flooded with lymphatic fluids and there is an absence of toned muscles that offer a squeezing massage to keep the flow active. These children are more susceptible to disease because of their underactive lymph flow. Next time your children watch several hours of television, think about their stagnant immune system.

❖ Meditation teacher Gunilla Norris says, "When we sit in stillness we are profoundly active. Keeping silent, we can hear the roar of existence." Once you hear the roar, act on it.

❖ William Blake wrote this line in a poem: "If the Sun and Moon should doubt, They'd immediately go out." Have parts of you gone out?

❖ The chakra situated at the base of the throat is the energy center called Akasha Tattva. If this energy is overactive, you will find yourself with the constant desire to tidy things up, to clean, to create order and to over-explain with logic. A culture might express this over-activity by using ritual, the ordering of gestures and sounds. Habitual or compulsive behaviors might express themselves, as will futile attempts to keep things from changing.

There will be a loss of vitality and flexibility. Change is the supreme law of the universe.

❖ Neck tension can be seen symbolically as a fear of failure. A stiff neck literally finds you unable to look in another direction. A single-minded version of reality and a single version of success require that you look straight ahead, never veering from your course of action. You will fail to entertain alternatives, and you will act quickly believing that success is assured. But hurry is no substitution for skill and you will find that the motivation to succeed is a poor substitution for integrity.

❖ Author Jack Kornfield suggests we develop a mature spiritual language and discontinue citing phrases that set one thing against another. What we name medicine may be poison and what we call tonic may be toxic. Listen to how you talk to yourself. Do you say you have to work 60 hours a week to "keep up?" Are you "keeping up" by over-consuming, buying unnecessary things and calling them necessary? Are you saying you are being responsible by owning more and more things but deep down you know you are living irresponsibly?

❖ There is a communicative web between all creatures on the earth. We have failed to listen to the messages from our tropical forests. We have failed to respond to the signals from a once thriving marshland. We have not listened to their language because we have been so busy with ours. Instead of fasting from food, take a fast from talking. Practice voluntary simplicity by adding no needless noise to the world today. No motors, no television, no radio. Listen to the earth's noises: birds, wind, waves, and feet touching the ground. Pablo Neruda's poem "Keeping Quiet" has these wise passages (parts not quoted remind us not to confuse silence with total inactivity):

Now we will count to twelve
and we will keep still
for once on the face of the earth,
let's not speak any language;
let's stop for a second
and not move our arms so much.

It would be an exotic moment
without rush, without engines;
we would all be together
in a sudden strangeness.

...If we were not so single-minded
about keeping our lives moving,

perhaps a huge silence
might interrupt this sadness
of never understanding ourselves
and of threatening ourselves with death.

❖   To help with heartburn, sleep on your right side to ease stomach emptying. Avoid tight waisted clothes and caffeine, which relaxes the stomach sphincter allowing food to travel up. Sit upright to eat, letting gravity keep food deep in the stomach and do not recline for a full hour after you eat. Honor the fact that your mouth sits higher than your stomach and should remain that way when both are in use.

❖   Practice choice every day. Don't become the type of person who medicates their illness in an effort to relieve symptoms only to go back to the poor health habits you had before. Choose to find the reason you're in pain, why you have a headache, why you suffer from nightly heartburn, and fix the cause rather than medicate the effects.

❖   Blind faith in technology, in the belief that material goods will make you happy and sedated by a lifestyle that is dictated by advertisements—these are all examples of what Thomas Moore calls, "psychological modernism." The uncritical acceptance of the modern world has led to accelerated scientific progress while neglecting to make the world a better place for everyone to live. Has the high-tech world paid any attention to the day-to-day existence of most of the world's inhabitants? One billion people live in slums. Has success in the technological world helped end famines? Does every child have an education or do a few children have computers in every classroom? It is an enormously different reality to own an Apple and own an apple.

❖   Negentropy is the opposite of entropy. It is freedom. The Buddhist concept of differentiation offers that one would free themselves from genetic and social determinism by controlling one's impulses and desires. By making choices, one finds integration and negates entrenchment.

❖   Be your own best friend. Talk yourself into going for a walk, tell yourself you are worthwhile, encourage yourself like you are someone you are fond of. You would never let someone squeeze your neck so tight you couldn't breathe. Don't let your muscles get so tight they are choking the life out of you. You wouldn't let someone tell you that you must eat a bag of cookies or that you must watch television all day. You wouldn't let someone tell you that you can't go outside today. Don't tell yourself such a thing.

❖   Faith is held together in the imagery of imagining (hope) and forgetting (forgiveness). Have a powerful imagination and remember Einstein's words, "Imagination is more important than knowledge. It is the preview of life's coming attractions." This is important, especially as questions about how the world works come closer together, and answers come farther apart. Imagination lies between the answers and the questions. It is said that science concerns itself with what is true and mythology concerns itself with what is more true.

❖ Aeschyleus wrote in the play Prometheus:
Prometheus: I caused mortals to cease foreseeing doom.
Chorus: What did you provide them with against such a sickness?
Prometheus: I place in them blind hopes.

❖ Tessitura is a phrase used by singers to note the place where their voice feels most at home. One person's tessitura may be as an alto, another as a soprano. All in all, it suggests a "sense of rightness" for that person's nature. As our voice finds its home, so might our sense of self. What makes up your life's tessitura?

❖ Dr. Paul Brand, a surgeon, and his wife, Dr. Margaret Brand, an ophthalmologist, spent most of their professional lives working with leprosy patients and found an unusual use for the strong masseter muscle in the cheek. Since leprosy destroys nerve endings, the patient has little to no sensation of pain in the affected areas, most often in parts of the body where nerve endings are near the surface. The bacterium seems to thrive in "cold" sections of nerves, such as where the ulnar nerve briefly surfaces at the elbow or the median nerve surfaces at the volar wrist. The eyelid houses one of those exposed, cold, nerve endings and thus, the patient fails to blink to wash and wipe away foreign objects and dust particles from the eyeball. Needing a muscle with a deep, warmer nerve, the Brands replaced the eyelid with a section of the masseter, keeping it intact with its "mother" masseter in the jaw. Having the patient chew gum all day, each bite on the gum told the new eye masseter to blink, thus protecting the eyeball. Use their example and employ the warm, deep parts of yourself to protect the cold, shallow part of you. Refuse to focus on the easy targets, to make shallow excuses, or to become cold and hardened. Perpetually opened eyes may see reality clearly but it is not healthy to stare reality down. Close your eyes and see the invisible.

❖ Emotions have a strong role in interrupting activity. Stopping to express our feelings can bring about control and can help deteriorate the linear progression of a situation. Emotions are a crucial control of motor actions. The neuroscientist, Damasio, calls the limbic or emotionally charged brain, a place of somatic markers where we have gut feelings. These gut instincts steer us away from options and pare down our choices to a more manageable few. But just as it can limit thoughts to make them manageable, it can limit them so much that we mistake them for the only reality available. "We might say the mind represents more than well-being, it also represents well-thinking...our thinking powers are either at the top of their game or can be taken there. Likewise, feeling sad is not just about a sickness in the body or about a lack of energy to continue. It is often about an inefficient mode of thought stalling around a limited number of ideas of loss." Increase the number of ideas you move around. Likewise, move around and increase the number of ideas you have.

CHAKRA SIX—TRUTH

BRAIN, NERVOUS SYSTEM, EYES, EARS

"To me it seems that those sciences are vain and full of error
which are not born of experience, mother of all certainty,
first hand experience which in its origins, or means, or
end has passed through one of the five senses."—Leonardo da Vinci

"I'm very brave generally, only today I happen to have a
headache."—Tweedledum

This area is where invisible information becomes perceptible. Our eyes, ears, and nose each receive information from afar and very literally, make "sense" out of it. It is where we experience insight, transformation, and the blessing of learning. It is here where something as simple as a tear or a smile can communicate the depths of what it means to be human. While our senses are the most personal content of our minds, they can also be the most culturally influenced.

The brain is composed of two hemispheres, the left and right brain, which communicate their specific functions, working together as the ultimate exchange organ to transform two types of information into one thought. The left brain houses language for the most part and is in charge of fine details, while the right hemisphere is the visionary brain, in charge of large spatial concepts. In a way, the right brain might set a goal and the left brain would outline the steps to make sure it happens. It is this movement back and forth between the two hemispheres that makes thinking an elegant dance.

In fact, the brain is often talked about as if it could move. At times our head is swimming or the mind is racing. Sometimes thoughts are running wild, or we might have a flight of ideas and even frenzied thinking. Other times, our brain is talked about like a force of nature, as when the mind is in a fog, or when we experience a flood of memories. We could be blessed with a lightning quick wit or have an idea that strikes like a thunder bolt and we might even see things through a dark cloud.

The eyes are the brain's window, a word meaning "wind's eye," in that a window allows us to see what is going on outside. A Buddhist concept of vision suggests that even emotions are represented in the eyes. While hatred and suspicion require the focused gaze on a single point of danger, trust shows the eyes widened to life's possibilities. Blame is the blasphemous position wherein one claims they can see like a God. Worry and anxiety are seeing and experiencing things that haven't yet happened and depression might be seeing a past loss in the present moment, as if it is occurring over and over again.

Linking our senses to our emotions might sound like mumbo jumbo, but our senses are notoriously unreliable at translating reality. Simply by placing your hand firmly against your eyeball, you will "see" light, even though your eye is closed. Tactile pressure is translated into the only language an eye understands—light—and so it very literally, speculates. It feels like it saw light and so that is what it tells the brain. Enough unusual input and our systems can quickly become disoriented.

In the case of tool use, an object becomes an extension of our sense of touch. We feel the feel the tip of a screwdriver on the screw yet we have no sense receptors there. In that case of dry ice, we feel the extreme cold as hot. We can push easily through the surface tension of water but to a bug, that tension is a major force in its life. And while gravity is imperative to us, a fly on the ceiling is impervious to it. Sensations are relative.

In the 1940's, a malady known as "railroad spine" attacked train passengers in debilitating numbers. Increased anxiety, sleeplessness, headaches, loss of appetite, and a profound feeling of dread were part of the rail experience and were thought to occur from the confinement and disorienting speed of the trains. People had never moved that fast before. While confinement is known to heighten our senses, with swaddled babies deprived of movement showing a sharpened sense of hearing and vision, it also adds to explosions in kinesthetic thresholds. Deprivation of movement can heighten anxiety, and in the case of the train passengers, was thought to be so disorienting, it could lead to madness and damage to the nervous system, hence the name "railroad spine." The antidote was to focus on an object inside the train in an effort to remove the incoming visual onslaught. By renting a standardized railroad book called, *Penny Dreadful*, named for their cost and the malady they would cure, a passenger could avoid motion sickness. By sticking their nose in a book, passengers forfeited the view out the railroad window but also avoided the incoming sensation that they were moving.

This same malady occurred in the first decade of air travel, with the remnants still present in every airplane we ride in today—the vomit airbag. Since we were used to traveling only as fast as a train could go, airplane speeds over-whelmed our sensory processing systems, causing nausea and vomiting in nearly every passenger on every trip. As we change our relationship to space and time, our insides take a tad longer to adjust to the reality our brains invented. In other words, our brains can make us move faster than our bodies can understand. With increased exposure, motion sickness can be integrated, much like a figure skater can learn to tolerate spins. Given time, our senses can catch up to the input.

Science tells us that the health of the eyes has to do with a fine-tuned sense of timing and rhythm, even when it comes to a simple thing like blinking. The eye blink is in charge of keeping the slate clean, shutting out information as much as it is taking it in, with our entire visual system shut off 50 milliseconds before the lids close. When we say that babies "take it all in," there are statistics to prove it. A two-month old baby blinks less than one time a minute, a five year old six times a minute, and a twenty year old, twenty-four times a minute.

The eye blink also regulates hormonal levels. Dopamine, a hormone in charge of smooth, coordinated movements, is released with an eye blink. Sleep, a prolonged eye blink if you will, cuts down on dopamine because the difference between rapid eye opening and eye blink has been removed. Of course, during sleep we are in very little need of a hormone that is in charge of how fast we move. Parkinson's patients, with their low dopamine levels, blink too seldom and schizophrenics, with high dopamine levels, blink too often. Impaired cognition and eye fatigue while working on a computer's visual display terminal is measured by increased eye blinks.

All of our senses are rhythm transformers. Our eyes take light waves and translate them into images. Even though there is a wide range of pulsations between the body and the outside world (waves of light pulse between 390 trillion and 780 trillion times per second, while the cells in the body pulse at 1,000), the retina bridges this gap. That gap is how we translate the world into color, as we pick and sort among the pulsations of a spectrum. Then these translations are themselves encoded in the brain via an optical hologram, where widely separated regions of the brain become synchronized. When ready to retrieve that same information for a second time, neural neighbors interact and entire functions can be reconstructed from a very small piece of information.

This is an amazingly ecological and economical memory storage system and in some people, quite refined. People with "synesthesia," can transfer one sensory experience to another through close association or "neighboring." You might neighbor when you say a high note on the piano is "tinny" (something you hear), or "bright" (something you see), or "sharp" (something you feel). In some cases, senses can take each others' places, as when the sounds of a very low pitch are "heard" through the skin (<60 cycles per second) which occurs within electrostatic fields—we can feel the vibration of bass sounds. True synesthetics make up 10% of a population and may see sounds, describing a low note as dark or a high note as yellow. Some can smell pain or taste touch depending on which holograms are communicating back and forth. Einstein, probably the most celebrated synesthetic, saw pictures when he thought of math problems. Such phenomenon offends our rational mind, defies notions of cause and effect, and makes us question the reality of what we perceive.

While synesthesia is an example of increased association, we usually sort through possibilities and narrow down our attention to information that "makes more sense." For instance, we sort through the thousands of possible sounds a human voice can make and narrow the choices down to a few cultural variants. Genetically, a six-month old baby can make every sound in every language on earth. But four months later, two-thirds of that capacity is cut away through alterations in cerebral tissue. The brain cells that are useful, that is the cells that recognize the language native to our culture, thrive. The ones that fail to prove their worth, that is cells that are never reinforced through hearing, will experience apoptosis—cell death. Choice becomes the brain's preferred economics once again. It chooses a small number of useful sounds to store in memory.

Not only does our brain become biased through reinforcement, but our behavior also changes through a sorting out of unpopular or superfluous information. "Epigenetic rules" are defined as any regularity that bias behavior in a particular direction. As human beings, we have an epigenetic propensity toward language that does not exist in animals. We require a greater range in audio-visual skills in order to have language, which is at the cost of a decreased sense of smell and taste. This propensity then feeds back and rebounds in a richer vocabulary for describing hearing and vision with nearly ? to ¾ of all words in any language applying to those senses. Less than one-tenth of any language, in any culture, describes smell or taste.

The senses dictate our behavior in the way we talk and the way we talk is dictated by the culture we live in. Once again, cultural evolution, or memes, alters the make-up of our brain through a series of selection, adaptation, and extinction. And most of that cultural information comes to our brain through the holes in our head.

Our head is considered a "mobile turret" upon which all long-distance sense organs are mounted. While it is easy to see that the majority of communicative signals produced by animals are linked with the movement of the head (both vocal and non-vocal in that animals also communicate their emotions with their teeth, horns, or antlers which are mounted on the head), it is not well known that such is the case for humans. While we think we can direct our eye gaze to the left and right without moving our head, our posterior cervical neck muscles remains subtly linked with our direction of visual attention.

Place your fingers against the back of your neck just under the occipital shelf of bone at the skull. Your fingers should be placed on either side of your spine, tucked firmly under the bony shelf as if ready to play the piano. Now, without moving your head, jerk your eyes to the left and right. You should feel the distinct movement of your sub-occipital muscles, at the ready for a motor response from the head, merely from the input of movement from the eyes. This is an example of how brain functions, including the senses, are descendants of motion.

Motion is involved in almost every aspect of human experience with even our thoughts relentlessly moving from one topic to another. Emotions and thoughts shift and as Ratey notes in *User's Guide to the Brain*, "Language is essentially a complex semantic dance by the mind and the tongue, a sophisticated form of motion that allows us to manipulate the contents of the world without laying a hand on them. To improve our brains, we have to move our bodies, take action, get going."

As it turns out, our muscular coordination, our attention center, and our spatial orientation of our near senses (proprioception, vestibular and kinesthesia are internal sensations) and far senses (hearing, vision, smell, and tactile are from external information) all take place in the cerebellum, literally "the little brain." The cerebellum is responsible for our balance, posture, coordination, and rhythmic shift of our attention. It connects and feeds back to other layers of the brain so that when we move, an emotion might be displayed and vice versa. When we are happy, we smile. When we smile, it triggers happiness. The voluntary choice of smiling can activate the involuntary system in the brain.

Paul Ekman and Richard Davidson study the brain patterns of smiling. They found that there is different brain activity between the fake smile and the genuine smile (there are eighteen types of smiles!). The muscles around the eyes, which pull the cheeks up, are only engaged during real smiles. Ekman says, "Muscles around the eye do not obey the will. The movement only occurs with genuine emotion." This detection system—looking at the eyes as they pull the cheeks—is a window into what the brain is really thinking. It is real evidence that a smile can signal when people are lying; for instance, saying they feel good when in fact they are miserable inside. As Ekman says, "The public display can betray the private thought." John Gottman of the University of Washington, found happily married couples display the real smile when they see each other, while unhappily married couples smile only with the lips. Their motor response (a fake smile) indicates their meager emotional connection. Another of Ekman's findings is that the emotional system is unified; you cannot have a profound expression on your face and have a small physiological response. The package goes together and the motor activity of smiling can dictate that the brain feel happy.

Some people are better at reading emotions than others and can translate ultra-rapid displays. These people can understand micro-emotions—small changes in the face. They do better at reading people but also are more open to new experiences, are interested and curious about things in general, and they are conscientious, reliable, efficient, and attentive. Advanced meditators fit this group with an enhanced speed of cognition, more accurate perception of rapid stimuli, and better attunement to emotions. With this sensory onslaught however, they remain increasingly calm.

Psychosomatic medical specialist, Dr. Tod Mikuriija of UC Berkeley offers biofeedback research that looks at attentiveness as it translates into brain waves from visual stimuli. He noted that those engaged in focused "hard eyes" had both right and left hemispheres of the visual cortex pulsing at 16 cycles per second or "beta wave state." Soft eyes, unfocused and relaxed, found the right hemisphere continuing at 16 but the left reduced to 12, an "alpha wave state." The right, intuitive brain took over and dominated the logical brain. Relaxing our eyes can change the way we think.

Visual requirements for activities vary greatly. The eye and brain functions employed in television viewing put demands on different parts of the brain than those used in reading. Kate Moody in her book, *Growing Up on Television: The TV Effect*, notes that this variation "causes incalculably different kinds of cognitive development at the expense of reading and writing aptitude." She warns of the effect a seemingly innocent toddlers program called "Teletubbies" might have on young children, as they watch characters whose stomachs are TV screens. What are we promoting when we feature the television as part of our anatomy? Are we diverting the child's eyes away from the cartoon character's face, which in the case of the Teletubbies, don't move, and toward their embodied television screen, virtually a screen within a screen?

Television could be seen as technology that prompts a developmental disadvantage, especially when it robs us of the ability to read facial cues and places us face-to-screen with visions of grandeur (from an inundation of sports feats, adventures, sexual exploits, and advertisements) with no opportunity to practice and gain competence in them ourselves. Being sedentary not only makes us un-fit, it robs us of sensory input.

Johann Heinrich Pestalozzi of the Swiss Pestalozzi Institute, created his *Fundamental Principles* in 1770, wherein he enlisted the senses in all learning procedures for his school. He prohibited desks and lines on paper and required drawing on large, slanted slates to promote creative, non-linear thinking. He prompted students to observe and experience events for themselves and talked of observation or '*anschauen*' as that absolute foundation of all knowledge. His '*begreiflichkeit,*' or "intuitive beholding," called for a grasping of all the senses as the necessary steps toward thinking. He called imagination, the "oldest mental trait." One of his students, one Albert Einstein, would go on to intuitively behold a new theory of reality termed, The Theory of Relativity.

It seems that our brains did not evolve to understand themselves, but to perform specific tasks determined by evolution. We pay attention to what keeps us alive and procreating. We'd be wise to heed the phrase "pay attention," which reminds us that when we pay attention, we are spending a piece of our life and putting memories in our brain's bank account. Our choices, therefore, need to be conscious. If we continue to be led willy-nilly by short-term choices, we are partners in replicating cultural memes like the ridiculous, futuristic ideas of a Teletubbie, or primitive genetic drives such as eating fat and salt every time we come across it. An ancient survival mechanism might help if you live a nomadic life and kill a bison once a month, but not when the grocery store stocks 70 varieties of crackers that have more fat in one handful than an entire bison-burger. There is a mismatch between the old and new world and for those of us trying to "make sense" of those worlds, we are often trying to make sense of genes that have lost their usefulness or use memes that simply never made any sense.

Take the case of the keyboard I am typing on this very moment. In 1860, the QWERTY keyboard was invented (named for the upper left row of letters), with one function in mind—to slow the letter hammers so they wouldn't jam. By 1873, the typewriter was considered a feat of "anti-engineering," employing a series of design tricks to slow the typist. It scattered common letters over the keyboard, especially on the left, usually non-dominant side. Our weakest fingers were made to perform the strength moves, by having the little finger hold down the shift lock for capital letters, hit the return, or strike the often-used comma and period. In 1932, trials of an efficiently designed keyboard allowed the typist to double the typing speed and reduce muscular effort by a whopping 95%. But, by that time, the QWERTY typing meme was firmly entrenched. Designers could not get the new meme through to the public and QWERTY persists even with adjacent technological computer breakthroughs that should kill a meme from the 1800's, just by mere association.

When we have the sense of wanting to "get away from it all," we are really longing for the environment our senses were designed to make sense of. Studies show that if given a series of pictures of cities, deserts, forests, plains, and beaches, a majority of people will pick plains and meadows surrounded by forest. It appears that any other environment we live in requires great adaptation not just in our physical survival strategies but in our mental strategies, too. We would have to constantly rationalize city life as much as we would have to physically modify desert life.

As Richard Brodie says in *Virus of the Mind*, "If you want to survive, you're in good shape—you will survive until you die." But what if we want to thrive? The answer lies in our ability to devote our mental resources, called choices, and align them with a course of action that "makes sense" to our senses in a new way. When we flood our vision with so much information it all becomes meaningless, or even worse, lacks priority, we are left pursuing ridiculous or artificial dangers. News bulletins of another earthquake in South America, is interrupted with news of a famine in Pakistan, which is superseded with statistics of the spread of AIDS through Africa, while we are made painfully aware of the immediate need for whitener, fluoride, and plaque busters in our toothpaste. What we do then, is the only thing we can do—we replace our toothpaste. Rarely do we take into account that we are putting bleach in our mouth, eating a toxic chemical that would kill our goldfish if put in their bowl, and triggering our already exhausted immune system to attack plaque three times a day instead of just manually flossing. Next time you are in the grocery store, feast your eyes on the choices of toothpaste before you. As you ponder such a wasteful, attention stealing, artificially charged array of "choices," don't be surprised if you think what I think: Shame on us. Tom's Toothpaste. Case closed.

Researchers find that this flood of information leads to "inattentional blindness." When we are not ready to pay attention to something in our visual field, we distance ourselves from a critical level of thinking. It is then that we regard our inventions and technologies as inevitable forces of nature that use us, rather than objects we designed to be tools for our use. We become the tools to technology. We pay attention to things that don't deserve it and apply critical decision resources that we can ill afford, never really seeing the toothpaste conundrum for what it is—trivial. What we don't notice may be killing us, even if it is only killing our spirit.

It seems we fail to notice what is in front of us and insist that what we can't see doesn't exist. And yet, it's in the invisible patterns that meaning and value can suddenly rise to the surface. Just as a culture like the Siberians fail miserably at sorting colors of yarn they have never been exposed to, and the scientists studying them failed to appreciate the twenty-four patterns of reindeer fur, we can't understand something we have never trained our senses to value. Watching a television show like *Fear Factor*, we see contestants gag and heave when eating foodstuffs that other cultures consider delicacies. Many inlanders have never considered buffalo testicles as food while some island cultures live in near starvation, never considering fish as a food source. It's all in how you look at it.

Mathematicians study knots by looking at spaces knots don't occupy. These empty spaces are called "not knots." K. C. Cole asks, "Is a hole a presence or an absence? By definition, it's an absence; but without holes, bread wouldn't rise, soda wouldn't sparkle, hemoglobin couldn't carry oxygen through the blood, bees couldn't make honeycomb and doughnuts wouldn't exist." Let's explore some of those invisible patterns that might hint at ways to be more fully human.

Darwin's book, *Origin of Species* is considered the most widely known, yet unread book on the planet. In it, he discussed physiognomy, the study of face reading, and found it to be the "most compelling channel of communication save speech" and that the ability to "read" emotions on the face occurs with great accuracy across every culture. An angry grimace is an angry grimace whether you are in the Outback or in Hollywood.

Although there are only fourteen bones in the face, there are over one hundred muscles in, or attached to, the head and face. Unlike anywhere else in the body, muscles in the face are not attached from one bone to another, but are attached to bone at one end and the skin at the other end. Thus we can smile and frown, furrow our brow, and wink. We display emotions in the face, not our knees or our elbows whose muscles are attached bone to bone.

There is a huge variation in the location, shape and prevalence of facial muscles among humans, more so by far than any other musculature. Slight defects give us charming "deformities" like dimples and crooked grins and some people have a greater capacity to express themselves with movement in the face than others. Most of us also practice what is called, "holophrastic expression," where an emotional experience, especially a critical one, is unconsciously transformed into a sub-literal expression. In other words, we subconsciously translate a negative emotion into a linguistic phrase as is evident in the expression, "it was a slap in the face," said after someone has insulted us. Another common expression is "my jaw dropped," when someone has surprised us.

Flexibility of the forehead and eyebrows is thought to express either tension or relaxation and those with expressive brows, are often creative interpreters of events and situations. Elain Halfield and John Cacioppo, authors of Emotional Contagion, call these expressive people "senders." Some people, they found, have enormous influence over others and by expressing their emotions in their face, the emotion becomes contagious. The carriers infect those around them who are susceptible, with the mechanism of spread the same as spreading a cold virus. The closer and more frequent the contact, the more chance of infection.

The authors note the occurrence of a "super reflex," a physiologic ability or specialized trait seen in people with a powerfully persuasive personality. These people are in tune with the world and can draw others into their rhythm, dictating the terms of the interaction. They possess high degrees of synchronicity, and a keen artfulness in "global seduction." Movements, silences, volume, pitch, eye blink, and mouth shape, all fall into balance and these senders may even equalize the speech rate, matching the number of sounds per second to coincide and infect the susceptible person. They also have a gift in latency, that period of time which lapses when one person stops talking and the other starts. They are the people who promote the motor mimic in us, infecting us with their body language, accent, tone of voice, facial expressions and emotions.

Malcolm Gladwell, in his book *Tipping Point,* designed a test to determine who is a connector. He lists 248 surnames from a telephone book and a point is awarded for each person one knows with that name. Connectors have unusually high scores. He found that in every walk of life, there are a handful of people who are connectors, people with the knack for making friends and business connections. They are the meme spreaders, the people who tip you off about a great house, tell you where to buy the best organic tomatoes, and the ones who set trends that you want to mimic.

And as nature so often has it, connectors are not a unique function of society, but a genuine physical property. It is how the world works. Systems, from molecules in a cell, neurons in a brain, highway and airway routes, the network of directors and actors, companies linked by joint ownership, to food webs that quantify how species feed on each other; all rely on links that are web-like. Connectors or "hubs," are responsible for a bulk of the work in the system, serving to connect weak links into a strong cluster. By employing collaboration, a few extra links to connectors can drastically transform how information is spread. When Columbus traveled to the Americas, he suddenly linked a Queen to an Indian by one degree of separation. These working acquaintances make up the bulk of interconnectiveness and form long bridges and collapsing separation.

The American Journal of Sociology published a paper in 1973 by a sociologist named Granovetter, titled "The Strength of Weak Ties," wherein he noted the power of acquaintances over and above the influence of close friends. While close friends tend to travel in the same, tight circles, it is the connectors who travel between circles and have weak, external links to the outside world. New information comes from activating these weak ties.

A subtle urge to connect and to synchronize is pervasive in nature. Synchronicity is responsible for the pacemaker cells in the heart, the chirping of crickets, the schooling of fish, and the matched menstrual cycles of female roommates. In his book *Linked,* Albert-Laszlo Barabasi discusses many more network similarities, and the topic of small worlds and degrees of separation are eloquently laid out. He questions how crickets synchronize their chirping. Do they pay attention to the cricket next to them or to their favorite cricket? It turns out that they pay attention to the connector, just as humans will synchronize hand clapping during applause.

There are those people who are considered socially awkward, unable to read social signals, facial expressions, and body language. Scientists find that these people can't shift their vision from eye to mouth and back in order to "read" a face. Severe cases exist in the autistic. The cerebellum, the part of the brain that coordinates rhythm, is impaired in people with autism, either too large or too small. It is thought that many autistic children fail to speak because they never imprint their first experiences with deep emotion and match that emotion with words.

In cerebellar strokes, motor planning is lacking, making activities of daily living filled with effort so that even figuring out how to get dressed becomes a chore. They also display flat and non-expressive facial features. People with attention deficit are thought to have cerebellar dysfunction, since they cannot coordinate a smooth, rhythmic shift from one task to another. Rhythmic gestures and facial expressions are imperative in successful social interactions, as is the rhythmic coordination of attention from one task to another. One function of culture is to coordinate and limit the number of gestures one must synchronize in order to "get along" with everyone.

Formalized gestures can be found in dance and "sign talk," or sign language, where hand movements are used to communicate without words. This is language for the eyes. Indian classical dance uses a sacred vocabulary of hand gestures called *hastas,* to tell stories about the Divine, allowing the dancer to experience the deity in person. *Mudras* are hand gestures used in yoga and are considered an established language in India to communicate esoteric concepts. The 108 gestures embody emotions, with the word "mudra" meaning "to seal joy" in Sanskrit, as they seal a spiritual message into the body. Gestures are understood by a part of our brain that responds to shapes, that is the lower right temporal lobe, which is not a site for language acquisition. While we switch to the left hemisphere in early childhood for speech, we retain our right brain connection for understanding the expressive movements of our hands into adulthood.

It is known that language, through the use of gestures first, formed from bodily action before being formed as speech. Brain-imaging studies show that gestures happen in "deeptime," the moment before we become conscious of our own thoughts. Gestures lend nuance to speech and are found to be more prevalent, the more abstract the thought we are trying to convey. While words represent thought, gestures embody them, and are the shapers of thought, merging the left and right brain.

We also read gesture in the face. Dr. Martin Skinner and Dr. Brian Mullen wrote in the journal *Psychology,* that the left side of the face is more expressive than the right and the left eye more accurate. Studies show that we often misinterpret emotions if we can only see the right side of the face, yet we are fairly accurate in reading the left-only side. Face reading is used in medicine by geneticists who look at eye and ear shape to diagnose chromosomal deformities and syndromes like Fetal Alcohol Syndrome and Down's Syndrome. In 1989, the British Heart Foundation claimed a link between the ear lobe and heart disease. A diagonal crease across the ear lobe at an angle of 45 degrees was seen most often in those with hypertension, diabetes and heart disease. Geneticists find kidney disease in those with misshapen ears as both the ear and the kidney form at the same time in utero.

Modern human language is a mix of eye and ear communications—it is aural-gestural. What we know of the ear is that it changes all information into sound. Even tinnitus, the crazy-making ringing of the ear, is not really noise, but an electrochemical signal generated in the brain. The brain, not knowing what to make of the nonsense signal, interprets it as sound. The vestibular system, located in the ear canals, connects the senses, blending all information into the sense of balance and coordination. Should the crystals in our inner ear become dehydrated or stuck to one side, our sense of up and down will be severely challenged. Although the world is not spinning out of control, it will certainly feel as if it is. Vertigo, while in no way representing reality, is a debilitating experience. Our senses then transform the moment and offer richness, and sometimes falsehood, to how we experience the present.

Marshall McLauhan noted that sensory input is the key to civilization itself when he said, "All human tools and technologies, whether house or wrench or clothing, alphabet or wheel, are direct extensions, either of the human body or of our senses…and give us new leverage and new intensity of perception and action." The brain invents the tools and the tools, in turn, expand the brain. Joseph LeDoux, a neuroscientist at New York University, found that sensory signals from the eyes and ears travel first to the amygdala, the reacting and emotional part of the brain. A second signal is sent to the neocortex, the thinking brain. So, there is a preeminence of "heart over head," as Daniel Goleman notes in *Emotional Intelligence.* Evolution has given emotion the central role in human function. "Our emotions…guide us in facing predicaments and tasks too important to leave to the intellect alone—danger, painful loss, persisting toward a goal despite frustrations" and in order to psychologically survive, we must at times ignore rationalizations. One has to wonder what would happen to a culture that consistently chose rationalizations over emotions. Would that culture bury emotions in order to get to work everyday, drive in rush-hour traffic, and purchase material goods that are destroying the environment?

Tool invention is a key player in advancing culture. It is a tangible meme wherein its use is apprenticed from one hand to another. J. M. Balkin notes in *Cultural Software,* that the Talmud recites a list of objects God brought into being on the final day of creation. At the end of the list of necessary items—items needed for miracles later on—was a set of tongs. A tool. He notes, "As the Talmud tells us, tongs can only be made with other tongs." It is a toolmaking tool. As are we. Tools are extensions of our senses, our arms and legs, of our ideas, and of each and every cell in our body. Diane Jacobs, a Vancouver physical therapist writes, "Cells were the first tool users, having learned to extract molecular energy within their boundaries to carry out tasks. Proteins move messenger molecules to complete tasks and once done, it recycles its left-over parts."

Tools change the world we experience and change our ability to experience the world. Language is no doubt the most influential tool we have created, allowing us to act on the world without touching it. Text in the *Upanishad* has one recite the vow, "*ritam vachmi, satyam vachmi*," which expresses the idea that we should speak words that strengthen both cosmic truth and worldly truth. Abusing the power of language, robs us of the energy to speak deeply. It is thought that observing silence for a day will allow us to re-gain vitality in speech and practice *Vaikhai*, the use of wise speech.

The brain has a "use it or lose it" nature, requiring a continual source of input to establish neuronal connections and competency. That continual source of input, as we have said, comes into the brain via the eyes, ears, and nervous system. Knowledge and sensations are food for the brain. The brain is the most expensive tissue in the body, requiring more calories than any other organ. Energy comes to the brain in the form of glucose, but since the brain has no storage space for glucose, the body must transport a continuous supply to keep the brain healthy. The brain then, is totally dependent on the swift and efficient movement of body parts for its food. In this way, a sluggish body can make for a sluggish mind.

Cell loss and cell growth in the hippocampus are major concerns when it comes to the aging brain, with many of us fearing dementia and memory loss more than heart attack or cancer. The hippocampus is not only responsible memory, but for appreciating the context of events. For instance, we appreciate the sense of home because that is where our family lives and where we find security. To someone with an impaired hippocampus, home is just a house. It has lost its significance. The hippocampus shrinks with the stress of depression or Post-Traumatic Stress Disorder, illnesses wherein we are sad when the situation is not sad or afraid when the situation does not warrant fear. Emotions are out of context.

One contributing factor to cell loss in the hippocampus and prefrontal cortex is the effects of chronic stress. Stress increases "bad" hormones like glucocorticoids, which inhibit new cell growth in critical areas of the brain. Stress also increases the heart rate and blood pressure, while suppressing energy intensive systems like the reproduction and digestive systems. It's a wise body that knows it "can't afford" to make a baby or digest a meal when there is danger lurking. It wisely slows those systems down, conserving energy until the stressor passes. But, what happens in a culture where the stressors don't stop? Will there be uncontrolled cell loss? The good news is that there are amazingly simple ways to counteract cell loss and attain cell growth.

Relaxation promotes cell growth by increasing seratonin, a "good" hormone that works to repair and build brains during fetal development and in adults, during sleep. Exercise can also promote cell growth. Neuroscientist Fred Gage of the Salk Institute for Biological Studies in California, reported that rodents with access to a running wheel showed twice the brain cell growth as their sedentary siblings. However, exercise in and of itself is not always a good answer, as not every activity is created equal.

In rehab medicine, exercise is often prescribed to rid a patient of aches and pains and to strengthen weak muscles. It would be difficult to recall a patient who didn't ask their therapist, "How often should I do that exercise?" and "How many times a day should I do that exercise?" What they are telling us is that, were they even to have the discipline to do the exercises (and that is highly unlikely), they would have no idea when they would do them, and no idea how it would fit in their day. It tells us the task is too artificial and would require sustained will power. If we were to encourage functional movement for rehabilitation, say baking bread, the patient would be done when the bread dough was thoroughly kneaded and they would bake it in time for dinner. Exercise for the sake of exercise is out of context for living in a body that thrives on meaningful motion. Herein lies the genius behind Occupational Therapy—a form of rehabilitation that concerns itself with how we occupy our time with meaningful activity.

We should be warned that our pursuit of rote exercise can serve to exaggerate the very stressors we are exercising to reduce. We clock our workouts, set fitness goals that measure lifted weight, record increased strength, and give gold medals to split second time gains. In fact, exercise can make you sick. Studies have taken those with high blood pressure (BP) and had them work out on exercise bicycles. While BP was lowered in many, about one-third of all men showed an increase in BP and stress hormones. Findings indicated that these men are thinking about their problems during the workout, essentially hard-wiring stress into the motor cortex. A simple tweak of the exercise routine, placing those men on real bicycles where they are distracted by nature, lowered the blood pressure. It is a good idea to place awareness on what you are thinking about when you are exercising. If you are degrading yourself with inner comments like, "I'm so fat" or "I hate jogging" while you are running, any cardiovascular benefit is over-ridden by the psychological and eventually, physiological stress.

Richard Petty, a psychology professor at Ohio State University, studied the influence of body movement on our thinking. He found that nodding our head "yes" or "no" not only sent body language to others, but to ourself. If we say something positive but nod our head "no," testing showed we didn't fully believe our own statements. The movement served as a "self-validation," confirming or negating our own thoughts. "If we are nodding our heads up and down, we gain confidence in what we are thinking. But when we shake our heads from side to side, we lose confidence in our own thoughts." He notes that body movements can even affect our belief in deep issues very important to us. In effect, the motor movement "wins out" and influences the brain more than the language we use, or even the thought itself.

Moshe Feldenkrais noted that the best intentions, when enacted compulsively, yield the opposite results. He suggests reading the body for signs of stress. The clenched fists, tense eyebrows, locked jaw, and taut low back are expressions of what he called "an impotent effort." This negative body language counteracts will power. If our "self," or our body, is stubbornly refusing to do something, we are disturbed. We should feel just as awkward in disturbing ourself as when we disturb someone else. In nagging ourself, we fail to listen to the body's cues for what it finds beneficial and which tasks it finds harmful. If learning to learn is the stuff the brain is made of, then learning to listen to our body can be the most important business of life.

Feldenkrais taught that a sensitive, well-behaved person should regard the feelings of others including the self. He used the example of someone who is unable to refuse any "reasonable" request asked of them. They are the people unable to say "no" or the people who can only say "no" by using pain as the way out. We may say, "I can't visit my grandparents because the drive will flare-up my neck," when we really mean to say, "I don't want to visit my grandparents." We are attempting to be nice or good in the eyes of other people, but are actually straying from our desire to be nice, by being "not nice" to ourselves. Resentment follows as our own behavior consists entirely of actions we force ourselves to do. This continuous string of resentments is so damaging to the self that Feldenkrais said "society would regard (such a perpetrator) as criminal should such harm be done to another person." We might ask ourselves, "If I am so nice, how come I'm not nice to me?" And in the same breath, "If running is so good for me, how come I hate it?" The answer just might be that we are engaging in impotent efforts and actions that get us nowhere.

When choosing an activity, certain features are proven more beneficial than others. The endorphin system, those natural opiates that give us a sense of well-being, respond best to monotonous repetition of low level stimulation but not so low that it is boring or easily mastered. The steady rhythm of walking, the intense concentration when you engage in a loved hobby, even a repetitive caress, can flood the brain with endorphins. Primates spend nearly 20-40% of their awake hours in grooming themselves and one another, which has been found to lower their heart rate and increase endorphin levels. Primates that do not groom others, partake in a fatal lifestyle as they quickly harbor infestations that lead to infections and imminent death. Life as a primate is really about "You groom me and I'll groom you and together we survive." Perhaps it suggests we humans would be wise to offer each other reciprocal massages. Interestingly, massage soothes the vagal nerve, releasing food-absorbing hormones such as insulin and glucagon.

Brad Hatfield at the University of Maryland found that the trance-like concentration of an archer increased the alpha brain waves in the left side of the brain, the area where we experience contentment. Even good parenting changes the brain. John Gottman led research in modifying vagal tone, a cranial nerve that regulates heart rate and sends signals to the amygdala from the adrenals. If primed with high vagal tone, the adrenals secrete catecholamines and adrenaline which signal "flight or fight" or stress responses. He tested the vagal nerve tone in children as they played with their parents. Those experiencing adept parenting showed low vagal tone, a sign of calm. In other studies, emotionally sound infants soothe themselves by treating themselves as their caretakers have, and learn to lower their own vagal tone. We are reminded again of the "tend and befriend" response wherein mothers and children calm each other during times of stress.

Certain types of movement can enhance certain brain functions. Muscles moved slowly and consciously are represented in the neocortex part of the brain. Walking, Tai Chi, Qigong, Yoga and bodywork, all serve to develop supernormal refinement of the proprioceptive capacities of the neocortex, the thinking part of the brain. It is the part of our brain that unites experiences into a feeling of wholeness. Yoga, the very word meaning "to yoke" together, can literally re-member us, pulling together lost parts of ourselves. It can remember what the body has forgotten.

Eric Hoffman measured brain waves after Kriya Yoga and found a 40% increase in alpha waves in the right temporal lobe, often referred to as "The Relaxation Response." Additionally, the National Institutes of Health (NIH) found a decrease in the stress-inducing hormone, cortisol, after yoga and an increase in the soothing hormone, prolactin, with Kriya yogic breathing. The message is, pick an exercise or an activity that sings to you, that makes you think good thoughts, and feel good feelings. Walking is always, always a good choice. We were built to walk. Every location of every muscle and every shape of every bone offers perfection in walking. Our bodies were not designed to lift weights, nor swim, nor cycle, nor sit. Our bodies want to walk. And with the body as in life, we will find that what attracts us is in our own best interest.

The word "motivation" is from the Latin "*movere*" meaning, "to set in motion." Motivation directs the emotions and decides how much energy will be assigned to a given stimulus. It is simply the pressure to act. Internal motor activity, such as an increase in heart rate, a squirt of an excitatory hormone, an electrical impulse to the face causing a muscle to smile; all serve to play out emotions through the body. Likewise, motor expressions of our body can change the chemicals in our brain, which alter our emotional state.

The supine position, which is lying down on our back, calms the nervous system enough to allow the brain to be less inhibited. Thus the effect of the psychiatrist's couch, where patients are more apt to reveal their emotions than if seated. This lordosis response, which can be witnessed in the female sex posture, activates the periaqueductal gray matter, which is connected to the reticular formation of the medulla and the spinal cord. The posture assumed by the spinal cord can signal the brain to relax.

A pheromone in boar's breath is irresistible to female pigs and the mere whiff of it finds the female freezing into lordosis. Truffles, the beloved fungi of gourmets, contain a "mimic molecule" of the same smell and female pigs will dig a yard deep to unbury it. Once found, they signal to their human companion by assuming the lordosis position.

Even the way our head is positioned on our shoulders can change information going into the brain. Centering our head is important, as the organs, which report the position of the head in relation to the earth, are located directly above the mastoid condyle behind the ear. A study in the October 2003 Neuroscience showed that muscle fatigue in the neck extensors affected the mechanism of postural control by producing abnormal sensory input to the central nervous system giving subjects "a lasting sense of instability." Changes in the plane of the head are "recorded" by the vestibular and labyrinthine sense organs in the inner ears, which then send information to the eye muscles. If the head is held off-balance, the eye muscles fatigue which further confuses the proprioceptive and vestibular system. In other words, you're dizzy. If the world seems to be spinning, you're less active; thus posture has changed your behavior and has changed the perception of whether you are coming or going. In the case of feeling dizzy, our physiology overwhelms our psychology. In the case of hyperventilation, our psychology can overwhelm our physiology. This feedback system, where our actions change our emotions and our emotions alter our motor responses, is exactly why we in no way resemble a computer.

Cognitive scientists are seduced by using the model of a computer for the human brain, even going so far as to call the brain "wetware," a continuum of the computer components, "software" and "hardware." This fails to recognize that cognition is often swamped by emotions that will change the motor expression and vice versa. Using the example of a chess game between a Chess Master and a computer, the computer might win the game but it cannot have tenderly remembered that its father taught it to play, cannot have acknowledged that the ivory chess pieces were elephant tusks that once roamed the Serengeti, and cannot have marveled at how the last move flirted with danger.

We are so influenced by outside stimuli that it pays to be well versed on the varying effects of different types of input. Norman A. Donald in, *Things That Make Us Smart,* suggests we look at the difference between a television ad and a newspaper ad and how they influence our sense of time and space. The TV ads are time-paced; that is they force us to watch them assuming we play the usual passive watcher. The newspaper ad is self-paced, in that we can ignore the space or turn the page. Television ads offer one thing to look at and are primarily an auditory medium; the newspaper ad has other articles and distractions on the page and is a visual medium. Television ads demand you devote your time, and newspaper ads, your space. One is event paced in that once it is off the screen, the image is lost except to memory. Reading allows reflection and one can spend as much time as is warranted with the image. Television controls the user; the user controls reading. That is a difference that can make all the difference.

The real problem with technology that controls the user is that the medium violates its affordances. Recorded business messages are a good example of technology violating the benefit of the telephone—it's a service that is good for the business called, but infuriating to the caller. We like the telephone because it allows us to talk to someone faster than if we were to travel to see them. The benefit is the "right now" part of the tool. The way we understand how it is used and any feeling of success in its use, is undermined when we have to listen to a series of taped directions to route our call. More and more of us prefer to leave a taped message, delighting in the time savings and glad to avoid the personal contact. What does that say about us?

We used to be able to see how technology worked—that is, the physical properties afforded the use. We could fix our own cars, take apart a clock, or sharpen a pencil. With that pencil, one could see that it writes, can tap it to make noise, and could turn it to erase. It is not difficult to discover its many uses. A computer, however, belies direct understanding. The "tool" bars have no physical or spatial relationship to what we know of as a tool, so it is difficult to learn its use. You can't press a lever, watch it turn a cog, and see it strike the page. As Donald says "There is no natural relationship between the appearance of the object and its use." Suffice it to say that our children will never be able to take apart the family car to see how it runs, nor tinker with the computer to see what makes it tick. They will not have the opportunity to use their hands or their brains in that way and we had better hope that this oversight doesn't stand in the way of their curiosity—for curiosity appears to be what motivates us to go on.

Helen Keller said, "No pessimist ever discovered the secrets of the stars or sailed to an uncharted land or opened a new heaven to the human spirit." An optimist, then, is curious and from that curiosity, expects something good to happen. Creative people do things their own way, not because they should do something, or do the thing the way they were taught—they do things for their own sake.

As Freud noted, "There are two types of people in the world—those who can enjoy desiring and those who need satisfaction." Creative people enjoy desiring and are rewarded by the pursuit of a goal, as much as the completion of it. Craving occurs when an object takes on tremendous significance. In healthy cravings (for creativity, innovation, compassion), the nucleus accumbens is activated, which is an area rich in dopamine. Dopamine, besides being responsible for smooth, coordinated movements, is also another reward hormone. In dysfunctional cravings (addictions), there is an unhealthy, uncoordinated link between increased wanting and decreased liking. The reward and the pursuit are mismatched. Addicts show low dopamine levels.

Linus Pauling, a two-time Nobel Prize winner and the genius behind the benefits of Vitamin C, believed his curiosity to be the one force behind his success. Curiosity is a hunger that prompts the brain to seek nourishment from ideas and new tasks, and more importantly, keeps the brain plastic (growing). Curiosity and new learning can be considered the occupation of an infant as it develops and explores the world around it. Robin Dunbar in, *Grooming, Gossip and the Evolution of Language* states, "During the last stages of pregnancy, the foetus's brain is growing very rapidly and consumes 70% of the total energy the mother pumps into her baby via the umbilical cord—and she, of course, has to provide all that. Even after birth, the brain still accounts for 60% of the infant's total energy consumption during the first year of life."

Thomas Aquinas thought that pessimistic people had a "contraction of the mind," or a "one-sided brain." Richard Davidson, a psychologist out of the University of Wisconsin, studied pessimists and optimists. He found increased activity in the left frontal lobe of cheerful people and increased right frontal lobe activity in negative people, when shown funny movies. Cheerful people showed "great delight," while negative people were only "mildly amused." Further studies showed that events can have an amplifying or muting effect on the left or right brain, as well as tonic versus toxic effect. Relaxation techniques (low arousal) are good for anxiety (high arousal), while exercise (high arousal) is good for depressives (low arousal).

Not only personality, but also which side of the brain is active, determines how one interprets what is stressful or pleasant. Pleasant and unpleasant experiences are not the problem, it is the chasing of one and the running away from the other that creates tension in the mind and leads to exhaustion. The internal ping-pong of the mind as it goes about liking and not liking every single event that happens during a day, can lead to constant irritation and suffering. Unexpressed anger activates the pessimistic, right frontal lobe and the amygdala, where distressing emotions are experienced. Anger, coupled with sadness or frustration, also activates the right frontal lobe. Anger with restraint, activates the left frontal lobe where we experience positive emotions and increased attention. The left frontal lobe is also where we solve math problems, enjoy music, or feel satisfaction when we attain a goal.

Our basic mental state can be strengthened by exposure to restrained emotions, just like we strengthen our immune system by repeated, small exposures to pathogens. When we notice emotions come, we need to detect them early and acknowledge them. Get to know them. Transforming anger into a problem to be solved is like solving a math problem. Anger is then further transformed, possibly into compassion.

Buddhist psychology notes that emotions are destructive if they cause harm to yourself or others. There is a subtle harm evident as well. If emotions distort our perceptions of reality, our mind is prevented from ascertaining reality. If we see objects as 100% attractive, we desire them. But this obscures a deeper assessment of the nature of things. A car is attractive and convenient but it pollutes and kills more people than war. If we expect ourselves to be 100% perfect, we are taking part in a deep delusion. The rhythmic movement of thought is denied and our ability to chain thoughts together is lost. We are thinking through the lens of black and white desiring. Emotion, from *"emovere"* means something that sets the mind in motion. But we have to be mindful of which side of the brain we move things into.

Vilayanur Ramachandran, a UC San Diego neurologist, studies right brain strokes. People who have a right brain stroke have left-sided paralysis and often exhibit a phenomenon called "neglect," where they are unaware of their left side. They may neglect to move it even though they might have muscle function and intact sensation. Ramachandran found that the right side of the brain is suppressed by the stroke, which is the area where we find "normal negativity." If they could use the right brain, it would understand the reality of being paralyzed, and ironically, they'd attempt to move it. But they have only a functioning left side of the brain.

The left side of the brain is profoundly dominant in manics, those who feel constant elation. The left side is also enhanced in those who are "chronic optimists." So in right brain strokes, the happy left brain is allowed to reign unchallenged, thinking everything is rosy. It is good at useful deceptions. The brain denies there is paralysis on the left side of the body and so "neglects" it. These people can have a perceptual neglect for objects as well and are unable to see the left side of their dinner plate or unable to shave the left side of their face. It is a constant effort in rehab to teach caregivers the complexity of this disorder, as it is difficult to understand how the brain could not acknowledge a whole side of the world. After all, we only understand left and right because we have a body, not because we have a brain. Caregivers have to be trained to attend to the left side for the person, even going so far as to turn their plate around to offer the food on the left side of the plate, to the side of the brain that can acknowledge it. Oftentimes, someone with neglect eats only half the meal and the caregiver thinks the patient is full. As the weight goes down, the only remedy remains in turning the plate or in placing all the food on the right side.

If we were to a have a stroke on the left side of our brain, with right-sided paralysis, we are most likely to lose our ability to speak. The job of speech is to story tell our lives, usually leaving out unimportant details, at times even skewing reality. The right side is realistic, which in reality is, pessimistic. In this way, a right paralysis (left brain damage) knows they are paralyzed and sees no hope in trying to recover.

It seems the left side of the brain likes stability and when reality does not match its version of what is real, it will confabulate. The right side of the brain knows reality all too well and will think of ways to avoid trying. A healthy brain can utilize what is called the "Kuhnian Paradigm Shift," wherein the right brain forces the left to completely revise its version of reality. Seeing a stroke patient suddenly realize they are hopelessly paralyzed after months of disability can be a sobering event and it can happen if the right brain convinces the damaged left brain that it is ill or vice versa.

Genes can alter our perception of the world by endowing us with one hemisphere dominant over the other. Practicing certain behaviors over and over again can do the same thing. Debbie Crews of Arizona State University and John Milton of the University of Chicago, study patterns of brain activation in golfers and find the better the golfer, the less brain activity just prior to making a shot. The key difference between amateurs and pros lies in the left hemisphere of the brain. Amateurs showed more total brain activity. Details, worries, and memories of bad shots overwhelmed them. The pros focused, quieting the left hemisphere. This would create alpha waves, which can overrule the pessimistic right side. Crews says, "How you think is probably more important than what you think."

Although the gene might in fact be faulty, we could end up with a desirable trait such as optimism. Much like sickle cell anemia protects against malaria, schizophrenia protects against arthritis, cystic fibrosis in its mild form protects against typhoid, and multiple sclerosis protects somewhat against estrogen-driven cancers, our illnesses may be useful to the survival of the species.

Manic persons, for instance, are endowed with creative energy, a tendency to ignore rules, standards and conventions, engage in rapid decision-making, instant partnerships, and a craving for stimulation. They are great assimilators of incongruent information and so it is of no surprise that manics show a predominant occurrence in famous authors, artists, and musicians. Manics require less sleep, denial is the favored defense mechanism in the face of failure, and they are full of plans. Additionally, they are impulsive enough to carry out those plans despite obstacles. A manic might not lead a comfortable life but they certainly have benefited society as a whole with their symphonies, paintings, and novels. In his book, *Origins of Genius*, author Simonton tells us that some degree of mental illness occurs in 28% of scientists, 60% of composers, 73% of painters, 77% of novelists and a whopping 87% of poets.

Even headaches may have an evolutionary benefit in that they often occur during ovulation in women. A migraine may be nature's way of inhibiting intercourse during periods of peak fertility, maintaining the family's status quo. Also, as Frank Vertosick MD notes in, *Why We Hurt: The Natural History of Pain*, since "migraines can occur after a stressful event, they may be an adaptive mechanism forcing us to rest...or may teach us to avoid conflicts and stresses that might be harming us."

Randolph Neese, a psychiatrist who writes on evolutionary medicine, describes the "cliff effect," wherein certain mutations of disease are beneficial except when they come together in one person. Gout is a cliff disease. Uric acid protects joints from premature aging unless one gets too much, which results in painfully swollen, gouty joints. Occasional headaches protect the sufferer from additional exposure to stressors. Migraine headaches are too much and are a protective mechanism gone amok.

Throughout history, headaches have prompted bizarre tactics from doctors. Ancient health practices used the "Doctrine of Signatures," believing that a plant showed its medicinal properties by its shape. The walnut, the meat of which looks like a brain, was widely used for headache. Thomas Cydenham, the founder of clinical medicine and epidemiology, suggested a long horseback ride. He would tell his patients to ride to another town to a headache specialist, who in reality did not exist. He found that the round trip horse ride and the resultant angry outburst cured the headache.

This brings to mind the meaning of the word "placebo" which is "to please," most often thought to refer to "pleasing the doctor." The placebo effect lies not in the potion but from the process—a process that utilizes intention. The doctor simply invites or allows the patient to do what they are already capable of: to control silent body functions, to grow or destroy, and thereby to lead itself to wholeness. In wanting to please the doctor, the patient complies by curing himself. It is the effect made powerful by our willingness to bow to external authority in lieu of internal responsibility. The intention to change is given to the outside judge.

Intention is a powerful force in science as can be seen by the existence of double-blind studies. Because of the power of intention to skew information, neither the tester nor the tested can know which study group has been given the placebo versus the medicine. If intention had no power, science would not need the double-blind scenario. It is such a strong indicator that intention and choice must have a huge survival benefit.

Another powerful brain dysfunction that has an evolutionary benefit is poor short-term memory. In fact, it is not a breakdown of function, but is a desirable mental operation. To function, we must be good at forgetting and as good at it as we are in remembering. Of the millions of sensory inputs that demand our attention every day, only a fine trickle will manage to gain our attention and of those, even fewer will deposit themselves into our memory banks. And it appears we long to forget in a big way.

Enhanced forgetting is the mechanism of any psychoactive plant, from the legal glass of wine after work, to the use of illegal drugs that "take the edge off." Some forms of religious ecstasy also serve to enhance cognitive function by impairing it, and include fasting, meditation, trances, chanting, sleeplessness, spinning, inversions (upside-down postures), deep and restricted breathing, and even self-flagellation. But nothing works quite like the anesthetizing effects of deep mediation, for there will be one "germ of insight," metaphor, or leap of faith that breaks our mental habits and transforms our mental and cultural givens. Anything that alters our mental functions is a meme buster.

Buddhist psychology offers antidotes to the seemingly concrete reality of destructive emotions. Love is an antidote for hatred. Education is a cure for ignorance. Meditation is considered an antidote for all destructive emotions, as they are experienced as catalysts, transforming themselves by practice, into compassion.

We can at any time be immersed in a world where the commonplace appears profound, where time has slowed or stopped, where we can lengthen the time between awareness and response, where an experience is lived as if for the first time, and one forgets all of life's familiarities. We can choose meditation or medication. Carl Sagan noted in a once anonymous article in *Marihuana Reconsidered*, that one has "devastating insights about the natural life" while intoxicated. He took copious notes to record the truths experienced on the night he imbibed, so his morning self would remember that the ideas were something to act on. John Nash, winner of the Nobel Prize for his game theories, and a schizophrenic, suggested that rational thought was unwelcome at times. He said, "Rational thought imposes a limit on a person's concept of his relation to the cosmos."

Andrew Weil notes that every culture excepting Eskimos uses some kind of psychoactive plants to alter their cognition with wine invented long before the wheel was even a daydream. Marijuana, he contends, is an "active placebo" as it triggers the mental state we call "being high." Historians note that different cultures ascribe different powers during that high. Even different time frames attribute varying powers to the same drug. Marijuana was considered to foster violence in the 1930's, but apathy today. The German historian, Wolfgang Schivelbusch, suggests that coffee, while once strictly taboo, became acceptable because it aided mental labor and increased the drinker's capacity to work harder. There are side effects such as paranoia attributed to smoking pot, but studies have shown that the paranoia exists only in cultures where legal restraints foster paranoia about getting caught. Even with drug ingestion, cultural precepts can alter the experience on drugs.

Some drugs are useful to the human experience. The uterus has a large amount of receptors for cannabinoid, our body's version of its own natural marijuana. The chemical serves to control pain during childbirth and helps with the required forgetting a woman must experience to give birth a second and third time. Cocaine has a link in determining who we want to remember and who we might forget. The same part of the brain that is stimulated by cocaine is stimulated when we view a loved one over a mere acquaintance. Perhaps by surrounding ourselves with loved ones, we might perpetuate a natural addiction and sense of well being without cocaine use.

Being in tune with our natural chemistry can only come about when we find an ease in our movements, which serves to coordinate our psychology with our physiology. In *The Private Life of the Brain*, Susan Greenfield finds that normal dopamine levels allow the brain to make sense of incoming information. Very low dopamine levels lead to depression, as the brain becomes super-rational and unable to be brainwashed or seduced by incoming information. Slightly low levels give a feeling of pleasure as the incoming information is allowed in but too swift for the brain to rationalize away. If nothing else impacts the senses, pleasure will fade due to the return of rational thinking.

At its opposite, excess dopamine finds the brain flooded with sensory input and pleasure will morph into fear—the information too rapid, too novel and too unexpected. The rate at which one novel stimulation jostles out another one, determines whether we feel pleasure, calmness, or fear. Rhythmic movement such as we might find in walking, dancing, drumming, and even sex, contains no huge surprises and transitions are gradual and in context. One sensory experience that merges and is slowly displaced by another is healthy. It's all in the timing and we will find in the next chapter that timing and rhythm are everything.

HOW TO EVOKE TRUTH

❖ This chakra tells us to allow the world to touch us, just as we touch it. Our senses unite the outer world with the inner world of living in a body. Don't lose touch with your reality. If energy is too high here, light and noises are overwhelming. If too low here, the system is shut down, unable to let information in. One person will feel life is too much and the other will feel it is not enough. Get to the point where life is just right.

❖ The tissues of the eye are thought to most closely resemble brain tissue. The muscles of the eyes are nearly identically replicated in the shoulder. The sphenoid bone, with its two sockets for the eyes, very closely resembles the pelvic bone. The two bones even show the same inclination in anterior and posterior tilt as we breathe in and out. Both the sphenoid and pelvis house endocrine glands with the sphenoid home to the pituitary and the pelvis, home to the gonads. So the eye has an unusual relationship with the substance of the brain, the rhythm of the muscles in the shoulder, and the bony back-and-forth of the pelvis. Giving your eyes beautiful things to look at can affect your entire anatomy. Make sure the first objects you see upon waking are beautiful. Arrange a shelf near your bed with objects that sing to you.

❖ Good vision relies on minute muscular adaptations. Tension across the orbit can result in a narrowing of the entire facial region, with chronic tension in the socket and eyeball. Prolonged immobility and narrowing from chronic squinting, compresses and distorts the shape and adaptation of the eyeball. Age-related vision problems stem from a gradual loss of flexibility and tone in the eye muscles. Robert Abel in, *The Eye Care Revolution* suggests we try eye-relaxing exercises. Open the eyes and keep the head and neck still. Picture a clock face, raising the eyeballs up to 12; hold one second, then lower to 6 o'clock. Do this ten times without blinking. Next, rub the palms together to generate heat and gently cup your hands over your eyes without pressing. Now, picture the clock again and rotate eyes from 9 o'clock to 3. Continue the entire pattern until you have done 8 o'clock to 2, and 7 to 4. He notes that the simplest way to break eye stress is to take a deep breath, cover your eyes, and relax. This can lower the blood pressure in the eyes by 20%.

❖ If you do computer work, take eye breaks every half hour or so. Point to a faraway object. Shift your focus from fingertip to object and back ten times. This offsets habitual focus patterns, which degrade the ciliary body's natural flexibility. Shifting counteracts this stiffness by taking the organ through the full range of focus. Or try gazing at the tip of the thumb with the arm extended. Move the thumb slowly toward tip of nose. Pause one second and reverse. This aligns inner and outer focus allowing a soft gaze at the world.

❖ Swami Sivananda, a yogic physician, considered sight the most abused of our five senses. The first chapter in Yoga Asanas (postures) describes eye exercises. The purpose of eye asanas is the development of insight, with the focus not so much on stretching and contracting the eye muscles, but in promoting relaxation. Swami Sivananda shares his theories with a much-celebrated ophthalmologist, William H. Bates, who thought that relaxation was the single most important element of eye health. Relaxation can offer dramatic eyesight and cognitive improvement, as sight is a huge "consumer" of brain energy. Vision occupies almost 40% of the brain's capacity, which is why we close our eyes to sleep, rest, and relax.

❖ We will not always be able to understand the way the universe works. Our senses aren't that reliable. Buddhist thought reminds us that our mission is not to clear up the mystery, but is to reveal the mystery clearly.

❖ The mind is composed of food. The coarsest food parts are eliminated through the digestive tract. The less coarse food is turned into flesh and sustains the body. The subtle aspects of food feed the nervous system and brain. Coarse water is urine, less coarse is blood, and most subtle is breath. Ludwig Feuerbach, a German philosopher, was thought to be the first who said, "Man is what he eats." But there is an Indian maxim that notes, "*Yatha annam tatha manah*" meaning, "as one's food, so is one's mind."

☙ Buddhist psychology suggests three ways to experience emotion. Express it, repress it, or avoid situations where it arises. The concrete example of gas in our stomachs is used and monks say, you can fart, you can hold it in, or you can avoid the food that caused it. Don't harm others, don't harm yourself, and have a dialogue with your intelligence so you can make thoughtful choices.

❖ The mind digests new information by using metaphor, a Greek word meaning, "to transform energy." When reason works well, it works in metaphor, taking two separate concepts and finding the slimmest, oftentimes the most creative, similarity. There is preference for metaphor in biology with each side having its own complexity. Muscles are a type of paired opposites. The biceps and triceps for instance, are arranged on the opposite sides of the arm bone and are the agonist and antagonist to each other, as one relaxes to allow the other to stretch. Muscles cooperate and reciprocate just like a marionette paddle that lifts one side while depressing the other side of the puppet strings to mimic walking. The words neuron and nerve are from the word meaning 'cord.' Neurospastos means puppet, in Greek. Move through your opposites.

❖ Read poetry and notice how powerful word play can be. Sigmund Freud said, "Wherever I go, I find a poet has been there before me." Complex theories can arise from word play, as Julian Jaynes notes in his book, *The Theory of the Bicameral Mind*. "Metaphor is not a mere trick of language…it is the very constructive ground of language."

❖ Hatha yoga is constituted by 84 classical sets of asanas or postures, from the 840,000 natural body positions. The play of opposites calls for the very muscles that assume each posture, to relax in order to hold the pose. How many different positions do you get into a day? If it is under ten, you have 839,990 more to delight in.

❖ A chess master plays the game of opposites. It is said that a real master spends more time thinking about the board from his opponent's perspective, than his own.

☯ Understand the transformation of fear into its opposite. If you were to suddenly fall into the ocean, you would use exactly what is frightening you the most, to help—you would take support from the water and swim to shore.

❖ The movement of muscles comes from a pulling action. In our mind, a moral purpose can have an "attractive" power that moves us, by pulling us forward. An attractive power found in a moral journey can move us. It can call to us, impress us, or inspire us. A pilgrimage is then a walk linked to a larger purpose. We are all offered a calling but we can hear it or not, and respond to it or not. Which do you want to do?

❖ The over-scolding voice convinces us to under-perform. If we have good energy in this area, we will quiet the over-protective voice and seek the risk in creativity and imagination. We will acknowledge the shadow side of us as a guide rather than something to fear. Entertain the ideas in Rumi's poem "The Guest House." "This being human is a guest house/Every morning a new arrival/A joy, a depression, a meanness,/some momentary awareness comes/as an unexpected visitor/Welcome and entertain them all!/Even if they are a crowd of sorrows/who violently seep your house/empty of its furniture,/still, treat each guest honorably./He may be clearing you out for some new delight./The dark thought, the shame, the malice/meet them at the door laughing,/and invite them in./Be grateful for whoever comes,/because each has been sent/as a guide from beyond." The sixth chakra is where we no longer fear outside visitors or obstacles. We gain detachment when this energy center is healthy. Carolyn Myss notes, "Detachment does not mean ceasing to care. It means stilling one's fear-driven voices." She suggests improved posture, that is, the inner posture of detachment where the sense of self is complete. Strive toward wisdom over intellect.

❖ Think of your imagination as fed by what you cannot see. When asked how much brighter the sun is than the moon, studies show most people will estimate it is twelve times brighter. In reality it is 100,000 times brighter than the moon. Sometimes what we perceive is limited compared to what we can imagine. In the moon study, our perceptions are incorrect and our wildest imagination, correct.

☯ Treat toxic thoughts as if they are poisonous plants. Buddhist psychology says there are three ways to handle a poisonous plant: you can pull the plant out of the ground, you can pour boiling water on it, or you can do what the peacock does. The peacock eats the plant, transforming the toxins into the most beautiful feathers on earth. Each solution is like a key: one is iron, one is silver, and one is gold. Each opens the door. Use the golden key of transformation.

❖ There is health in chaos. A healthy heart and brain are more chaotic than diseased organs. If we have no flexibility in our thinking, perseverate on one thought, or experience a depressed mood that fails to lift, we might never appreciate the value of chaos and change. Some of us have a tendency to "awfulize," where we escalate minor problems toward the worst possible conclusion. The body struggles to understand the difference between events that are actual threats to survival and events that are present in thought alone. If we always think of the worst-case scenario, the body just might "think" the worst is really happening. Such chronic stress and "learned helplessness," lowers norepenephrine, the contentment hormone and increases cortisol, the alarm hormone, making the body feel as if it is fighting for survival. Psychologist Martin Seligman calls for "the dance of development," wherein one takes control over their reactions and interactions to avoid messages of threat, alienation, and helplessness. We fail to dance if we continually participate in "regressive coping." We forever back away from challenge and commitment, dwelling instead on repetitive emotional reactions, triggering the hormonal signals that serve to perpetuate the cycle. Dance through life.

❖ Western culture tends to value intellect over wisdom, tuition over intuition, and the university over the universe. The body symbolizes intellect over wisdom when it is held in poor posture, which places the forehead as the highest part of the body. In Western medicine, this posture is thought to cause neck, shoulder, and jaw pain due to the misalignment of muscles and bones. In Eastern thought, the intellect center is held higher than the crown, the source of wisdom. Chakra theory proposes that increased energy to one area supports growth. If the intellect center were held too high, too much energy would support overgrowth in the form of excessive thinking and mental excitation. Too little energy or exhaustion from holding it too high would trigger poverty of mental expression, as in dementia or apathy. Larry Dossey notes that even a lopsided pursuit can lead to imbalance. "The desire for wellness, if it is a disguised need for power over disease, is much more than a desire for healthiness: it is a veritable risk factor for becoming sick." Place your wisdom center higher than the intellect center. The crown of your head should be higher than your forehead.

❖ Slow down your efforts to always see the reason behind the ways of the world. Wait for the process to appear to you much like an artist waits for inspiration. Respect periods of waiting. Humans are unique creatures on the planet with the ability to pause between stimuli and response. Be the type that chooses your response and throw your full weight at it with confidence and insight. Heed these words from Ronald Sukenick, "In order to see some things others don't, you have to be blind to some things others aren't." Be blind to negative emotions. See another reaction that's not so apparent at first. Practice patience; the next time you are at the grocery store, practice slowing down by choosing the longest line at the checkout. Then practice with your emotions.

❖ Pleasure can be an antidote to harmful stressors. ARISE, or the Association for Research Into the Science of Enjoyment, studies the effects of pleasure as it increases levels of antibody and immunoglobulin A, strengthening the immune system. It has found that feelings of guilt lead to absentmindedness and sufferers are prone to more errors. Those that are pleased with their reactions to past events feel as if time has slowed down, and they make far fewer errors. Find delight in the way you handle things.

☯ Buddhist thought says there are eight paired winds: praise and ridicule, joy and suffering, gain and loss, credit and blame. If you are unaware of them, they will blow you like dry leaves. Know what moves you.

❖ In Chinese medicine, there are layers and levels of illness. Level Two shows symptoms at the chi level. These are the stubborn, chronic symptoms that won't go away. The time ratio between how long you feel good and how often you feel bad is shortened. Soon, you are sick all the time. This level shows our senses changing with itchy or watery eyes, blurred vision, stuffed sinuses, asthma, and dry, scaly skin. If the disease penetrates deeper into Level Three, the blood is impaired. The circulation of the spirit is threatened and it wanders aimlessly through the body. We are restless or listless, agitated and sleepless. Our behavior goes inward and transforms into worry, pain, and fever. Arthritis, diabetes and lupus are placed in this level, as it takes a blood test to diagnosis these ailments. Level Four displays quiet symptoms and the patient withdraws. Cancer, AIDS, stroke, depression, and failure to thrive, occur here. Pay attention to your symptoms when they are on the surface, express your emotions early, and keep the toxins from reaching deep inside you.

❖ Pain is often described in association with metaphor. The words piercing, stabbing, burning, and punishing are heard in pain clinics as patients describe their pain. These words tell us that they feel as if they are being tortured and rehab therapists will attempt to dissociate such a link. Since it takes time to forge association, therapists will employ the distracting qualities of movement. If the body is allowed to sit and anticipate, pain will increase. In fact, when we are initially injured, our body instinctually uses movement to distract the brain, giving the body time to seek help. If we slam our hand in a door, we rub it, shake it, and press on it. In other words, we use friction to create heat (rubbing), vibration (shaking), and deep pressure (pressing). Each of these "modalities" forms rapidly dispersing neuronal firings to compete with the source of pain. Each takes the same pathway as pain and literally gives the brain something else to sense. If the brain has to attend to the sensation of vibration, it doesn't have as much room on the pathway to give to the sensation of pain. A therapist is wise to use graded exposure toward painful activities, at first moving the patient in a pain free arc. Then, gradually widen the arc until the brain no longer links movement with pain. If you are a therapist, read the phenomenal work of David Butler. His book, *The Sensitive Nervous System* should be required reading in all therapy schools and the book *Explain Pain,* required reading for patients. Read about graded exposure, novel stimuli, diversion, and a return to dance-like neural gliding. Learn to identify your pain, not identify with it.

❖ Sometimes things are other than they seem. Take the simple notion of putting ice in a drink to cool it. Ice cools not by conduction alone but mostly by melting. In other words, ice does not convey coolness to its neighbor; the ice absorbs heat from its neighbor. The result is a meeting in the middle. Don't assume that outside events are influencing you. Assume that there is a meeting in the middle and you are able to influence events as well.

 Imagine the fire in you drawing others near, allowing them to transcend their ordinary existence. Bring ideas out of the dark and liberate them into the light. Be a catalyst.

 Empower yourself with the idea of water. When likely to be defeated by fire, escape into steam. When likely to be contained and clouded by air, transform into rain. When about to be defeated by grief, become a tear. When you need more shape, become an iceberg.

 Let the earth in you unite people into villages and nations. Provide caves and hollows in which to live and offer great harvests to transform those around you.

❧ Believe that the air in you can unite all things. Chuang Tzu (369-286 B.C.) said, "There is nothing which heaven does not cover."

❍ Try Trikonasana: Triangle pose is the play of opposites. In this pose we establish a solid foundation to allow us to fly. We stand firmly on our feet in order to grow away from the earth. We find the muscular balance to become lighter and less serious. We rest into the back of the body to liberate the front.

❍ Try Anja: Forehead Lotus. This posture energizes the insight chakra, the eye that sees the future. Anja in Sanskrit means "authority" and it commands the vision of unlimited power. We should lead with the forehead, not hold it up as high as we can. It governs all other chakras except the crown lotus, which should always be above it. Chakras use the lotus or flower image to signify the part of a plant that is incomplete, the fruit being the final product. The flower contains possibility.

❍ Try Ardha Matsyendrasana: Half Lord of the Fishes Pose. This position integrates the right and left sides of the body. As you twist around, imagine you are polishing inner gems. The important sequence in this twist is to begin with the body. The last to join in the twist is the head, which is meant to remind us that we don't always need to lead with the head. Intellect cannot solve all our problems.

❍ Try Child's Pose, quickly move into Cobra Pose and end with Bow Pose. The child begins life in the fetal position which is soothing, but is seen as a position of retreat when we are older. By lifting into cobra, you recreate a snake's first impulse to lift its head up and look around at the world it inhabits, just as an infant would raise its head. Cobra pose tones all of the cranial nerves of the head and relaxes the thoracic spine, resetting the autonomic nervous system. Now with a sense of calmness and confidence, sure of the things you are seeing, move into Bow pose and show you are prepared to strike out into the world, sure of your aim. It is like the toddler taking their first steps.

❖ There is a Tibetan saying: "If you are too clever, you could miss the point entirely." It is remindful of a Chinese fable of a sage at a well, pulling a rope up hand over hand. A clever young man asks him why he works so hard when there is a pulley. The sage says, "If I use a device like this, my mind will think itself clever. With a cunning mind I will no longer put my heart into what I am doing. Soon my wrists alone will do all the work. If my heart and whole body are not in my work, my work will become joyless. When my work is joyless, how do you think the water will taste?" Beware of an overly clever brain. Use all your parts when engaged in an activity. Use tools only if they make sense, not because they make things easier.

❖ There is a Greek phrase, *kalos kagathos*, which means that something is both good to look at and manifests goodness in action. It includes things that are beautiful to the senses as well as virtuous. Become *kalos kagathos*. Live beautifully while keeping the world beautiful.

❖ Some say the sense of hearing allows us to act on whispered wisdom. Listen for the little voice in you that is trying to tell you about your true nature. Listen to children that want to tell you secrets. What are the secrets you tell yourself about how you should live?

❖ Daniel G. Amen, MD, author of *Change Your Brain, Change Your Life,* writes about metacognition, which is the act of thinking about your thoughts. As a psychiatrist and neuroscientist, he suggests that we should continually challenge our thought patterns and change from negative, to positive input. Question your ANTS, an acronym for Automatic Negative Thoughts. "You don't have to believe every single thought you have. Many thoughts lie to you. They scare you." If you don't question your thinking, you will believe everything you think.

❖ In the book *No Enemies Within*, Dawna Markova suggests that the demons in your head are agents of your own evolution. They've becomes successful because they have replicated. She says an agitated mind is like a shaking bowl of churned up water. To stop the turmoil, you don't have to smooth out the water, you just need to find a way to hold the bowl still and the water will settle by itself. Agitated thinking cannot be quieted until the body is held still in meditation. But don't allow illness to be the only sanctioned form of inner exploration. Explore your mind when you feel well.

❖ Jokes and riddles are examples of playful thinking. They require that we think outside of logic, free from artificial answers, and free from the tyranny of looking at things from one perspective. Once we hear the answers to a riddle or the punch line to a joke, we are so surprised by the alternative way of thinking, we smile. We realize that many beliefs are simply figments of our imagination and an agreed upon perception of reality. As the comic Lily Tomlin says, "After all, what is reality anyway? Nothin' but a collective hunch."

❖ See yourself as you really are. Wake up and smell the green tea. Look at yourself and the life you live. What form of yourself are you failing to envision? Larry Dossey says in *Beyond Illness*, "Perhaps the question we should ask ourselves is not 'Am I healthy?' but 'Am I as healthy as I know how to be?' I believe that for most all persons the answer would be an unequivocal no. Almost everyone knows how to implement a higher order of healthiness. And if a 'no' answer doesn't make us unmistakably uncomfortable, it is likely that we haven't squarely asked it. Answering 'no' means that we have hidden from ourselves. We have shunned an inner wisdom."

❖ The Hawaiian word "Aloha" is from "alo," which means "meeting face to face" and "ha," which means "of the breath of life." When we look into each other's faces, remember, we are witnessing the breath of life. When we look in the mirror, we should relish the fact that we are faced with the breath of our life. Don't ever scorn that face.

❖ If you feel overwhelmed with sensations and thoughts, ask yourself "when am I not anxious," or "when am I not confused?" Learn to notice what is scarce. In rehab, we ask patients, "when does your back not hurt?" "In what position does your foot feel good?" Once you find that place, you work from there.

❖ Timing is everything. Practice activities that make you a "temporal millionaire." If the body can be disoriented from riding in trains and airplanes, orient it to a slower pace. Which activities make you lose track of time? What brings on flow, that feeling of performance trance? Which activities regenerate you and bring you relaxation? Do those things often.

❧ Stephen Levine said, "Wanting is the urge for the next moment to contain what this moment does not." Live each moment and fill it with choice. Instead of busying yourself with wanting, act toward what you want. Our most unused gift is choice. Decide literally means "to cut." Like a sculptor who works in subtraction rather than addition, cut the wanting away and live. We've all heard the quote, "The unexamined life is not worth living." Julia Cameron says, "The unlived life is not worth examining." If you are always wanting what you don't have, you are living a life that is not your own.

❖ The word "song" means sensation; Sing and become sensational. "Art" is a form of the verb "to be;" Create and become.

CHAKRA SEVEN—HARMONY

MUSCULAR SYSTEM, SKELETAL SYSTEM, SKIN, AND FASCIA

"It would be a simple enough thing to do if only simplicity were not the most difficult of all things."—Carl Jung

"Nature is an endless combination and repetition of a very few laws. She hums the old well-known air through innumerable variations."—Ralph Waldo Emerson

"A system which takes a risk yet survives deserves more credit than does a system which survives but has taken less risk."—Stephen F. Barker

"The understanding of atomic physics is child's play compared with understanding child's play."—David Kresch

The skin, the first barrier to disease, is the largest organ in the body and along with the fascia, is responsible for holding us together in one harmonious whole. The muscular system is responsible for the movement of the body through space, moving it towards that which is pleasurable and away from that which is deemed dangerous. Most of us think of our skeletal system as providing integrity to the body, but many animals like worms and octopus, move across the earth or through the water without a skeleton. It's the skeleton that is useless without muscles, not the other way around. The two systems of muscles and bone are often linked by one name into a co-dependent system, called the musculoskeletal system. Ideally, rehabilitation therapists would consider the even more holistic term, myofascial-skeletal system as critical in our development as "movement medicine" specialists.

These integrated systems are our connection with the world and the embodiment of grace as we move ourselves through that world. They are the body's version of the "big picture," the very representation of our relationship between life and death, and the physical go-between as we stand between heaven and earth. They are the shelter; the outward home for the inward inhabitants.

The Puritan view of the house was "borrowed" from the standards their God used in constructing the body. Tracey Kidder in *House,* says the Puritans thought "the house is the human imitation of divine handiwork. A roof was like a head, rafters were like bones, posts were shoulders, clapboards were skin, windows were eyes, doors were mouths, a threshold was lips, and a chimney was the breast in which lay the heart, which resembled the hearth which contained the flame which stood for the soul." While this serves as an attractive metaphor for a house, there is a structure that is built using the body as a design template. Architect Buckminster Fuller, coined the term "tensegrity," from tension integrity, to refer to structures that maintain their wholeness by balancing continuous tensile forces through the structure, as opposed to leaning on continuous compressive forces. His inventive geodesic dome is such a structure. Our body is another.

As it turns out, there exists a huge variety of tiny natural systems constructed using tensegrity. Carbon atoms, water molecules, viruses, bones, and cells are tensegrity systems that are the building blocks of larger systems. By providing the maximum amount of strength using the smallest amount of material, tensegrity systems are economical and allow structures to "live lightly on the earth."

The large myofascial-skeletal system, which makes up our support structure, or our home, employs an ancient communication network between each system—that of simple pulling, lifting and resting, stabilizing and mobilizing. But we should not be fooled into thinking the muscles hang from the skeleton and shove it around by merely pulling two insertions closer together. A tensegrity structure might find a muscle pulling outwards, but it does so by stabilizing against the opposite muscle that pulls inwards. As long as the two forces are balanced, the structure is stable. All of the elements—the fascia, the skin, the muscles, and the bones, rearrange themselves in response to a stress. The more stress, the more members that come to lie in the direction of the stress. This can vary according to individual make-up, prior injury, or cultural adaptations.

Our skin color and contours vary between cultures, perhaps as varied as the houses the citizens of the world live in. But it is seldom realized that our myofascial-skeletal systems can be different from culture to culture depending on lifestyle, work, and habits of movement. The French sociologist, Marcel Mauss, taught that there existed a "triple viewpoint of movement" according to the ways different cultures learn to use their bodies. The triple consideration consists of the physical, the psychological, and the sociological; all style-dependent factors in body movement. In *Techniques of the Body*, he notes that some cultures dive with their eyes open, march with their legs straight, carry objects on their heads, hips, or in their arms, and nurse infants, sleep, and sit in different positions. By using the body in habitual patterns, a culture will alter their muscular and skeletal systems and deteriorate in different ways as they are exposed to patterns, age, accident, and illness.

Cultural variations in shoes, for instance, can change the structure of the feet. Chair use can change muscle length, leading to undue joint wear of the hips and knees, while squatting can actually reduce wear in those same joints. Learning how to write at a chalkboard can produce more legibility in handwriting as the shoulder muscles become better stabilizers. By seating our children at desks earlier and earlier in their development, we will be perplexed as to why they write with so much finger movement and so little legibility. We write from our shoulder, the entire forearm and hand remaining stable in legible handwriting, gliding across the page as a unit. A generation who learned to write at a chalkboard will show greater legibility.

Even the position used for birthing can have profound future effects on muscles and bones. Obstetricians Lamaze and Leboyer, each developed positional birthing methods that affected a baby's neuromuscular response, increasing both the baby's overall health and the physical survival of the mother. Western birthing methods often rely on medications to induce mid-day births and positioning the mother on her back, thus placing priority in the comfort of the physician, not the mother or baby. Using natural birthing methods and allowing the mother to squat to utilize gravity, requires that the physician be present when the baby is ready to be born and to assume a squat position themselves. Apparently, that's not what the doctor ordered.

Cultural variations in movement and positions all seek some temporary gain. The hobbling movement of a woman in high heeled shoes may give the temporary benefit of added height, muscular calves, and a vulnerable and thus seductive physical presence. But high heels contribute to the permanent loss in the range of motion in the ankle and knee, painful weight-bearing through the arch of the foot, and undue wear on the balls of the feet. This shortens the plantar fascia of the foot and allows the loss of integrity that would be found in a normal center of gravity. Tipping the skeletal system up on its toes will keep every bone from its proper weight bearing position, depleting it of calcium-gaining forces. You can use gravity to signal a calcium deposit in your bones or you can move improperly and have to ingest extra calcium. It's up to the cultural variants you respond to.

To check your foot health, stand upright and wiggle your toes back and forth. If you are able to freely wiggle the toes, then your feet, ankles, and knees are properly weight-bearing. Should your ankles and knees be inflexible, with your toes clutching the ground for support, it points to the fact that the energy between you as an individual and the Earth you stand on, is impaired.

The temporary hygienic gain from Western toilets can be great but the individual cost can be great as well. Freedom from diseases borne of poor hygiene might indeed be the temporary gain of a Western toilet but we had better be prepared for its contribution to permanent losses such as incontinence, constipation, hemorrhoids, and the extravagant waste of our fresh water.

The temporary comfort gained from chairs leads to future and long-term discomfort. In a process called "weeping lubrication," synovial fluid is squeezed in and out of the cartilage in our joints through movement. This forced pressure of lubricating fluid lifts the two bony surfaces apart, creating space to move and acts as a pillow against painful bone-on-bone degeneration. Since the joints have no blood or lymph fluid supply to nourish and wash away waste products, only maximum range of motion will lubricate the joints, and for the hips and knees, maximum range of motion can be found in squatting. Sitting in chairs limits range of motion, especially in the hips and knees, thus exposing them to malnourishment which leads to early wear and tear, eventual pain, and even artificial replacement. When Swami Venkatesananda was asked what the unhealthiest thing we exposed the body to on a daily basis, he replied "Furniture."

Niels Diffrient, an industrial designer featured in *Discover* says, "Ideally a person should work standing or lying down. Sitting is a compromised position…it really is kind of like an athletic endeavor, and it should allow you to move and equally important, you should be aware of your body's condition." Sitting in a chair requires constant effort, yet we label the activity "rest." It is an athletic endeavor without cardiovascular benefit and without the healing benefits of real rest. Diffrient notes that instead of designing better furniture, "designers should get more broadly involved in designing work itself."

Skeletal muscles are built to move and the structure of their blood supply tells us so. Skeletal muscles have an increased collateral blood supply since they reside in moving parts. Mechanical bending of a joint can kink an artery so a collateral artery is needed to ensure that at least one artery remains open no matter what the position of the limb or joint. If we sit in positions that cut off the collateral supply, say, by having the back of our thighs press against a chair for hours on end, the circulation to our legs can be severely hampered.

Living in a cultural vacuum where there is little knowledge about how temporary comforts thwart our future health, serves as a set-up for poor body awareness. We literally don't know what ails us. Worse than that, what ails us is what we have chosen in the name of comfort, ease, and success at work. When we are off balance physically, it is difficult to find our emotional compass, our spiritual center, and our life's true path in the process. What must the body think when it tells us it's uncomfortable in a chair and we choose to sit longer? Sore shoulders, a stiff neck, and low back pain are the yellow warning flags sent by the body to initiate movement. But yet when plagued by such pain, we sit longer, or choose bed rest. A dribbling bladder or strained defecation is telling us the bowel and bladder are getting the wrong positional messages and yet our solution is to sit longer on the toilet. Wrist pain tells us to get off the computer but our solution is to impose ergonomic comforts which only allow us to work for longer periods. Cars pollute the air and crowd our towns, with roads and parking lots where plants and trees could grow. Finding such an environment stressful and coughing on the air, our solution is to get in the car and drive to a park or to the shore, leading to the demand for more roads and more parking. It seems we just give the body more of what ails it. As Marta Beck states in her book, *Finding Your Own North Star*, "I believe that your body knows a lot more than your mind about the life you're supposed to live."

The oldest form of bodywork, Hatha Yoga, specifies asana and pranayama practices as the first two steps in returning to our true nature. Practicing an asana (position) and breathing through that position (pranayama), requires an internal focus to keep the mind still while the body moves. It is different from other forms of exercise because of its firm basis in intention; the intention to value ourselves enough to maintain a lifestyle conducive to our life's purpose. Hatha Yoga teaches one to live in the world while maintaining certain ethics and honoring the integrity of the body. While health is not tied to physical well-being or an absence of symptoms in Yogic tradition, it does pivot on the idea of wholeness—an intentional, aware relationship with pain, disease, and death.

The first step toward wholeness might be to understand the choices we make or the temporary fixes we opt for and then take responsibility for the consequences of those choices. Without that awareness, we suffer breakdowns, not only of the muscles or the bony support systems, but of our emotional support system. Many of our emotions, such as phobias, anxiety, and anger are no longer reliable advisors. We are afraid, anxious and angry about everything. They are maladaptations to repressed, healthy adaptations. Darwin in *Descent of Man*, concluded that "the highest stage in moral culture is when we recognize that we ought to control our thoughts." Choice, then, becomes our keenest survival strategy. In *Darwin's Ghost*, Steve Jones warns against sloughing off responsibility for our well-being and well-thinking, especially when we blame our genetic make-up for our ills. "To say that genes are in control of our behavior has no more intellectual content than to claim that people go to work because their legs drag them to the office."

If you are feeling that ordinary solutions no longer hold value for you and that money and success hold no attraction any longer, you may be in the midst of a spiritual crisis—a feeling of waiting for something to wake up inside you. I can guarantee that our muscles and bones are waiting for just such an awakening. They are telling us so. They are the body's messengers, trying to communicate the "big picture" through the obstructive screen of mundane events and temporary choices. They are waiting for an inspired life full of movement and the path not taken. They are telling us to make a choice.

Illness might serve as the only catalyst—a last resort—for spiritual transformation. Were we to listen to the pain felt in muscles, we would be privy to an early catalytic warning. I tell my patients they are very wise to put their stress in their muscles for though uncomfortable, they are not yet damaging their organs with high blood pressure, stomach eroding ulcers, and cancer cells gone awry. The muscles can be used as our first warning sign, the yellow flags telling us there is a higher level of integrity that guides our choices. Even muscles, in order to move, must have one end inserted higher than the other. In order for us to get through life gracefully, we have to find a higher order, a vision that pulls us. It is the opposite of pushing ourselves. Hatha Yoga tells us that there is a higher purpose and we can practice with our body.

That higher order can come to us in understanding and fully honoring the adaptive response found in our body's "yellow flags." Freud taught that taking responsibility for the truth about ourselves would require people to be honest— to confess to the instincts that are at work in them. While he spoke most often about the psychological instincts as a psychiatrist, he was first a neurologist and knew the body had instincts of its own. These instincts of knowing what is best for its survival, are what we so easily ignore and often counter-act. The first confession of truth to ourselves is that, sometimes, sickness is not the opposite of health. Sometimes it is a healthy adaptation.

Western medicine prides itself on eliminating symptoms; the quicker the better. People gravitate toward doctors who help them in this social adaptation, often at the expense of physical adaptation. Taking medications that adjust the symptoms does not always adjust the disease and the little picture wins out over the big picture once again. Additionally the body must adjust to the side-effects of medication (even bed rest has side-effects) and thus the body requires more and more adjustments to maintain status quo. Evolutionary medicine, as outlined by Randolph Neese and George Williams in, *Why We Get Sick*, explains the adaptations and the underlying usefulness of symptoms.

Medications that quiet coughs and sneezes, stifle powerful forces that can send viruses and bacteria away from our body at one hundred miles an hour. Medicine that dries up mucous membranes dries up the sticky fluid that might trap viruses. A runny nose serves to rid the body of virus germs or send them through the GI tract to be killed by stomach acid. Likewise, pills that quiet a fever silence the only heat that can burn and destroy a viral infection.

During the tuberculosis epidemic in the '40's, many patients who were treated in sanitariums with cutting edge medical care, died. What perplexed doctors was that many sicker people, who had not had treatment, lived. Little did they know that their medical intervention was the killer. In the sanitariums, TB patients were noted to have extremely low iron in their blood and so were administered iron supplements, and lots of them. It turns out that iron is exactly what TB bacterium feeds on. Our blood, in all its wisdom, was locking up the iron, putting a coating of protein around it to starve the TB bugs, an adaptation that should never have been interfered with no matter what the patient's laboratory tests looked like.

Diabetes, a lifestyle disease in the U.S. and countries experiencing a nutrition transition, occurs when increased access to processed foods collides with genes weaned on poverty. Jared Diamond, an evolutionary biologist, notes that low birth weight, coupled with lifestyles of excess, are a formula for diabetes if one becomes obese as an adult. Diabetes benefits a society that experiences periods of scarcity with its ability to respond to huge fluctuations in blood sugar levels. Without the fluctuations brought on by scarcity, the disease becomes full-blown, placing the satiated person at a huge health risk.

Stomach ulcers are blamed on *Heliobacter pylori (H. pylori)*, and not stress, lifestyle, or excessive worry. Yet half the people on Earth are infected with *H. pylori*, with only 10-20% of those people experiencing peptic ulcer. *H. pylori* must have lifestyle triggers that cause it to ulcerate only some of its hosts. Since ulcers and the bacteria are decreasing secondary to antibiotic administrations, we may be losing the protective properties of *H. pylori*. It protects against esophageal cancer, asthma and reflux, as the chronic but mild inflammation of the bacteria in the mucous lining produces a reservoir of disease-fighting cells, which neutralize stomach acid. Without *H. pylori*, we produce the full amount of stomach acid and it is thought that we may soon have the first generation with full stomach acid on Earth. In the process, we are losing a symbiotic relationship that has protected 80% of us.

The increased incidence in skin cancer, despite nearly two generations who have had sun screen applied since they were infants, is cause for investigating the role of adaptive responses. Sunburn is an adaptation; a message to get out of the sun after an hour, which is just the right amount of time to allow for a healthy dose of Vitamin D, which is just right for processing calcium, which is perfect for building bone. Also, it gives us just the right dose of melatonin to trigger a good night's sleep. That light sunburn is a warning to put on a hat and some loose, long sleeves, keeping us protected from the sun for the rest of the day. Sunscreen, however, permits us to stay uncovered for hours at a time, exposing us to deep penetrating rays, the ones that change our DNA. Taking away the protective, adaptive mechanism of a simple sunburn by wearing sunscreen, is all the permission we need to substantially increase our risk of cancer. Sunscreen changes our behavior which then changes our gene expression.

Another adaptive response is the emergency reflex, know as fight or flight. When faced with danger, our body prepares to fight the offender or flee from it—either way, the body wants a motor response. With that motor response, emergency chemicals like adrenaline and glucose are disintegrated naturally, the big muscles used for running or fighting able to quickly metabolize waste products. Unfortunately, most of our stressors are not physical and do not, in fact, require that we run or fight. One would risk their job should they punch an irritating co-worker or run screaming out of a frustrating meeting. But the body under stress knows no difference from work ethics and survival reflexes. It wants a motor response. With reflexes "put in motion" and the body struggling with a passive experience, there is no outlet. What was once adaptive, is now injurious. Our aggressive feelings, irritability, and pent-up rage eat us up inside. It's as if the motor response goes inward.

Even poor posture "tells" the body to get up and go. While seated in a chair at work with our head held forward off our spine (the computer posture), we are assuming the same posture that we use to get out of a chair—our head goes forward and the body follows. Our neck muscles are literally telling our body that the head is starting to go and the body should follow. Yet, we never get up from that desk. The body is still getting the message, possibly for hours at a time, yet it never follows the head. The body doesn't know the brain has determined it will sit for eight hours to get a paycheck—it only gets the primitive message that the head is about to go and so it stays at the ready. This accounts for the restlessness and agitation we experience after a few hours of sedentary, forward head posture work.

We have adapted our adaptations so much that we don't know if we are coming or going. Disease and pain are assumed to be abnormal but they are normal responses to abnormal activity, done for an abnormal amount of time. Making our computer chairs more and more comfortable, our bodies are quieted from their usual warning signal—it is unhealthy to sit longer than thirty minutes. Sitting for a meal takes twenty minutes. Then we are up. Even one sit-com is thirty minutes. Then we should be up and out of there. We even toss and turn naturally while asleep, so as not to stay in one numbing position for very long. We move even in rest.

Uncomfortable computer stations do bring pathology but what we must reconcile is that pain sometimes has an unappreciated benefit. Carpal tunnel pain is sometimes the body's only way to get us away from an abhorrent situation—that of sitting for hours at a time. Perhaps such muscular disorders are a way of signaling how many of us have meaningless, paper-pushing jobs. Perhaps excessive Worker's Compensation claims are a way of slowing down out-of-control capitalism.

Many diseases, as we have noted, have adaptive benefits. Sickle cell anemia protects against malaria. While malaria kills many children, sickle cell allows its "host" to live well into child-bearing years, thus preserving the species. It's not comfortable for the "host" but it serves a benefit. Mania is thought to serve society at large in that many artists, composers, musicians and authors suffer from bipolar disorder. Although not a comfortable life for the artists, society reaps huge benefits from their hyper-productive and creative lives. Multiple sclerosis "benefits" the patient in that they are very unlikely to get estrogen driven cancers such as breast and ovarian cancer. And sometimes, discomfort, illness or accident is the only way some of us will take stock of our lives, quit unfulfilling jobs, and live like there was no tomorrow.

It is wise to remember that when we are looking only for comfort, we deaden our ability to be fully awake. We have designed and resigned ourself to the negative side of normalcy when we adapt to something wholly dysfunctional. It's no wonder we often feel as if we are sleepwalking through life. The trade-offs we make, the self-betrayals, and the dishonorable way we treat our bodies, are all put in a tidy package called "normal." One can imagine a mother being deemed negligent for failing to lather her child in sunscreen, or allowing a 100 degree fever to go untreated. It isn't difficult to imagine being reprimanded for getting up from our computer stations every half-hour to walk a message over to a co-worker down the hall, rather than use e-mail. Instead we stay at our computer stations, tolerating sore shoulders and wrists and on the weekends, send our children out all day with their sunscreen.

What we call health just may be our sickness. If we dull our messages, we cannot hear the inner wisdom, and we are much like the man James Joyce wrote about when he said, "Mr. Duffy lived a short distance from his body." We need to live in our bodies and to do that, we need to listen to our body's messages. After all, those messages are made to change our behavior.

Take the simple phenomenon of thirst, which is outlined in Candace Pert's book, *The Molecules of Emotion.* A peptide called angiotension, mediates thirst and it immediately starts to change the way the body functions, first decreasing the vapor that is exhaled from the lungs, decreasing the urine excreted by the kidneys, and eliminating sweating, tearing, and salivation if it has to. At the same time, this peptide (a type of hormone) sends us into action on the outside. It alters our consciousness, our mood, and our behavior. It makes itself known so the body will seek water. It makes us leave our desk, stop the car, or walk for miles if it has to, essentially stopping any activity that is not involved with getting water. Our behavior changes all in an effort to appease this peptide. The unconscious and conscious body work together, conserving the water inside the body while moving to find more water to put in the body.

When this type of mind/body connection shifts into awareness, messages like thirst and pain can take on new meaning. The entire unit will work together to make things right, to have things make sense, to feel successful, and to feel whole. When parts of the unit or parts of the message are ignored, it's no wonder we feel unbalanced, at a loss, at wits end, and unfulfilled—we feel as if we are missing something. We are. This connection toward wholeness is the goal of energy practices like visualization, Yogic breathing, the relaxation response, and bodywork therapies as they bring up the connections lodged in the body's chemical and myofascial-skeletal network to make the system whole again.

Ida Rolf, who developed the intense Rolfing massage techniques, would see a patient with hip pain and remark, "I can see your brain in your hip." The limping and tip-toeing around the pain, placed all the attention and life energy in the hip. She wanted her patients to get their brain in their whole body. Feldenkrais found that many patients had a "terrifying sense of shakiness, fragmentation, and impermanence at the core of their sense of self. Some were so without a center that they did not even know that I would recognize them from week to week. They literally did not know that they existed in a continuous way in the minds of other people. So they felt compelled to tell me their whole story over and over again." For these people, their brains are not in their body, there is no internal safe harbor, and they feel a deep sense of panic, as if they are falling apart. Annihilation anxiety is a good term for this phenomenon. If we are not connected to a soothing sense of centeredness, we feel as if we will cease to exist.

Even our clothing can restrict our full potential and keep us from being whole.

In 1888, British Suffragettes created the Rational Dress Society to protest deforming fashions such as corsets. Terms like "tight laced" and "loose women" are corset metaphors, and referred to whether or not a lady was showing proper behavior. Citing that women were unable to take a deep breath and subject to fainting while laced in a corset, they sought a ban on such garments. They banned weighted skirts which did not allow exercise, and high heels which did not allow running or comfortable walking and even had to go so far as to demand that undergarments weigh less than seven pounds. The new activity for women during this liberating time was cycling and from that activity, we gained pedal pushers and bloomers—clothing that allowed freedom in pedaling.

Iris Young, in an essay titled "Throwing Like a Girl," believes that girls remain held back in a state of "inhibited intentionality." Constrictive clothing brings about shrinking behavior where girls are afraid to speak out or laugh aloud, so they whisper and giggle instead. She notes that tight clothes cultivate a body that says, "I am small and vulnerable, narrow and harmless." Girls learn early to take up little space and are subject to the "bonsai effect," unable to fully express their full potential because of the small container they put themselves in. Colette Dowling notes in *The Frailty Myth,* that "Girls movement patterns are often incomplete because they don't learn to generate torque when executing a throw, a swing or a tackle. Lack of torsion (which essentially is what is meant by "lack of follow through") results from failure to put the whole body into the motion. Girls often hold themselves back from full, complete movement…They learn to hamper their movements, developing a body timidity that increases with age."

Bodyworkers talk of "myopsyche," or muscle personality. If the muscle personality is disturbed, then movement will be clumsy, stiff, and uncontrolled. Mature posture is muscular equilibrium, where muscles stabilize each other and act as starting points for every new movement. The more stable the starting point, the smoother and more efficient the movement. Motor maturity is practice for spiritual maturity: our capacity to be open, to forgive, to let go, and to grow deeper.

Spiritual maturity finds us untying the complicated knots, untangling conflict, and undoing our struggles. It is the capacity to come into joy, to rest, and to feel blessed. Dogen, founder of Japanese Zen said, "The human mind has absolute freedom as its true nature. There are thousands upon thousands of students who have practiced meditation and obtained this realization. Do not doubt the possibilities because of the simplicity of the method. If you can't find the truth where you are, where else do you expect to find it?" He thinks the sage in us can be awakened by practicing meditation. The Suffragettes thought that, as a first step, women could become awakened by practicing rational dress. Buddha said, "Only within our own body, with its heart and mind can bondage and suffering be found, and only here can we find true liberation." Liberating ourselves from constrictive clothing is surely a start.

Another area where confusion between what constitutes liberation and restriction is in the idea of play. Play, as any child knows, involves some risk, as Theodore Roosevelt told us when he held a White House reception honoring the formation of the Playground Association of America on April 13, 1906. The Association's purpose was to prepare children "for challenges, opportunities, and risks of life" by creating "a new equilibrium between individualism and cooperation, initiative and caution." Seesaws were intended to cultivate an individuals "sense of balance" and "a certain feeling of responsibility" toward the other seesawer. Swings offered "tethered security while flying in the face of danger." Lady Allen of Hurtwood, the leader of the playground movement in Britain, encouraged risk-taking on the playground noting, "Better a broken arm than a broken heart."

Today, the National Program for Playground Safety warns of the dangers of play. Not only is the equipment, much of it installed after John F. Kennedy's

Council of Youth Fitness promotion, in question, but so is the earth itself. The Federal Handbook states, "Earth surfaces such as soils and hard packed dirt are not recommended because they have no shock-absorbing properties." Additionally, "grass is undesirable because wear and environmental conditions can reduce their effectiveness." School districts in Philadelphia have eliminated recess, one in Southern California has banned running, and New York City has removed all low limbs to discourage the climbing of trees. We are essentially telling our children, "better safe than sorry." But is that what they hear? Lauri Macmillan Johnson, Professor of Landscape Architecture at the University of Arizona notes that if playground equipment is too boring, children make up dangerous games like crashing into the equipment with their bikes.

Philip Howard details our trend at making life safe in his book, *The Lost Art of Drawing the Line.* Afraid of liability and resultant lawsuits, America is resorting to detailed rules to protect business. Park City, Utah retreated from offering free bicycles to tourists to offset traffic, citing liability issues. Cities, many mentioned in his book, are disassembling playground equipment due to lawsuits that won big money for parents whose children were injured. Howard says, "Legal fear has become a defining feature of our culture…Instead of looking where we want to go, Americans are constantly looking over our shoulders." He notes that it has gotten to the point that making a mistake isn't what scares you—it's whether someone can sue you for that mistake. He notes, "Even the mortar boards at Yale University come with a written warning inside the graduation cap stating that throwing it could result in injury."

Julian E. Barnes writes in *The New York Times,* that the Consumer Product Safety Commission reports the rate of head injuries among bicyclists has increased 51%, even as helmet use has risen and bicycle ridership is declining. "It's puzzling to me that we can't find the benefit of bike helmets here," notes Ronald L. Medford, the Assistant Executive Director of the Safety Commission's Hazard Identification Office. They can't find the benefit of bike helmets because it's the use of bike helmets that lead to more risky behavior. Specialists in risk analysis are cited in the article as saying that "the increased use of bike helmets may give riders an inflated sense of security and encourage more risk."

There is a parallel to the helmet theory in the car industry with the invention of the anti-lock brake. Government and industry studies in the mid-90's showed that "as drivers realized their brakes were more effective, they started driving faster and some accident rates rose." In Dr. Steven Berglass' book *Reclaiming the Fire,* he notes that psychologists and economists have explored the notion that in mandating safeguards, one can expect a psychological "boomerang effect." "The paradoxical yet empirically validated theory of *risk homeostasis* (his emphasis) maintains that the more government creates safety nets for businesses and individuals…the more likely people will seek out the exhilarating feelings of risky activities, enterprises, or investments." Berglass explores the phenomenon of self-handicapping in business leaders. He suggests that people who seem to parlay every move they make into a success, often turn to performance inhibitors such as alcohol, illness, accidents, and even angry outbursts in order to sabotage their low-risk skill set. It seems that if business becomes too safe, people will make it dangerous with risky behavior, perhaps as a substitute for that risky feeling we get when we play.

Play offers us a time when we quiet the internal mental noise, and as children know deep down in their bones, it is the brain's favorite way to learn. Carl Jung said, "The creation of something new is not accomplished by the intellect but by the play instinct acting from inner necessity. The creative mind plays with the objects it loves." In *Homo Ludens*, Johan Hvizinga looks at the study of play. "Play creates order, is order. Into an imperfect world and into the confusion of life it brings a temporary, limited perfection." Play requires freedom, the freedom to be a child, to be "off from work," to be free of what inhibits you.

Diane Ackerman traces the word play in her book *Deep Play*. The word "'play" comes from the Anglo Saxon "*plega*" meaning singing or dancing gestures, clapping or quick movements. More ancient etymologies show the Indo-European word "*plegan*" meaning to risk, change, and expose oneself to hazard. Pledge, peril and plight are all related to the word play and indicate a tight engagement and risk in an activity.

Ackerman describes two escape routes to play, one horizontal and the other vertical, that are directly linked to being in a body. The word "ecstasy" means "to stand outside of." When we are gripped by the passion of ecstasy, it is considered a horizontal event, occurring as we stand beside our self on the ground. Rapture however, implies the kind of play that is vertical, where we are seized by a force and elevated as if caught in talons. Words like ravenous, rabid, ravage, rape, usurp, and raptor are all related to rapture, literally meaning "to be carried aloft." Both words for escaping into play describe what happens to the body. It either gets carried away or stands apart from its usual self.

In most of the healing arts, this sense of play, of being carried away and living outside oneself, is taught in the context of "letting go" and in that letting go, we find more of who we are. The question Yoga asks, says Richard Miller Ph.D., a clinical psychologist, is "how do I get larger and larger to embrace all my energies? How do I make room for what I am pushing away?" We make room by letting go.

The playful act of juggling was studied by Austin at MIT, who found that the accuracy of the toss depends on when you let go. Errors that seemed to be errors in direction or speed of the toss (that is, errors in space), were really errors in the timing of "letting go." If the internal clock was no good, the motor skill was no good. Austin suggests that the biggest mistake in juggling is the throwers infection by the "one-height bug." Having an inflexible routine, by expecting the ball's position to be accurate if it is always thrown at the same height, is a recipe for disaster. "It should be distinctly surprising, even to a computational theorist, that getting better at juggling for the most part involves building better and more sophisticated error compensations."

Another finding of the juggling study was that this letting go, and allowing actual versus expected motor patterns to emerge, often requires a mentor. The novice saves endless repetition by gaining advice on predictable mistakes. One must let go of their ego to allow a teacher to give advice and it becomes clear that seeking advice is, in and of itself, a skilled motor response—one has to seek out a mentor or be found by one. Like a rehab therapist plays a role in constructing new motor patterns for disabled patients, a mentor serves to remind us all of our natural abilities to let go of old or useless patterns.

Annie Dillard in *Pilgrim at Tinker Creek* writes, "We let our bodies go the way of our fears...Why do we lose interest in physical mastery? If I feel like turning cartwheels—and I do—why don't I learn to turn cartwheels, instead of regretting that I never learned as a child? We could all be aerialists like squirrels, divers like seals; we could be purely patient, perfectly fleet, walking on our hands even, if our living or stature required it. We can't even sit straight or support our weary heads."

We could all find that sense of play by learning to turn cartwheels, juggle, or dive into a wave. We could learn to swim, ride a bike, dance or jump rope. But first, we have to let go. In rehab, many of our sessions in restoring the proper muscle energy for good balance, first include a lesson in learning how to fall. Likewise, cyclists learn the best way to survive a crash, and parachutists, how to roll their landing to avoid injury. Another predictable training technique taught in rehab clinics is, regretfully, how to get up off the floor without help. I say regretfully, because it is surprising how many people even in their forties, are unable to get up off the floor without climbing up on furniture. Their lack of flexibility prevents them from sitting on the earth and they couldn't play in the mud if they wanted to. If they were to let go, they would fall and they couldn't get up.

Jack Kornfield offers, "We already know how to let go—we do it every night when we go to sleep, and that letting go, like a good night's sleep, is delicious. We begin to trust the natural rhythm of the world just as we trust our own sleep and how our own breath breathes itself...We survive because there are natural periods of ease—lasting longer than our grasping and fear." This ease can come in the form of play, in trusting that your body can get up from the floor, or in having faith that you could learn to turn a cartwheel, or dance on your tip toes.

The proper use of a muscle, joint, and nerve and the skills they afford, translates into emotional commitment, lifestyle habit, and a sense of well being. Lack of flexibility can then negatively affect your sense of living well. The habit of sitting in a chair that shortens and weakens musculature can be seen to have both physical and mental consequences especially when a chair is the only permitted place to sit. The chair essentially takes responsibility for where we sit in a room and what muscles we use or not use. Stephen Cope, in his wonderful book, *Yoga and the Quest for the True Self,* cites the Western model of medicine as splitting the awareness of the outside and inside of the body. Skin and muscles are available to awareness and volition, while our insides remain outside our volition and hence outside our responsibility. "We banish feelings we don't want to face to inside the body where they manifest as disease. Then disavow responsibility, seeing the disease as an outside invader." Stanley Keleman notes in *Emotional Anatomy,* "Without anatomy, emotions do not exist…To be an individual is to follow the urges of one's own form, and to learn its unique rules of organization." The unique organization of the knee, for instance, allows the activation of emotional and spiritual centers in the brain, with knee pressure activating the centers in the brain that store spiritual and religious thoughts. The knee connects our outsides with our insides and our top to our bottom. As Diane Jacobs, a physical therapist in Vancouver notes, "it takes us out of a hierarchical perception of our body into a more kaleidoscopic perception, where there is no up/down/in/out, only a shifting pattern and a balance of parts."

There exists an ancient method of healing called "toning" that serves to restore the patient to such harmonic patterns. It's as if there was a cosmic symphony of which your heartbeat is perhaps one of the instruments. Julia Cameron writes in *Vein of Gold,* that toning is a spiritual tool where the voice opens the heart. Cameron has studied the body's energy centers or chakras and reminds us that each chakra has a vowel or "seed sound" which calls to it and allows it to do its job more forcefully. By singing the vowel sounds, a vibration is felt, first with the mouth open and then with it shut. "The mouth has now become a 'sound cave,' a portable spiritual site that resonates," states Cameron. The vibration reverberates into the chest cavity and surrounds the heart, thus stimulating the chakras to function with more clarity and harmony.

Johann Wolfgang Von Goethe said that "architecture is frozen music," so perhaps the animated body might be music in action. Don Campbell, another researcher into the body's harmonics suggests that "if the body can respond so decisively to music, it must in some sense be music." This, of course, is not a new idea.

The Pythagoreans of Greece had the Music of the Spheres and the ancient Chinese had the Primal Sound, an inaudible but ever-present divine vibration. The Egyptians lived by the careful listening of the melodic Words the Gods and the Indian spiritual tradition had Nada Brahms, where the creator and the whole cosmos is sound. As Mickey Hart, the drummer for The Grateful Dead and drum historian writes, "In the beginning was noise. And noise begat rhythm.

And rhythm begat everything else." Whirling dervishes and Sufi dancers both employ spinning counterclockwise with their arms in specific directions as a form of worship. Believing they are in harmony with the cosmological rhythm of atoms and planets, they find dance as the source of higher consciousness.

Where does science stand on this issue of rhythm and vibrations? Well, it seems the next revolution in physics lies in the science of harmonics. While music and auditory vibrations may possibly be the critical factor in the next revolution of the spirit, according to sound therapists, there is also music in the air according to leading physicists. In fact, sound is what is holding the universe together.

Physicists have come to agree that the building blocks of nature are no longer particles, but vibrating strings of some fundamental, unknown "stuff," according to K. C. Cole in *A Hole in the Universe*. She notes that physicists have identified about 1% of the matter in the known universe. They know the shape of that universe (flat) but what is the other 99% that is holding it together? That "what" is string theory, also known as superstring theory and more recently M-theory (M-theory stands at any one time for magic, mother, mystery, matrix, or membrane theory). The M-theory states—the universe is held together by a song.

Cole notes, "As described by M-theory, the entire universe arises from the harmonics of vibrating strings, membranes and blobs in eleven dimensions. These unseen dimensions curl around one another in strange, convoluted shapes, forming holes, knots and handles…Depending on the exact geometry of the vibrating string, it will produce different harmonic chords, just as a piano produces a different sound than a flute…In a sense, the resonant patterns are equivalent to the particles, the universe the symphony they sing." And the world's leading physicists agree on the string-theory and they find it, well, beautiful.

John Schwarz, Caltech physicist said, "It looked a little crazy (string theory), but I felt such a beautiful mathematical structure had to lead someplace." String theorist David Gross notes, "It's not just that it's mathematically beautiful. It's physically beautiful."

While the universe may indeed be held together by a song, the body, in fact, was the first musical instrument, as Curt Sachs notes in his *History of Musical Instruments*. "Instrumental music…began in general as a percussive act of the body: slapping the buttocks, the belly, the thighs, or clapping the hands, or stamping the ground." The act of percussion, of making something, anything, vibrate is the only universal cultural artifact and is found everywhere on Earth. While every culture does not enjoy fire, the wheel, or even domesticated animals, drumming is found in every culture.

Like any ancient culture, harmony is what the universe is made of. "The drum is sacred. Its round form represents the whole universe, and its steady beat is the pulse, the heart, throbbing at the center of the universe," says American Indian,

Nick Black Elk. The enchantment we all seek is music, as the word tells us in its Latin origins. From "*incantare*," enchantment means to "sing magical words or sounds." Michael Drake in his book, *The Shamanic Drum*, says that "the drum's pulse synchronizes the left and right hemispheres of the brain. When these hemispheres begin to pulse in harmony, there is a change in the actual physiology of the brain waves that produces a high state of awareness."

The Hindus believe that as long as Shiva Nataraja dances and beats her drum, the world will continue to exist, and the Chinese myth of P'an-ku tells the origin of the universe, as he pounded on the cliffs of Chaos to sculpt the planets. These myths suggest that a drummer was the architect of the universe. Mickey Hart, historian of drumming throughout cultures, says there is "an almost organic compulsion to translate the emotional fact of being alive into sound, into rhythm, into something you can dance to." He notes that the body, flooded with adrenaline from the pounding that mimics a "flight or fight" heartbeat, responds to percussion in a primitive manner. With nothing to flee from or fight, it dances. Hart notes that repetitive, physical work is often wedded to drumming, such as the carpenters hammer. In the introduction to his book *Planet Drum*, he poetically links drums with science noting, "Science has taught us that we live in a rhythmscape in which everything is pulsing in time with everything else. Every atom, every planet, every star is vibrating in a complex dance. We live on planet drum."

In some cultures, the drum links the present with the netherworld. The Kaluli drummers of Papua New Guinea and other shamans use the drum as a "trance tool," with percussion able to carry them out of their body to align with the vibrations of the dead. This alignment, either in this life or with, perhaps the dead, is what Dutch scientist Christian Huygens called "entrainment," when in 1665 he discovered a law in physics that holds if two rhythms are nearly the same and sources are in close proximity, they will fall into synchronicity. Nature is efficient, it is thought, and it takes less energy to pulse together rather than in opposition.

Whether there is truth in this phenomenon may be explained by an increasing number of scientists who say that our health and behavior may be caused by waves of electrical changes in weather systems. In other words—vibrations. Shifts in temperature, humidity, cloud cover, wind speed, and barometric pressure are studied by biometeorologists or bioclimatologists, scientists who study mind-body-weather phenomenon.

Michael Persinger, a neuroscientist, clinical psychologist, and preeminent biometeorologist, says that while statistics would be too invasive to test, "medical conditions from angina and arthritis to hip fractures…have been statistically linked to weather." He warns that we are especially vulnerable to weather insults because of our physically constant weather conditions in a building and our lack of weather exposure. Our culture of working indoors and our sedentary habits away from work, serve to protect us from weather yet in the long run, make us more susceptible to weather changes. Persinger states, "One thing we do know about biological systems is that they tend to respond to contrast. And one of the things that fluctuates most these days is the weather." One of Persinger's students, Rod O'Connor, found that the incidence of sudden infant death syndrome (SIDS) is higher when geomagnetic storm activity is very low. It is known that SIDS deaths are connected to low levels of melatonin, an internal clock hormone that mediates the production of nitric oxide, a transmitter integral for breathing. O'Connor believes that weather events can depress nocturnal levels of melatonin and nitric oxide.

There are few arthritic sufferers who would doubt the weather's effect on pain. They are walking barometers with their joints swelling much like a barometer's fluid levels rising and falling. In Germany, Deutscher Wetterdienst, the German National Weather Service, has issued daily bio-weather bulletins for over ten years. "Cloudy with a chance of migraines," or "damp with a chance of insomnia," are common forecasts. The Weather Channel also shows a daily "aches and pains index" in the winter and the world's largest weather gatherer, Weather Services International, has a biometeorology page on its Web-site.

It seems we are tied to the earth's vibrations and seek to entrain with them. A Babatunde Olatunji, a Nigerian drummer says, "Where I come from we say that rhythm is the soul of life, because the whole universe revolves around rhythms and when we get out of rhythm, that's when we get into trouble. For this reason, the drum, next to the human voice, is the most important instrument. It's very special."

As it turns out, our entire body is made of communication systems, the voice being the only one we can hear. Most importantly, these communication systems can be in a state of ill-health or in survival mode, or find health and resume their specialized "social" function: Contraction (myofascial-skeletal system), secretion (endocrine system) or conduction (nervous system). Signal transmissions are what the nerves use to transmit information. Neurological diseases like Multiple Sclerosis, diabetic neuropathy, polio, nerve compression syndromes, Parkinson's, and leprosy are the interruption of these transmissions. Slow waves of DV current run along the nerves, constantly signaling either generation or regeneration. It has been referred to as the body's "integrating pacemaker."

Michael Levin at Boston's Forsyth Institution and Harvard University found that when an embryo consists of four cells, an electric gradient begins to switch on genes that distinguish left from right. This signal tells the heart to form on the left, the liver to form on the right, and accounts for other asymmetrical features of the body. But the electric gradient also accounts for the symmetrical features as well. It tells one arm to form to the left and to be matched by another on the right. These gradients are now being studied in unwanted tissue differentiation, for instance, in their role in cancerous tumor formation.

As it turns out, our myofascial-skeletal system has a similar generation and degeneration communication system that is electrical. When stress deforms or moves a muscle, it deforms or moves the cells within that muscle, stretching the bonds between molecules. This creates an electric flow called piezo-electric charge that is "read" by the cells and causes the connective tissue to respond. If you squat for 75% of your day, the hip would build up bone to withstand the stress. If you sit for 75% of your day, the unstressed hip would not build up bone. The electric cellular charge meets the demand by "talking to" osteocytes, the building blocks of bone formation. If it gives information to release osteoblasts, new bone will be laid down. If it gets information to eat bone, the osteoclasts will come into action. Interestingly, osteoclasts cannot eat bone that is piezo-electrically charged and that charge comes from muscle movement.

This accounts for joint shapes throughout cultures. While a lifetime of hard labor shows auto-fused thoracic spines in the Aztec and Egyptian laborers, thin hip bones show up in a sedentary culture like the U.S. The piezo-electric charge is evident in all connective tissue and too much stress or too little stress changes the tissue's shape.

A forward posture will eventually stiffen muscle tissue as it fails to replace itself with new elastic fibers. Fibroblasts orient themselves along the line of piezo-electric charge which, of course, is high along the lines of tension. The muscle stiffens, becoming malnourished due to lack of circulation, which in turn leads to tissue toxicity and pain. The ease of the pull needs to change or a reopening of the tissue needs to occur. Regardless, the tissue must restore its elasticity. Bodywork will identify and correct both the maladaptive habits and the tissue impairment. Holistic communicating systems, seen in practices like bodywork, Yoga, and relaxation breathing, can restore the body's harmonic patterns.

In the myofascial-skeletal system, timing is everything. Coordinated movements are impaired when diseases like Parkinson's, cerebral palsy, and arthritis hamper our ability to move in fluid, dance-like patterns. As Olatunji notes, "When we get out of rhythm, that's when we get into trouble." But it's not only the major diseases that place our timing and coordination at risk, it's our very lifestyle. When we fail to be as active as we were designed to be, we fall out of sync with our body, and muscles loose their agility and ability to fully experience our environment. When we use technology to increase efficiency, we work faster than our body was designed to move. Tired after a day's work, we forfeit a rich social life and decline leisure pursuits. It seems the farther away we get from our body, the less we know of the world.

John Cage tells of visiting Harvard University's anechoic chamber, a place void of any sound. He sat down in the chamber expecting complete silence but heard two noises. When he asked the engineer what the noises were, the engineer told him the high one was Cage's nervous system in operation and the low one was his blood circulating.

Our noisy world prevents that kind of link to our own body. Technology prohibits our understanding of many physical phenomenon in the same way. At times, movement itself is unperceivable as when we are flying in an airplane. We don't really feel the wind in our hair or the whoosh of air past our ears as we are passively moved through the air at break neck speeds. We feel as if we are standing still, that is, until we hit an air pocket and the forward trajectory is briefly interrupted. That small change can have a profound effect on our perception of movement. A moment ago we felt as if we were sitting still and suddenly we feel as if we are plummeting to Earth. Neither sensation is accurate.

We trick ourselves all the time with gadgetry, especially when we measure it. A year, for instance, is not a measurement of time really; it's a distance, the distance the earth moves around the sun. Even the terms "sunrise" and "sunset" don't really explain the truth of the event, as the sun is neither rising nor going down.

Measuring and timing things can get complicated. Einstein noted that if you sit with a beautiful girl for two hours, it will seem like two minutes. If you sit on a hot stove, two minutes can seem like two hours. That, he said, is relativity. Relativity also tells us that a year to a one-year old baby is a lifetime, but to a fifty year old man, it is 2% of his life. The phenomenon of how things are measured constituted an early, profound memory for Einstein after his father showed him a compass when he was four years old. "That this needle behaved in such a determined way did not at all fit into the nature of events. Something deeply hidden had to be behind things." Einstein realized that one could affect the world without direct touch. He realized that the invisible could direct the visible world.

Just the act of measurement is an attempt to make visible something that is invisible, for every tool of measurement is a conversion device, a translator between different realities. Scales, thermometers, watches, and gauges attempt to place equivalence between two separate events. Weight, fever, time and heat are converted to volume, temperature, space and pressure; all concepts that allow us to trust what we cannot see. The gauge, developed during the Victorian era, was a way to monitor what was not only unseen, but dangerously volatile. Internal heat and pressure could now be calculated and monitored to avoid explosions. The natural world was tamed during the Steam Age, sometimes called the Age of the Gauge, with the gauge symbolic of the convertibility of the invisible.

Before we understood relativity and before we had gauges, scales and clocks, we measured things according to natural occurrences and events we could experience and see for ourselves. If we moved fast, our body adjusted because it could feel itself moving. Every cell in our body knows we are running but few cells know we are flying in an airplane. (This is especially true of our liver, the organ that misunderstands flying more than any other and accounts for the toxic feeling of jet lag.) As we saw in the preceding chapter, the only way to tolerate a train ride was to read rather than look out the window and essentially, pretend like you weren't on a train. Today, to avoid jet lag from a long airplane trip, one should start living and sleeping according to the time zone of the destination. That is, we should pretend days earlier, that we are already there. And we certainly don't have to travel to experience a type of jet lag as Daylight Savings Time will pack as big a punch to our internal clocks, if not bigger, than a trip across the U.S. by plane.

This type of reality conversion was highlighted in the late 1800's when local, or what was called Solar Time, became a problem. Solar Time is only convertible by the people who live at each particular longitude and latitude. They see that the sun is high in the sky so it must be noon. Once rapid movement between towns became common due to rail travel, the railroad could not convert the separate realities of 144 official Solar Times in North America. Train wrecks were daily events and clocks set in rail stations might read Erie Time, New York Central Time, or Vanderbilt Time. To know the arrival time of your train, a passenger would convert the time standard of the train he arrived on to the local time of the station he now boarded from and then convert that to the local time of the station of his destination. The natural world of Solar Time brought on technical inertia. Everything came to a standstill except for the Earth moving around the sun.

In the book, *Time Lord*, Clark Blaise tells of Sanford Fleming's creation of Standard Time and notes that Fleming fought for the "rational authority to cast off the dead weight of natural thought." This "dead weight" was Solar Time. The 1880's were called, The Decade of Time, with Standard Time a symbol of progress and rationality as clocks, now linked by artificial, invisible meridians, in turn linked industrial invention to our consciousness. They changed the way we thought about time and space. Now, time zones changed as if the Earth stood still in order for technology to advance.

From the 1830's onward, the rate of travel on land and water increased a hundredfold. Blaise quotes the cultural historian, William Everdell, saying, there was "a change in the rate of change" with a revolution in time, spawning an uneven transmission of knowledge from one generation to another. Time was domesticated and information sharing was tamed, able to spread at the speed of the signal, not at the speed of human contact.

While mechanical time gained form in the making and marking of meridians across the globe, the human experience was robbed of the gift of space. Obedience to a clock will always be independent of, or at the expense of, the immediate experience. While the technological world took shape, our natural lives atrophied.

To understand how our preoccupation of time changes the way we think, talk to a child. Young children don't understand an event unless it happens in the present moment. To talk to them about the past or the future, is to alert them to the rhythms of life that are too distantly spaced for them to comprehend. While a parent is clock watching, measuring everything from sleeping times, feeding times, anticipation of disasters, and the successful mastering of developmental milestones, a baby is busy internalizing those events, paying attention only to the feel of the present moment. What parent doesn't remember when their child finally understood the admonition, "We'll go to the park in a minute?" It is the day that everything didn't have to happen right now. But it was also the day that our child learned to tame their natural rhythm. As Michael Smolensky says in *The Body Clock*, "we pay more attention to watches we wear on our wrists than to clocks we acquire in the womb."

Flood waters, snow fall, leaves turning red, or the shape of the moon used to tell us when to plant, when to rest, and when to play. Even play is tainted when we keep statistics of teams and award medals for the skier who is faster by 1/100th of a second. We play by the clock with the clock ticking at a pace that only benefits the orthopedic surgeon who will fix the broken knees and shoulders of elite athletes. Excellence in play becomes excellence in sports and excellence in sports is often at the edge of healthy human anatomy.

Our body was our first measuring device, not the clock. The clock is supposed to be our tool, not the other way around. When we measured with our body, we knew the world in a different way. Body measurements are called Rules of Thumb, our bodies helping us appraise a situation and giving us a "feel for the subject." Some examples, several taken from the book *Rules of Thumb* by Tom Parker, include:

* When a pig conceives, make a notch just above the moon on your fingernail. When the mark grows off the end, the sow is about to give birth.

* A clay pot has soaked in enough glaze when it has been submerged for four heart beats.

* The first joint of the thumb to the thumb tip is a "human inch."

* The foot is, well, a foot.

* A pace, the longest stretch one can make between one step and the next, equals a yard.

* Continental drift is occurring at the rate your fingernail grows.

* If the wind rustles leaves but can barely be felt on the face, it is blowing at 4-7 miles an hour.

* Corn must be knee high before July 4th to give a good crop.
* To build a fence strong enough to hold cattle, each section must be an arm length long plus the width of the fingers.
* A safe snowshoe must be the size of encircled arms, your fingertips just touching each other.
* A safe pitch to a ladder can be measured by standing erect with the toes against the ladder beam and arms straight out. If your hands fall comfortably on the ladder rung in the grasping position, it is set for climbing. If the fingertips touch the rung, the base is too far from the building. If the heel of the hand touches, the base is too close.
* You should be one step away from a power source for every 1,000 volts. Ten steps for 10,000 volts.
* If you inhale rapidly and the moisture in your nose begins to freeze, it is 10 degrees F or colder.
* The resting pulse is usually equal to the external temperature you find most comfortable measured in degrees Fahrenheit.
* Goldsmiths keep the gold in the fire until they can see their face in it.
* To measure water for rice, rest the tip of the finger on top of the rice and add enough water to reach the first joint no matter what size the pot.
* The distance from your heel to the articulation of the calf muscle is an indication of jumping ability. For athletes and dancers to be good jumpers, the distance needs to be equal to or greater than the length of the foot.
* Your wedding ring size should be the same number as your hat size.
* The closed waistband of your pants should wrap around your neck. That is, your neck should be half the circumference of your waist.
* A hen is an egg layer if you can fit three of your fingers in its cloaca. One finger, it is not a layer and two fingers, it may be.
* To determine the center of a low pressure system, stand with your back to the wind with the right arm extended sideways. Move the arm forward 45 degrees and you will be pointing to the center of the low system. If you are pointing west, bad weather is due.
* Hold your wrist near the inner corner of a brick oven. It is hot enough to bake bread if you can only hold it there for a quick count to twenty.
* Paint and seal all wounds in a pruned tree that are larger than your thumbnail.
* Hold your palm facing you at arm's length with your little finger on the horizon. The width of the hand covers a 15-degree arc above the horizon.

* To size socks in a store, wrap the bottom "foot" around your fist. If the heel and toe just meet, it will fit your foot.

* Water the garden if the soil is dry past the depth of your index finger.

* Wrap a pencil-sized stick of clay around your index finger. If the sample cracks, the clay is not plastic enough to throw a good pot.

* A child is old enough to enter school when he can cross his arms over his head and grasp his ears with his opposite hands.

* In the very early morning, stretch your arm straight out in front of you. Place your open palm toward you while facing west. If you can see the lines on your hand, it is then you can consider it sunrise.

Our body is not only a measuring device; it has its own internal clocks. Our liver, as we've noted, is particularly affronted on a long airplane trip. When its internal clock is unappreciated, we will feel groggy, sluggish, and hung over. In this case, the hangover is not after drinking too much alcohol but by drinking in too much time. Our liver doesn't understand moving across so many solar zones. The body is not valued during the activity of flying.

Carl Jung noted that, "There must always be a high and low, hot and cold etc., so that the equilibrating process—which is energy—can take place…The point is not the conversion into the opposite but conservation of previous values together with the recognition of their opposites." In other words, we are often in error when we measure things, because either the thing measured becomes invisible or the body is not taken into account in the measuring. Activity must literally make sense to the body. Activities that are done out of context or are meaningless, leave the body attempting to understand incomplete information. Imagine the body trying to make sense of lifting weights for 20 repetitions. No real activity takes place other than the strengthening of an isolated muscle. There is no wood chopped for the fire that will cook the food for a meal that will feed those muscles. In lifting weights, there is no real work done. Activities that offer enjoyment just for the sake of the activity itself, like music, play, art, and dance are usually relegated to others to do with the bulk of us happy to just observe. We work repetitive jobs to buy tickets to sporting or musical events (or watch them on TV), rarely participating in them ourselves. When we say we enjoy music, it is most often that we listen to recordings, not play the instrument ourselves. We watch experts move.

Music and dance are a kind of motion through time and space that the body understands. Alan Watts said, "When we make music, we don't do it in order to reach a certain point, such as the end of the composition. If that were the purpose of music, then obviously the fastest players would be the best." We are not tied into time, or speed, or repetition. We are engaged in rhythm, coordination, vibration, and movement.

Dancing is one of the most shared cultural phenomenon in the history of the world, practiced by almost every culture. Dance is performed to a culturally agreed upon melody, usually drumming, so that every body in the tribe responds emotionally and physically in a like manner. Philosopher Anthony Storr notes that dancing "harmonizes the emotional mood of a group," and the ancient Pythagorean philosophers claimed dance was the "reconciliation of the warring elements" in the soul. Harmonizing our emotional lives and the reconciling the troubles in our souls should not be minimized by passively listening instead of doing.

While dance is paired with greater individual and group coordination, playing a musical instrument is known to impose greater communication between the left and right hemispheres of the brain. Neurologist Barry Bittman studies the effects of hand-drumming and finds a heightened level of immune cells, called natural killer cells, circulating in the body. He suggests that the rhythm between the hemispheres signals the brain to decrease the production of cortisol, a stress hormone, and leads to biological change. Drumming synchronizes the brain and as the brain waves begin to pulse in harmony, our physiology is altered, producing a higher state of awareness. In this way, physiology is paired with action and action is linked back to consciousness. The activity makes sense to the whole body.

If there were one lesson in this book, it is that variety in our actions can change the way we think and can not only save the world, it is the probably the only thing that can. We need what might be called "A Spiritual Ecology," a healing of the human spirit that in turn offers the healing of the planet we have aimed to destroy. Our genes, if left in charge of our future, will assuredly use and abuse, consume and conspire, and will do this according to known brain priorities. That is, the brain is hardwired to respond to primitive triggers such as the alert to danger, the mission to build shelter, to hunt and succeed at all costs, to problem solve despite the long term outcome, and to take advantage of opportunity when it is in front of us (mate, eat, consume). Our brains are certain the world is unfriendly and that all the odds are against our survival. We panic trying to get ahead of the survival game. But by trying to stay alive, we may be killing ourselves.

This book is not a call to return to native or tribal ways. It is a call to change human behavior through choice. There is little to no evidence that native tribes conserve game or fruit, with many native cultures cutting down whole trees to gather a few pieces of fruit or driving entire herds off cliffs to consume only a half dozen carcasses. Native tribes are conservationists simply by virtue of their material poverty. They have no huge house to stock, no car to pollute, and no malls in which to purchase items they don't need. There is probably little environmental ethic in our species. We are in fact, driven by genes and memes to consume, with primitive cultures' ecologies confined by technological limits, not by virtue. "We are a species that has evolved to survive starvation, not to resist abundance" says surgeon Alul Gawande in *Complications*.

Dawkins, creative inventor of the meme concept, urges us to rebel against the tyranny of selfish replicators (whether they are genes or memes) and be aware enough to overcome such tyranny. Instead of arranging institutions that capitalize on human selfishness, we should arrange them to bring out human virtue. Pope John said, "The seriousness of the ecological issue lays bare the depth of man's moral crisis."

We need to realize that small habits have big consequences. Just as numerous, individual car trips to the store have resulted in a polluted world, numerous, individual walks to the store may result in saving that world. We need to develop conscious habits when confronted with choices during everyday experience. We need to evaluate which options and which activities promise harmony. As the Chinese metaphor prompts, we need to "Choose the most harmonious alternative."

We need to provide individuals with complex experiences, free from sedating, bland, mundane existences. We have failed to make complex choices and it has become difficult to know what to do now when the stakes are higher. According to Mihaly Csikszentmihaly, who wrote *The Evolving Self,* we are in need of "transcenders," people who act as sages. A transcender joyfully invests energy in complex goals; has a life dedicated to complexity; contributes to the future through harmonious present choices; nurtures harmony; and contributes to evolution by leaving complexity in a culture. He reminds us that Buddhist teaching is revolutionary as it marks the introduction of a positive psychology. It is a radical rethinking of the route to happiness.

We can no longer condone a brain that has ignored it lives in a body. In the same way, we can no longer condone individuals that ignore they live on a planet. The mind is a physiologic process that has lost track of its function and human beings are in the process of losing track of their place in nature. With two opposite tendencies that mark our evolution, that is changes that lead toward entropy (exploiting resources) or toward harmony, we have to make a choice. Otherwise, we will find ourselves living in a Woody Allen world where he recites, "More than any time in history, mankind faces a crossroads. One path leads to despair and utter hopelessness, the other total extinction. Let us pray that we have the wisdom to choose correctly."

Unfortunately, sometimes both entropy and harmony are present in a situation. When we decide which fish to consume, we are pressed to choose between the entropy of depleting the fresh fish lifecycle or purchasing farm raised fish which uses antibiotics to control for overcrowded, unnatural environments.

Breeding cattle cuts down on hunting wild game but depletes rain forests and the contained herds consume most of the world's supply of corn.

The bridge between the two forces may lie in the Buddhist concept of differentiation. It aligns perfectly with the evolutionary theory of harmony, which is achieved by changes as they increase both differentiation and integration. If there is only differentiation, we have someone who contributes to the culture but is not compassionate—say by feeding the masses but over-fishing the oceans. With integration only, we have someone who is compassionate but does not contribute to the culture—for instance by protecting the oceans but using chemicals to breed farmed fish.

As we have seen throughout this book, it is not a requirement of evolution to be complex; in fact, it will usually choose the simplest means available whether the change is spread through genes or memes. But to secure a livable world, we must move toward complexity with every muscle in our body. To move toward complexity, we needed information on what drives us and what moves us. Hopefully, this book has offered that information in a context that feels right. In learning about how each chakra center of our body "moves itself," we can go forward in enhancing the complexity of our daily lives. We must cease to mistake accidental elements (bad memes) in our lives for essential ones (good memes). Any meme that spreads itself at the expense of harmony is to be questioned and replaced.

We can no longer condone the meme of the automobile or our excessive individuality at the expense of a sustainable world for that individual to live in. As Charles Allen said, "If the human race wants to go to hell in a basket, technology can help it get there by jet." We have been living according to past genetic and memetic commands and we must choose to live according to the future ideals of freedom, compassion, and harmony. The future is a weaker link, of course, being an abstraction, and requires a visionary who has no timepiece to strap to their wrist. It will require desire, a word derived from "*de sider*," or "of the stars." Someone with desire imagines the territory of a new world and in the words of David Whyte, someone who "breathes from the atmosphere of possibility itself."

We must go beyond our drive to merely survive life's difficulties and our preoccupation with cause and effect. We have entertained ourselves with an endless series of postponements—postponements that the earth can no longer tolerate. We must come to a complete stop before it is stopped for us. It might sound contradictory to state that we must come to a stop so we can progress. Physicists use the word "complementarity" to show how something like light can be discussed in terms of both a particle and a wave even though a single object must be one thing or the other. Light, then, became a "wavicle." It is like the lotus amidst fire, a Buddhist phrase describing the potential flower that blooms in difficult circumstances.

In this way, our mess becomes a gift. But only if we find the treasure that requires a forgetting of the individual self as we unite with something bigger than ourselves. This book has been an attempt to forget the technological self by exploring the self as it is represented in a body. As Philip Moffit quotes Buddha, "There is one thing, monks, that cultivated and regularly practiced leads to a deep sense of urgency…to the Supreme Peace…to mindfulness and clear comprehension…to the attainment of right vision and knowledge…to happiness here and now…to realizing deliverance of wisdom and fruition of Holiness: It is mindfulness of the body."

Moral courage is embodied as we "stand tall," "stand up for what we believe in," "stand firm," and "not take it lying down." We are obligated to take a stand. We are at the point that if we are to move into a future, it must be one of our choosing. We would be wise to name ourselves an obligate. An obligate is a species that depends on another species for survival. A beautiful monarch butterfly is an obligate of the rangy milkweed. A huge whale is an obligate of invisible plankton. It is not difficult to imagine that we are all obligates and obligated to everything on the face of the Earth.

By using up the resources of the world, we are using up ourselves. Perhaps we could change directions and be bigger than that. The great triumph of our existence will find us doing what is right for ourselves while doing the right thing for the Earth. In that way, we will discern which cultural creations serve the brain and which serve the heart and body as well.

HOW TO EVOKE HARMONY

❖ Tapa is an Indian word likened to behavior and is an unwavering determination, focus, heat, radiance, and devotion to a wave of energy bigger than one's fears, doubts, or confusions. Tapas are an essential part of the yogic path of self-discipline. Tapas share an ancient root in magic where the body was a cauldron for cooking up extraordinary powers (siddhis). Tapas burn away impurities and kindle a spark of divinity in each body. Ama (toxins) and samskaras (mental, physical, and emotional patterns from past actions) are purified through consistent Tapas practice. If your tapa is too attached to the outcome of an action, zeal becomes obsessive with only the ego stoking the fire. Adjust your temperature by watching your intentions and taking responsibility for the repercussions of your actions. Commit to staying in the fire of the difficulty. Pass through the fire with a daily commitment that can never be extinguished.

❖ Participate in clockless time. Attend a Quaker gathering or observe Navaho sand painting where there is arbitrariness between the beginning and the ending. Or make time move back and forth with no distinction by giving and receiving in the present moment. Realize that they are the same act, just in different directions. Make no claim to being owed once you have given. In that way, you are not transgressing out of the present moment, for to be owed is to live in the future.

❖ Sleep and rest have an incubatory rhythm inherent in them. Intense sleep can come after intense work. The rhythm of meaningful work and profound sleep can be called "body music." Neuroscientists estimate that our unconscious data base outweighs our conscious data base on an order exceeding ten million to one. When we "sleep on it" before we make a decision, we stall the time between awareness and reaction. There are millions of other answers in us besides the few immediate answers we usually resort to.

❖ "The trouble is," said the chief diagnostician, "we don't know what the trouble is—it is impossible to tell whether the patient has clockitis, clockosis, clockoma, or clocktheria. We are also faced with the possibility that there may be no such diseases. The patient may have one of the minor clock ailments, if there are any, such as clockets, clockels, clocking cough, ticking pox, or clumps. We shall have to develop area men who will find out about such areas." So wrote James Thurber in *The Thirteen Clocks*. What kind of "time disease" do you have? Do you wish for the day to end or the week to pass quickly? Do you only live on the weekends? Get comfortable with all the days of the week.

❖ Create sacred space. Create spaces that can be your sanctuary and be transfigured when you enter them.

❖ Joan Oliver Goldsmith, in her book *How Can We Keep From Singing*, notes that it is "creation's assignment to learn the notes, to find your music. The invisible instrument is the one instrument we must all learn to play…Listen to the sounds around you and as light taught Monet how to paint, the earth may be teaching you music." We can't hear the earth's music when there is so much engine noise. Press the "off" switch on devices and listen to the sounds of nature. U.S. lakes, the most serene body of water in our mind's eye, are full of motor boats and jet skis. That is, unless one side of the lake is bordered by an Indian Reservation. Then, only wind propelled or self-propelled vessels are allowed—sailboats, canoes, rafts, or kayaks. Visit such a lake and notice how it enjoys you as much as you enjoy it.

❖ Practice Ting Jing, the Chinese phrase for "listening to the energy." By listening, we gain awareness that allows us to finally feel what is wrong and what is unharmonious. Ask yourself if you control your environment with one mood. Are you always angry with what is wrong in your life? Or are you apathetic and don't care about what is wrong? Do you practice denial that anything is wrong with your life? Listen to how you talk and how you behave. You may be always striking the same note; anger, denial or apathy. Make more music than that one note.

○ In Chakra work, it is known that one chakra center is more active than the others and it generally awakens first. Overuse or abuse of one chakra can bring about disease to that area. Even if you evade disease, one chakra can overpower the others. In Western culture, intellect has overpowered heart. In Yoga, the brain is symbolized by the moon, which reflects the sun's light while generating none of its own. The brain is limited in what it can know on its own—it must reflect the light of the heart. Combine the knowledge and energy of each of the chakras.

☙ The trick in Buddhist practice is to become alert to how we restrict ourselves. *Chogyam Trungpa* is a Buddhist practice of watching the mind's ongoing commentary, often termed "subconscious gossip." To watch the gossipy restrictions surface during meditation is to begin the process of liberation. Self-knowledge is not an end in itself, it is a beginning and useful as a means of getting oriented. Once oriented, one can practice *Dudjom Lingpa*, a visionary account which states that mere realization will not bring freedom. A common example of mere realization versus understanding, coupled with action is: Even though we have food, we will not be satisfied if we don't eat it. Expand that to other examples: even though one has the vision to change their lives, they will not be changed until they live differently.

❖ Ask yourself this: Are you able to enjoy yourself without using gasoline and electricity? Can you "play" without employing the unnatural noise of cars, motorboats, jet skis, computers, televisions, stereos, or amplified instruments? Maybe your mother meant it when she said "play quietly." Can you enjoy yourself without having to buy something to play with? Can you go to your favorite place and enjoy it without taking anything but you with you? Remember, with a Hatha Yoga practice, the only thing you need with you is you.

❖ Awaken the sage in you. Take your own advice.

❖ Take a rest from consumerism. Bring nothing new into your house for thirty days except for food. That which is always present is often overlooked and begins to be perceived as nothing. Air, gravity, breathing, good health, food, and shelter all become nothing when taken for granted. Grant it your attention. Be grateful and re-member it into something. Artists make something new out of nothing. Artists practice creation. Rumi, the thirteenth century poet notes in *Work and Emptiness*, "Every craftsman searches for what's not there to practice his craft."

❖ Life is too short to engage in all the things that make it shorter. Enlarge your sensibility about choices and lace them with power. Accumulate your choices into conditions that will improve your relationship with the laws of nature. Passivity is poverty of movement. To fail to eat from the wide array of choices is to remain malnourished. Expand your choices. Move in rhythm to your environment. Eat a healthy dose of life.

❖ The skin is linked to the emotions like the surface of a lake is linked to its depths. They are one continuous entity. Bodyworkers realize that to touch the surface of the body is to touch the depths. It is a privilege and an opportunity, an adventure, and an exploration of things that have worked to remain hidden. It is with great honor and grace that they should be lifted.

❖ A Tibetan greeting never asks "how are you" but "how is your body?" How is your body today? How is the body of the earth you live on today?

❖ Thomas Moore suggests that our vocation should include time to pause from the pressures of daily living to wonder at being alive.

❖ Practice letting go of things. Start with one shelf. Decide whether each object brings beauty, meaning, or usefulness into your home. If it doesn't, let it go for someone else's use. Only objects that meet the criteria of beauty, usefulness, or meaning should be allowed in your sanctuary.

❖ Not every thought in your head is true. Not every inclination should be acted on. Practice free will and free won't. Will power and won't power. Turn them both into Skillpower.

❖ The Five Basic Moral Precepts of Buddhism are restraints. Most of the Ten Commandments are Thou Shalt Nots. Cutting edge neuroscience points to the power of mindful choice in refusing to act only on the commands of the amygdala, the part of the brain in charge of emotions. The wisdom of the pre-frontal cortex can be engaged by choice and waiting between response and action.

❖ Blaming others for your circumstances is allowing others to have responsibility for your circumstances. As you blame and ridicule, think for a moment—are these the people you want to be in charge of how you feel? If not, then don't blame them for your circumstances. Regain your identity: face the conflict, stand up for what you want, or be willing to happily go without it.

❖ To indulge in artificial needs only serves to detract from our true energy as we try to control more and more objects that our biological systems think are required for survival. Make a list of energy detractors—endless objects, grandiose lifestyle, and beliefs that no longer support the truth of your life path. When confronted with choice, develop the habit of asking yourself this question, "Will the choice add to my life path?" This will put a stop to soul searching, guilt, and remorse. The energy you will save can go towards real work.

❖ In Ancient Greece, the word "*opiso*" means both past and future. The Greeks thought themselves as standing still while time moved up behind them, overtaking them, and becoming the future. In Chichewa, an East African tongue, there are two past tenses: one for events that continue to have an effect on the present and one for events that do not. Know the difference and sometimes, choose to stand still. You might find your real life sneaking up from behind.

❖ Feldenkrais tells us the ideal standing posture is obtained not by doing something to oneself but by literally doing nothing. Indeed, the vast majority of muscles are at rest when we stand with an upright posture.

❖ When a patient sits before a therapist, there may finally be time to tell the story of an injury. But for the therapist, each patient brings a new set of symptoms coupled within a complex social and emotional history. Oftentimes a therapist must proceed without the luxury of science or certainty. They must function even if unready. They must work in good faith, with empathy and the intuitive use of patterns. This is called "the therapeutic use of self" and is a method of enjoining the therapist with the rhythms of the patients' story.

❖ Stopping the rhythm of events is distracting. In1995, National Football League owners voted to end the instant replay. Stopping the game to see "what really happened" interrupted the game and lowered the fans enjoyment. The quest for what was true distracted from the "now" of playing a game.

❖ The world is a dance of connections. Gases are molecules that dance through space, associating only when they bounce into each other. Crystals are molecules that are slow dancing, holding on to each other in an embrace. Liquids are molecules dancing between order and chaos. They come together into an ordered group then break apart to join others in yet another group. At transition points, like the point where water freezes or water turns to steam, the molecules are poised to choose between two phases. The point is often a point of indecision and the molecules may go back and forth, vacillating as they near the critical point of deciding. The molecules can lose their identity, neither choosing to be liquid nor, quite yet, gas. It is said that this vacillation resembles a community where someone is not quite an individual and not quite drowned out in society. From cell to self to society—it's all the same dance.

❖ Tipping points or transition points are the sites for varying phenomenon. Paul Treichel, a chemistry professor at the University of Wisconsin in Madison, notes how bubbles form in liquids. Molecules of dissolved carbon dioxide are evenly dispersed through a liquid in a closed container like a bottle with its cap on. Once the pressure is released, the gas molecules migrate to certain spots on the side of the glass to form bubbles. The molecules prefer surface areas with imperfections (pitted or scratched areas) which are called "sites of neucleation." As more CO_2 molecules attach, the unit grows until it creates its own tipping point, the point where the bubble breaks off and becomes buoyant. These sites are responsible for crystal formation in a solution such as sugar crystals in honey, the formation of raindrops in clouds, the formation of knots in a tired muscle, and the build up of plaque in an artery. This accumulation of energy can have far-reaching consequences and can work to change the form of an object for better or worse. Think of an idea in you that has had time to gather energy. Perhaps it's time for those ideas to take form. Let them crystallize, bubble to the surface, and reach their creative tipping point. Introduce them to the light of day. Gain control over destructive emotions by smoothing out the pitted imperfections they latch onto. Make the surface of your mind smooth so the emotion can come into awareness but then slip away.

❖ There is resilience in nature's designs. Robustness, from the Latin *"robus"* meaning "oak" is an increasingly studied topic in science. Interconnectivity, nature's tolerance of error even in drastic events like hurricanes or volcanoes, tells whether an event is robust or not. The interplay between robustness and vulnerability shows nature's ability to sustain function under even high error rates. Studies show that our ability to withstand and recover from even dire illnesses is linked to our interconnectivity. Social contacts can make you robust and offer healing even during times of high error rate. Dr. Dean Ornish cites numerous studies that show how social support is more important than health habits in predicting heart disease. Lonely, unconnected, rage-oholics with low cholesterol are more likely to suffer heart disease than those who are social butterflies with high cholesterol. Invite friends over for dinner. Join a book group. Go to church or take walks with the Sierra Club. Join a birder's group. Just join.

❖ The famed poet Rumi offers, "Out beyond ideas of wrongdoing and rightdoing there is a field. Meet me there." Nothing needs to be pushed away.

Happiness need not be the opposite of sadness. Both are part of our ecology just as sure as if they co-existed in the same field.

❖ Feldenkrais taught that we each have a postural signature, a unique posture that embodies our attempt to inhibit feelings too difficult to bear. Unconscious adaptations such as twisting away from life, limping along our path, brittleness, constriction, and holding our breath all hide away our mental health. That which remains unconscious will make events and circumstances seem to come to us as fate. If nearly 65% of communication is body language and our body is constricted, or as Feldenkrais termed it "internally strangulated," we are destined to remain incommunicado. As the strangulation continues, circulatory systems are inhibited, food supply to all tissues is diminished, and we die a slow death. Finding flexibility and balance is essential for physical and mental stability. Balancing the power between the right and left, front and back, and high and low aspects of the body creates symmetry. We conduct much of our lives asymmetrically which creates stress in the body. Parts of us work overtime; other parts are showing signs of atrophy. Our weak parts feel like a burden to us and are dragged around as a hindrance, often making themselves known with the language of pain. The healthier your body, the less body-conscious you become as it operates perfectly, not requiring your constant attention. Feeling healthier, you make healthier food choices and pursue activities that feel right.

❖ Maria Montessori who developed her theories into practice via Montessori schools, noted that every personality has its own way of doing things through their body; just look at handwriting, she suggested. In handwriting or any other expression of muscular movement, "man is put in touch with his world" while vegetative, sedentary lifestyles "only serve to keep him alive." It's the movement of muscles that keep us in relation to things. Practice your individuality. Move places you want to go. Make your own path.

❖ Muscle amnesia is a condition of a muscle forgetting how to work properly, how to do its job, and how to relax. Wilhelm Reich and his Science of Bioenergetics called this muscle memory "character armor," where muscles act other than they are. Instead of flexible, elastic muscle, they act as if they are bone, hard and full of defensive posturing. What have you forgotten how to do? Re-learn how to jump rope or dunk under waves. Take off the armor and live a little.

❖ Heed the words of Harriet Beinfield and Efram Korngold in their glorious book *Between Heaven and Earth*. "We want to live the life of our bodies and want our bodies to permit us to fully live our lives."

❖ Even repetitive exercising in rigid postures can lead to the stress of certain muscles and nerves. Chinese medicine finds that exercises to individual muscle groups can weaken the immune system by overstressing meridian or energy pathways. Tight, overdeveloped muscles sustain the attitude that life is hard and fraught with conflict. Exercise and experiences in life are like zeros in a long line of numbers; meaningless without a digit in front of them. The digit, when it comes to muscles, is flexibility. When it comes to life, the digit is peace of mind.

❖ Dr. George Vaillant in his book *Adaptation to Life* finds that mental health is the most important predictor of physical health. He conducted a 40-year study of Harvard sophomores and concluded that the lack of recreation time contributed significantly to relative degree of illness over the years.

❖ Daniel Goleman in *Emotional Intelligence* suggests that distressing emotions are as toxic a risk factor as smoking and high cholesterol. Express your emotions instead of storing them up until they explode. Candace Pert talks of the unifying nature of emotions. "They integrate physiology from the top of your head to the tip of your toes so the whole organism can act in a unified whole." She suggests we use all our states of mind.

❖ Germs remind us that invisible things can have visible consequences. Thinking that hidden emotions aren't dangerous can be a huge error.

❖ The Relaxation Response proved that negative conditioning is derailed by relaxing through breathing techniques, opening the mind to the formation of more productive habits. When under pressure, the relaxation response can be called on to weather the storm. Shakespeare gives us the image of boats out to sea. When the sea is calm, all boats alike show mastership in floating. In a storm, they are obliged to cope and only the seaworthy survive. Be the captain of your own ship, adept at calm and rough waters.

☙ Feel the earth in you as the point of reference for all the other forces of nature; the reference around which all other aspects of character are rooted. Pluck a blade of grass and see it as the center of the universe. Now pluck another and see it too as the center of the universe. There is enough space and time around you for both to be true. See yourself as the center of the universe. Now look at a homeless man and see him as the center of the universe.

☙ See the water in you buried in underground springs like a womb. Dig deep to find your resources. When you surface, take the form of the vessel that contains you and wonder at the power to conquer by yielding. As you are poured back into the river, know that you will always follow your destined course to the sea even though the journey may wind and turn.

❧ Be the fire that burns in the sun, telling the sap to rise in the trees, allowing them to reach for the star-clustered heavens. Be the sunlight that surrounds a forest so thick, it contains the dark wilderness itself.

❧ Imagine the air in you as the space inside the bowl, the emptiness inside a room, the vastness in the hollow of the lungs. You are the space that makes matter useful. You hold the space where all else moves. Surround it.

❖ Try the difficult postures of Hatha Yoga and show your willingness to risk tumbles and falls that are inevitable when learning something new. Learn to find the means of reliable support other than your feet; twist so you are looking backwards, support your weight with your hands, or lift your legs over your shoulders. When's the last time you sat on the ground?

❍ Try Tittibhasana: Firefly, where the urge to fly is played out. Practice flying with your mind or imagine yourself in this position, as it is very difficult to master. Imagine the effect you have on things far away even though you stand firmly on the ground. In physics there is a phenomenon called morphic resonance and springs from Quantum Non-locality or what Einstein liked to call, "spooky action at a distance." It finds that two photons or electrons that were emitted by the same atom remain somehow linked even if they are miles apart. Link yourself with people and places even though you are miles apart. Be a part of the spooky action that flies between the two.

❍ Try Sirsha Angusthana Yogasana: head to ankle pose. In this posture, every body part is aware of all the others. Get in this posture to be aware of all the other animals on Earth.

❍ Try Mulabandha: Root Bandha, a most simple yet profound Yoga posture. It is merely sitting still with legs crossed. In our restlessness, we fruitlessly attempt to prove our worth or disprove our worthlessness. This posture depicts the focus of the Yoga practitioner's attention or Kundalini. It is the conscious wisdom of Shiva, depicted as a snake awakening from a slumber, every muscle drawing energy to the top of its head to propel it forward. In this posture, we reach our full potential.

❍ Try Halasana: Plough Posture. This pose breaks up the ground to plant the seeds of new behaviors. We will need these new habits to meet the lives we are now living.

❍ Try Dandasana: Staff Pose. This posture supports all movements. Danda means "staff of the wanderer" and implies no attachments to one place or one existence. It is the cane we use for support as we move on and the staff that allows us to cope with new territory.

○ Try Shavasana: Corpse Posture. Swami Ambikananda Sawaswati says, "If Yoga contained only one of its forward bends, one of its backbends and Corpse Posture, it would still be a highly formidable body/vitality work system." Corpse pose is considered the most difficult Yoga posture yet it consists only of lying flat on the ground with outstretched arms. It is windless silence and the deep communication with the air as we release into the ground, feeling the full pull of gravity in us.

❖ Offer your bones something they long for—hug your muscles to your bones. Offer your internal organs something they long for—massage your organs by bending and twisting. Honor these parts of you as you honor that they will one day return to the earth. Take a walk along the beach and honor all that has washed on shore. Look only at the dead kelp. Spot small bones and feathers, and empty shells. Site the driftwood and the rock that has split in two. Honor all that has died and yet is as much a part of the ocean as that which is alive. It is all the same. Marcel Proust offers, "The real voyage of discovery consists of not in seeking new landscapes but in having new eyes." Walk the beach with new eyes.

❖ The science of Yoga teaches that the source of the universe is an unceasing sound or vibration. When is the last time you sang? What vibration are you offering up to the universe?

❖ There is a beauty that calls to us; a wholeness that we know exists. The Sufis call this "the voice of the beloved." We are born in this world with a song in our hearts, yet we might only come to know it by the feeling of its absence. If you are not hearing your song, if something essential is missing, step away from the ego with a simple gesture. Bow. Bow to the home you live in and thank it. Bow to a tree you can see out the window or a cloud in the sky. Start with a bodily gesture that says you are committed to gratefulness, simplicity, and awareness of the wonder around you. Bow to the air you breathe and remember it even when the wind doesn't blow. Breathe in and out, bringing the outside in, integrating your inner life with outer expression. Bow to the members in your family, perhaps just their pictures at first, thanking them for their community. Do this every morning to start a day of thankfulness.

❖ The clock was an invention to bring precise regularity to the daily routines of medieval monks, a marker invented as a tool to worship God. Spend that kind of time in the morning.

❖ Sleep is a time of repair and occurs in phases, each with its own rhythm. Every two hours, we change position, not in a fitful, restless manner, but as a rhythmical function to prevent pressure sores. We dream and have nightmares in order to act out issues too disturbing while awake. If we are worriers and can't fall asleep due to our busy minds, consider those racing thoughts as messengers that will circle and circle around you until you listen. The issues, if heard and acted on during the awake cycle, would not haunt us night after night.

❖ Epictetus, a Greek philosopher said, "Do you know that disease and death must overtake us, no matter what we are doing? What do you wish to be doing when it overtakes you? If you have anything better to be doing when you are overtaken, get to work on that."

❖ The Greeks had a word, "*temenos*," that meant "a place where extraordinary events can happen." Create *temenos*. Your thoughts and actions can make your body a portable paradise.

❖ Depression is a cousin of hibernation, a silence and withdrawal that conserves energy by stopping new information. In *The Private Life of the Brain*, Susan Greenfield notes that the world of depression is the opposite of the sensory world. Past events, rather than new incoming information, gain too much meaning. Associations are overdeveloped between memory neurons, strengthening and increasing the connections. Medications that are GABA enhancers will lower the number of neurons recruited and act as a chemical brake on depression. GABA receptors are estimated to operate as much as 30% of all our neuronal connections and can be recruited in what is known as the "kindling concept of depression." The brain, fueled by previous bouts, can be set off by smaller and smaller signals that provoke it, much like a once sprained ankle is easily twisted again with the slightest misstep. Engage in natural GABA enhancers like rhythmic movement, community, and a small glass of wine.

❖ Re-incarnation is thought to be for those beings that always choose the familiar. If we are unfamiliar with true joy, we will not seek a heavenly afterlife. Many of us will choose the familiar and return to earth again in another form. Change your pattern today. Take another route to work. Pick up your children early and go to the beach for a picnic dinner. Do something unfamiliar.

❖ The Japanese word for "begging bowl" is *oryoki* which means, "just enough." A beggar must be content at accepting whatever is put in the bowl. The word "perfect" stems from the Latin "finished" because when something is perfect, it is complete as is. Take notice of the things that are perfect in your life just as they are. Realize you have just enough.

❖ Robert Jourdain writes, "The nervous system functions the same way in all its reaches." He notes that anticipation primes the nervous system and offers ecstasy. It is the same in love making as it is in listening to music crescendos, as it is in chancing upon a new idea. Anticipate the look on your children's faces when you choose the following: When they walk in the door, act as if they have been gone for a week. Greet them as if you missed them and do it every time they come home. They, in turn, will anticipate and find ecstasy in coming home. Now act as if your spouse lights up the room when they walk in.

❖ Learn to draw the Chinese ideogram for human. It is a figure rooted in the Earth like a tree with hands stretched to heaven. We are nature, sustained by the power of the Earth and transformed by the power of heaven. Once we have learned to draw it, perhaps we could live it.

❖ Fung Yu-Lan in *A Short History of Chinese Philosophy* notes that Western civilization is historically seafaring and exploring, represented by the heroic pioneer. Chinese civilization is land-based, offering continuity and preservation of resources by an adaptive, heroic individual. Find both of these heroes in you.

❖ Practice self-recognition not self-improvement. There is nothing dangerous in our subconscious. Get to know the shadow parts of you. One quick way to recognize the parts you are trying so hard to hide is to listen to yourself the next time you criticize someone. If you are saying they annoy you because they are selfish, you are able to see selfishness because it is your issue mirrored back to you. You are annoyed because you are spending so much energy keeping the selfish part of you from coming out and here they are, expressing what you try so hard to repress.

❖ Practice Vastu, the ancient Hindu science of dwelling and placement. This 4,000 year old Vedic spiritual philosophy prescribes how structures should be designed so inhabitants reside in a positive environment. The energetic placement of objects and buildings is an extension of yoga and raga (music) and both find design elements inherent for inner peace. It is yoga for a room and mirrors the perfection to be found in the universe. Using a mandala depicting body parts as a grid, the center of the house is at Vastu Purusha's navel. This is where one would place the hearth or centerpiece of the home. Should one live gracefully within their surroundings, their last responsibility would be to die gracefully to complete the cycle.

❖ Practice *Feng Shui*, the ancient Chinese art of practical ecology. This philosophy prescribes how space contributes to how you feel. It honors the movement of wind and water as veins of energy that course over the earth. Placement of furniture and buildings places us in favorable relationships with these forces so we can derive the maximum benefit from our environment. Align yourself with the currents of energy. Honor the fact that you bring fire into the home and use the energy with balance and consciousness.

A simple balancing practice in *Feng Shui* is to use all four burners on the top of your stove equally, rather than repeatedly using the bottom right burner. The south-eastern corner of the house and of each room is the relationship corner. Ensure you don't have waste receptacles or recycling here and remove phones or other technology in that corner since they interrupt face-to-face relationships.

❖ In 1875-1920, the American Arts and Crafts movement's principle goals were to restore the "joy of labor" by a return to handcraftsmanship and to promote uncluttered interiors by a unification of all household objects in an aesthetic of "honesty." Rectilinear forms in furniture replaced "unnatural curves." Solid, native woods replaced imported veneers and unnecessary decoration was abolished. Construction was displayed rather than hidden so one could see how a piece was made. It was a unification of the useful with the artful and a return to Native American crafts, weavings, and rugs. Go through your house and give away what you no longer use. When you do chores like washing the dishes, relish the warm water, the clay that has been made into a dish, and the soap that so perfectly forms a bubble. Align with the artful in your tasks.

❖ Shaker furniture makers always made an extra chair for a home; made especially for an angel to sit in should they visit. When someone in your family is not present for dinner, remember them by honoring the chair they once sat in. Act as if they are seated with you. Don't talk about them just because they can't hear you.

❖ D. H. Lawrence said, "We have lost the art of living, and in the most important science of all, the science of daily life, the science of behavior, we are complete ignoramuses." Get smart about your life.

❖ Think of phrases we use referring to spatial or architectural power. "On the bench" (penalty for poor sportsmanship), "stay on the walkway," "stay off the grass," "stay in line," "straddling the fence," and "thinking out of the box." Read your state's requirements for a kindergarten student to advance to the first grade. You might see that it includes phrases like, "able to stand in line when told," "able to sit in circle time," "stays in their chair during work time," and "colors in the spaces." Kindergarten has lost its connection to its original sense—children's garden. Their time is structured and mapped out. Have you remained contained? What rules do you have on how to conduct yourself? What obstacles do you put in your way? What structure are you demanding of your body? Is it restrictive or do you have room to move in your life?

○ Look into Kundalini Yoga, a practice that uses the healing energy of vibrations conveyed by gongs and chanting. An outgrowth of Kundalini is *Sahaj Shabd* meaning, "at ease with sound." These practices use sound patterns to tune the organs and energy meridians of the body with the vibrations of the universe.

❖ If you are having difficulty believing there are vibrations and sounds or "songs" you can tune in to, imagine it is true even if you can't see it or test it. You can't see air can you? Yet it certainly exists. In fact, it's you who wouldn't exist without it. We live on the invisible.

❖ The physicist, Arthur Eddington said, "If you drag a net with two inch mesh through the sea, you will conclude there is no such thing as a fish that is shorter than two inches." The physicist Strominger said, "The history of physics is the history of giving up cherished ideas." Drag a smaller net through your mind and fish out a beautiful idea. Give up the cherished idea that you are here alone and believe that there is a universal vibration you are dancing to.

❖ The French pioneer of the steam engine, E. M. Bataille stated, "Is not invention the poetry of science?" His steam engine, by the way, was invented on a false conclusion about the conduction of steam. And yet, poetry prevailed. What if your life story was a poem rather than a forgone conclusion? Rewrite yourself.

❖ Poetry, it is often noted, is best when it's unclear. Poetry takes some deciphering and engages the reader in the act of creating meaning. Read or write poems. Get a book on Haiku and create some yourself.

❖ Mountaineer Marco Pallis tells us, "Only he who attains the summit and made himself one with it knows the solution of the mystery." When asked why he climbs, he says, "So long as there yet exists a step to be taken there are alternatives and hence there are possibilities of comparison, but at the summit all alternative routes become one; every distinction between them and therefore every opposition, is spontaneously reconciled. The summit itself not only occupies no space, although the whole mountain is virtually contained in it, but it is also outside time and all succession, and only the 'eternal present' reigns there." Think of alternative ways to live. Stand at the top of your life and see what is contained in it. Is it a mountain worth climbing?

☙ Ayurvedic medicine suggests that if you can't eat it, don't put it on your skin. This medicinal practice uses facial massage, herbal steams, and masks to cleanse the largest organ of the body—the skin. Vata represents space/air and is suggested for dry skin. Pitta is fire/water and is practiced for sensitive skin, while Kapha is water/earth and for oily skin. Do your skin a favor and wear comfortable, loose fitting clothes. Go barefoot often. Let the air touch your skin and the earth touch your feet.

❖ Pavlov noted a phenomenon that defies genetic coding. He called it "acquired characteristic inheritance" wherein we inherit the propensity to learn what others have learned. He found that mice take an average of 300 trials to learn to run to feed with the ring of a bell. However, offspring of those same mice learned it in 100 trials. The third generation learned it in 30 trials and the 4th in only 10 attempts. Inherit the work of others by studying ancient healing practices.

❖ Your life is a song. Compose yourself. Armando Ghitalla of the Boston Symphony Orchestra said "Some musicians play the notes, some the rhythm and some the music." Be someone who sees the whole picture and play the music you were supposed to play. Move the way you were supposed to move. And in the process, enjoy yourself.

❖ Thank you for reading Embodied Wisdom……Joy

Bibliography

Ackerman, Diane. 2000. Deep Play. Vintage Books, NY.

Amen, Daniel G. 2000. Change Your Brain, Change Your Life. Three Rivers Press

Appels, A, Hoppener, P., Mulder, P. Increased Vital Exhaustion Among Type D Patients with Clinical Implications: Ishemic Heart Disease. International Journal of Cardiology. 87 Oct; 17(1):15-24

Baldwin, Neil 1995. Edison: Inventing the Century. Hyperion NY.

Balkin, J. M. 1998. Cultural Software: A Theory of Ideology. Yale University Press, New Haven.

Beattie, Andrew and Ehrlich, Paul R. 2001. Wild Solutions: How Biodiversity is Money in the Bank. Yale University Press, New Haven

Beinfield, Harriet, Korngold, Efram. 1991. Between Heaven and Earth: A Guide To Chinese Medicine. Ballantine Publishing. NY

Beck, Martha 2001. Finding Your North Star. Crown Publishers NY

Berglas, Steven. 2001. Reclaiming the Fire. Random House. NY

Berry, Wendell. 1996. The Unsettling of America: Culture and Agriculture. Sierra Club Books. San Fransisco

Berry, Wendell. 2000. Life is a Miracle: An essay against modern superstition. Counterpoint, Washington D.C.

Blackmore, Susan. 2000. The Meme Machine. Oxford University Press. Oxford.

Blaise, Clark, 2000. Time Lord: Sir Sanford Fleming and the Creation of Standard Time. Pantheon, NY.

Bloom, Howard, 2000. Global Brain: The Evolution of Mass Mind From the Big Bang to the 21st Century. John Wiley & Sons Inc., NY.

Brand, Paul and Yancy, Philip. 1993. The Gift of Pain. Zondervan Publishing House, Michigan.

Brandon, Nathaniel. 1996. Self Reliance and the Acccountable Life: Taking Responsibility. Simon & Schuster. NY

Brewer, B. 1973. Trans. Techniques of the Body. In *Economy and Society*. Vol 2 No 1 pg 70-88.

Brink, Susan. Smart Moves in *U.S. News and World Report.* May 15, 1997. Pp 76-84.

Brodie, Richard. 1996. Virus of the Mind: The New Science of the Meme. Integral Press. Seattle.

Butler, David, Moseley, G. Lorimer 2003. Explain Pain. Noigroup Publications, Adelaide

Butler, David 2000. The Sensitive Nervous System. Noigroup Publications, Adelaide

Cameron, Julia. 1996. The Vein of Gold: A Journey To Your Creative Heart. G.P. Putnam's & Sons. NY

Caplan, Ralph. How Chairs Behave in Cranz, Galen. The Chair: Rethinking Culture, Body and Design. W.W. Norton & Company, NY

Caporal, L. R. 1986. Anthropomorphism and Mechanomorphism: Two faces of the Human Machine. Computers in Human Behavior, 2, 215-234.

Chiles, James R. 2001. Inviting Disaster: Lessons from the Edge of Technology and Why They Happen. HarperCollins Inc., NY

Cole, K.C. 2201. The Hole in the Universe: How Scientists Peered Over the Edge of Emptiness and Found Everything. Harcourt, NY.

Cope, Stephen. 1999. Yoga and the Quest for the True Self. Bantan, NY

Cranz, Galen 1998 The Chair: Rethinking Culture, Body and Design W.W. Norton & Company NY

Csikszentmihalyi, Mihaly. 1993. The Evolving Self, HarperCollins, NY.

D'Agnese, Joseph. Is the Weather Driving You Crazy? *Discover,* June 2000 pg 78-81. Vol 21. No 6.

Damasio, A. 2000. The Feeling of What Happens: Body and emotion in the making of consciousness. Harvest Books, NY

Damasio, A. 2003. Looking for Spinosa: Joy, sorry and the feeling brain. Harcourt, NY

Darwin, Charles. 1997. Descent of Man. Prometheus Books, NY

Dawkins, Richard. 1998. Unweaving the Rainbow, Houghton Miffin Co., NY.

Deacon, Terrance. 1998. The Symbolic Species: The co-evoluation of language and the brain. WW Norton and Co., NY

De Botton, Alain 2001. The Consolations of Philosophy. Vintage Books, NY

De Graff, John, Wann, David, Naylor, Thomas H. 2001. Affluenza: The all-consuming epidemic. Berrett-Koehler Pub Inc,. San Francisco.

Denollet, J. Type D Personality: A potential risk factor refined. *Journal of Psychosomatic Research.* 2001 Sept: 51(3); 465-8.

Diamond, Jared 1997. Guns, Germs and Steel: The Fates of Human Societies. W.W. Norton & Co. NY

Dillard, Annie. 1998. Pilgrim at Tinker Creek. Perennial Press. NY

Donald, Norman A. 1993. Things That Make Us Smart. Addison-Wesley pub Co., Reading Mass.

Dossey, Larry. 1984. Beyond Illness: Discovering the experience of health. Shambala. Boulder, Co.

Dossey, Larry. 1982. Space, Time and Medicine. Shambala, Boulder.

Dowling, Colette. 2000. The Frailty Myth. Random House. NY

Drake, Michael. 1991. The Shamanic Drum: A guide to sacred drumming. Talking Drum Publications, Bend Oregon.

Dugatkin, Lee Alan, 2000. The Imitation Factor: Evolution Beyond the Gene. The Free Press, NY

Dunbar, Robin 1996. Grooming, Gossip and the Evolution of Language. Harvard University Press, Massachusetts

Epstein, Mark. 2001. Going on Being: Buddhism and the Way of Change. Broadway Books, NY

Feldenkrais, Moshe. 1985. The Potent Self: A guide to spontaneity. Harper & Row, San Francisco

Feynman, Richard P. 1999. The Smartest man in the World: The pleasure of finding things out. Perseus Books, Cambridge, Massachusetts

Frattaroli, Elio. 2002. Healing the Soul in the Age of the Brain: Becoming Conscious in an Unconscious World. Viking, NY

Gawande, Atul, 2002. Complications: A Surgeon's Notes on an Imperfect Science. Henry Holt and Company, NY

Gerson, Michael MD, 1998. The Second Brain: The Scientific Basis of Gut Instinct and a Groundbreaking New Understanding of Nervous Disorders of the Stomach and Intestines. HarperCollins, NY

Gladwell, Marcolm. 2000. The Tipping Point: How little things can make a big difference. Little, Brown and Company. NY

Glausiusz, Josie. 2000. The Rhythm of Mind in *Discover,* vol 21. No 1.

Glover, Savion 2000. Savion: My Life in Tap. Morrow NY

Goldsmith, Joan Oliver 2001. How Can We Keep From Singing: Music and the Passionate Life. W.W. Norton, N.Y.

Goleman, Daniel and Gurin, Joel (eds). 1993. Mind/Body Medicine: How to Use Your Mind For Better Health. Consumer Reports Books, NY.

Goleman, Daniel. 2003. Destructive Emotions: How can we overcome them? Random House Inc. NY

Goleman, Daniel. 1995. Emotional Intelligence: Why it can matter more than IQ. Bantam Books NY

Gould, Stephen, 1996. Full House: The Spread of Excellence from Plato to Darwin. Harmony Books, N.Y.

Granovetter. The Strength of Weak Ties in *American Journal of Sociology*, May 73

Greenacre, Phyllis. 1971. Studies in Creativity. Emotional Growth, vol 2. NY: International University Press. Pg 399-615.

Greenfield, Susan. 2000. The Private Life of the Brain. Penguin Books, NY

Halfield, Elaine, Cacioppo, John. 1994. Emotional Contagion. Cambridge University Press, London

Hart, Mickey. 1991. Planet Drum: A celebration of percussion and rhythm. Harper Collins Pub, NY

Hiss, Tony. Man About Towns. *Sierra Magazine*. Nov/Dec 01 pg 62

Holton, Gerald ed. 1949. Albert Einstein, "Autobiolgraphical Notes" trans. By Paul Arthur Schilpp, Evanston Ill: Library of Living Philosophers in Albert Einstein: Philosopher-Scientist.

Howard, Philip. 2001. The Lost Art of Drawing the Line. Random House NY

Illich, Ivan. 1999. The Right to Useful Employment and its Professional Enemies. Marion Boyers Publishing Ltd.

Ingber, Donald E. 1998. The Architecture of Life. *Scientific American* January 1998 issue 1098.

Jacobs, Diane. 2003. Personal Correspondence, Vancouver, Canada

Jolande, Jacobi, 1962. The Psychology of C.G. Jung. Yale University Press; New Haven.

Jones, Steve. 1999. Darwin's Ghost. Random House, NY

Jones, W. Paul 2001. A Table in the Desert: Making Space Holy. Paraclete Press, Mass.

Jourdain, Robert 1998. Music, the Brain, and Ecstacy. Avon Books, NY

Juhan, Deane. 1998. Job's Body: A handbook for bodywork. Station Hill. Barrytown Ltd. NY.

Kleinman, Arthur, Straus, Stephen. Chronic Fatigue Syndrome: Proceedings of CIBA Conference May 12-14 1992. London: Wiley 1993:3.

Kornfield, Jack 2000. After the Ecstasy, the Laundry: How the Heart Grows Wiser on the Spiritual Path. Bantam, NY.

Kosko, Bart, 1993. Fuzzy Thinking: The New Science of Fuzzy Logic. Hyperion, NY

Kunzig, Robert. 2001. The Physics of Walking: Falling Forward. In *Discover* Vol 22 No 1 July 01.

Lakoff, George and Johnson, Mark 1999. Philosophy in the Flesh: The Embodied Mind and its Challenge to Western Thought. Basic Books, NY

LaBier, Douglas. 1986. Modern madness: The Emotional Fallout of Success. Addison Wesley Pub Com. Reading, Mass.

Leonard, George. 1978. The Silent Pulse: A search for the perfect rhythm that exists in each of us. EP Dutton NY

Lorch, Elizabeth, Anderson, Daniel. 1983. Looking at Television: Action or reaction?. In Children's understanding of television: Research on attention and comprehension. Academic Press. NY

Loori, John Daido. 1996. The Heart of Being: Moral and Ethical teachings of Zen Buddhism. Monny Myotai Treace Ed: Charles E. Tuttle Co. NY

Lynch, Aaron 1996. Thought Contagion. Basic Books/Perseus Group, NY

Markova, Dawna 1994. No Enemies Within: A creative process for discovering what's right about what's wrong. Conari Publishing, Maine.

May, Rollo. 1975. The Courage To Create. W.W. Norton & Co Inc. NY

Moffitt, Philip. The Body as a Spiritual Path in *Yoga Journal*, November 02, pg 53-59.

Montessori, Maria. 1967. The Absorbant Mind. Hold, Rinehart & Winston. NY.

Moody, Kate 1967. Growing Up on Television: The TV Effect. Times Books NY

Myers, Thomas W. 2001. Anatomy Trains: Myofasical Meridians for manual and Movement Therapists. Churchill Livingston, London.

Myss, Caroline 1996. The Anatomy of the Spirit: The Seven Stages of Power and Healing. Crown Publishers, NY

Napier, John. The Antiquity of Human Walking in Scientific American, April 1867.

Nathan, Bevis. 1999 Touch and Emotion in Manual Therapy. Churchill Livingstone, London.

Nesse, Randolph M, Williams, George C. 1996. Why we get sick: the new science of Darwinian medicine. Vintage Books NY

Ornstein, Robert and Sobel, David 1987. The Healing Brain: Breakthrough Discoveries About How the Brain Keeps us Healthy. Simon & Schuster, NY

Oz, Mehmet. 1999. Healing From the Heart. Dutton, NY

Palumbi, Stephen R. 2001. The Evolution Explosion: How humans cause rapid evolutionary change. W. W. Norton & Co. NY

Parker, Tom 1983. Rules of Thumb. Houghton Mifflin Company, Mass.

Pedersen S, Middel, B. Journal of Psychosomatic Research 2001, Aug; 51-(2): 443-9

Pert, Candace 1999. Molecules of Emotion: The science behind the mind/body machine. Simon & Schuster NY

Petty, Richard 2003. Nodding or Shaking Your Head May Even Influence Your Own Thoughts. *Journal of Personality and Social Psychology.*

Pollan, Michael. 2002. The Botany of Desire: A Plant's-Eye View of the World. Random House, NY

Porpora, Douglas V. 2001. Landscapes of the Soul: The Loss of Moral Meaning in American Life. Oxford University Press Inc., NY

Ramachandran, V.S. and Blakeslee, Sandra. 1998. Phantoms in the Brain: Probing the Mysteries of the Mind. William Morrow & Co. NY

Ratey, John, Johnson Catherine. 1997. Shadow Syndromes. Pantheon NY

Ratey, John. 2001. The User's Guide to the Brain: Perception, Attention, and the Four Theaters of the Brain. Pantheon, NY.

Rechtschaffen, Stephan. 1996. Time Shifting: Creating More Time to Enjoy your life. Doubleday NY

Ridley, Matt 2003. Nature via Nurture: Genes, Experience, & What Makes Us Human. HarperCollins, NY

Ridley, Matt 1997. The Origins of Virtue: Human Instincts and the Evolution of Cooperation. Viking/Penguin Books. NY

Robbins, John. 1987. A Diet for a New America. Stillpoint Pub. Walpole, New Hampshire

Rolheiser, Ronald, 1999. Holy Longing. Doubleday, NY

Rybcyznski, Witold. 2000. One Good Turn: A natural history of the screwdriver and the screw. Scribner NY

Sachs, Curt. 1940. The History of Musical Instruments. WW Norton, NY

San Francisco Chronicle July 29, 2001 Bike Helmets no guarantee by Julian E Barnes, from the New York Times

Saraswati, Swami Ambikananda. 2001. Healing Yoga: A guide to integrating the chakras with your yoga practice. Marlowe & Company NY

Saunders, Fenella. "Is Overeating An Addiction?" *Discover* May 2001, Vol 22, No 5, pg 14.

Schleppati, M., Nardone, A., and Schmid, M. Neck Muscle Fatigue Affects Postural Control in Man. *Neuroscience*, Vol. 121:2:277-285.

Schueller, Gretel H. 2001. Eat Locally in *Discover*. May Vol 22 Number 5, pg 70

Schwartz, Jeffrey, Begley, Susan. 2002. Mind and Brain: Neuroplasticity and the power of mental force. HarperCollins NY

Shermer, Michael 1997. Why People Believe Weird Things: Pseudoscience, Supersitition, and Other Confusions of Our Time. W.H. Freeman & Co. NY

Simonton, D. K. 2002. Origins of Genius. Oxford University Press.

Smolensky, Michael and Lamberg, Lynne, 2000. The Body Clock. Henry Holt, NY

Taylor, G. John. 1999. The Race for Consciousness. MIT Press. Mass.

Taylor, Shelley, E., 2002. The Tending Instinct: How Nurturing is Essential to Who We Are and How We Live. Henry Holt and Company. NY.

Travell, Janet G., Simons, David G. 1999. Myofascial Pain and Dysfunction: The Trigger Point Manual. Lippincott Williams & Wilkins, Philadelphia.

Vertosick, Frank T. Jr. 2000. Why We Hurt: The Natural History of Pain. Harcourt Inc., NY

Watson, James D. 1968. The Double Helix: A Personal Account of the Discovery of the Structure of DNA. Critical edition, edited by Gunther S. Stent. London: Weidenfield and Nicolson, 1981.

Whyte, David 2001. Crossing the Unknown Sea: Work as a Pilgrimage of Identity. Riverhead Books, NY

Wilson Edward O. 2002. The Future of Life. Alfred A Knoph NY

Wilson Edward O. 1996. In Search of Nature. Island Press/Shearwater Books, Washington D.C.

Wilson, Frank. R. 1998. The Hand: how its use shapes the brain, language and human culture. Pantheon. NY

Winfree, Arthur T. 1987. The Timing of Biological Clocks. Scientific American Books Inc NY

Yancy, Philip. 2001. Soul Survivor: How my faith survived the Church. Doubleday, NY

Zauner, Renate. 1980. Speaking Of: Children's posture problems and the injuries they cause. Delair Pub NY

Index

Abel, Robert, 190

Ackerman, Diane, 211, 241

Acupressure points, 124

Adam's Apple, 143

Addiction, 50-51, 54, 59, 69, 102, 154, 189, 246

Affluenza, 96, 242

Air, 45, 72,102, 127, 130, 146, 159, 195, 234

    As eight winds, 194

    Navaho wind, 134

Alcohol, 18, 31, 60, 63-64, 89, 99, 153, 156, 177, 211, 222

Alexander, Colin J, 23

Alexander, Matthias, 148

Allen, Woody, 224

Allergies, 83, 151

Alpha waves, 19, 181, 186

Alphabet, 177

Ambiguity, 95, 156

Amen, Daniel, 197, 241

American Nervousness, 60

Anger, 35, 40, 78, 98, 104, 110, 113, 116-117, 130, 138-140, 143, 147-148, 161, 185, 203, 228

Angina, 115, 117, 130, 215

Anja pose, 196

Ankle, 27,37, 201, 234, 236

    Ankle pump, 17, 23-24, 122

Anna Karenia Principle, 88

Antaeus, 38

Anxiety, 22, 61-65, 70, 83-84, 96, 99, 105-106, 116, 130, 132, 156, 167, 184, 203, 208

Apathy, 2, 22, 42, 189, 194, 228

Aquatic Ape, 137

Aquinas, Thomas, 39, 73, 184

Ardha Buddha Padmasana pose, 101

Ardha Matsyendrasana pose, 101

Arms, 21-22, 24-25, 40, 44, 82, 105, 117-119, 121-123, 125-126, 131-132, 142, 145, 148, 160, 162, 178, 201, 214, 221-222, 235

Arteries, 46, 56, 85, 104, 110, 115-116, 130, 155

Asana, 36-37, 160, 203

Aspiration, 143

Asthma, 65, 112, 121, 146, 194, 205

Automobile, 1, 8, 18-19, 21, 43, 225

Axelrod, Robert, 33

Ayurvedic Philosophy

    Bathing, 132

    Medicine, 239

Balkins, J.M., 8

Barabasi, Albert-Laszlo, 175

Barnes, Julian E., 210

Bateson, Gregory, 73, 75

Beard, George M., 60

Beatles, 6

Beattie, Andrew, 98, 241

Beinfield, Harriet, 232, 241

Benzer, Seymore, 89

Berglass, Steven, 22, 210

Bernstein, Nikolai, 38

Berry, Windell, 5, 87, 241
Beta Waves, 171
Bicycles, 179, 210
Bittman, Barry, 223
Black Elk, 83, 215
Blaise, Clark, 219, 241
Bland, Jeffrey, 59
Body
    Architecture of, 13
    Ecology of, 12
Bok, Derek, 39
Bonniet, Nardi, 71
Brand, Margaret, 164
Brand, Paul, 4, 164, 241
Breathing
    As silent thread, 133
    Hyper/hypoventilation, 105
    In rabbits and dogs, 115
    In Tonglen, 159
    Kriya yogic breathing, 181
    Throat breathing, 141
    Yogic, 69
Brodie, Richard, 8, 173, 241
Buddhist psychology, 2, 75, 128, 185, 188, 191, 193
Burnett, Frances, 129
Butler, David, 75, 195, 242
Cacioppo, John, 174, 244
Caffeine, 60, 63, 156, 163
Cameron, Julia, 198, 213, 242
Campbell, Joseph, 3, 37
Caplan, Ralph, 24, 242
Caporael, L. R., 24, 242
Carlan, George, 118
Carpal Tunnel Syndrome, 25, 120, 125, 206
Cavagna, Giovanni, 49
Chair, 8, 21, 23-26, 53, 55-56, 66, 119-121, 158, 201-206, 213, 238
    Rocking chair, 16, 24, 27, 56, 122

Stadium seating, 58
Chaitow, Leon, 112, 116
Chakra
    Fifth, 135
    First, 15
    Forth, 105
    Second, 48
    Seventh, 199
    Third, 78
Chakrasana pose, 101
Chaos, 34, 46, 193, 215, 230
Chinese philosophy, 237
Cinderella Syndrome, 82, 121
Clothing, 161, 177, 208-209
Cognitive Dissonance, 11
Cognitive Lock, 9
Cole, K.C., 28, 150, 174, 214, 242
Connective tissue, 37, 80-81, 217
Cope, Stephen, 213, 242
Cow face pose, 132
Cranz, Galen, 23, 24, 242
Crocodile pose, 132
Csikszentmihaly, Mihaly, 224. 242
Cummings, Nicholas, 85
Damasio, Antonio, 164. 242
Dance, 4, 45, 100, 130, 148, 160-161, 166, 170, 176, 193, 212, 214-215, 222-223, 230-231
Dandasana pose, 234
Darwin, Charles, 87,174, 203, 242
Darwinianism
    Medicine, 63
    Neural, 6
Dauvois, Michel, 146
Davidson, Richard, 170
DaVinci, Leonardo, 5, 28, 166
Dawkins, Richard, 6, 16, 152, 224, 242
Deacon, 138-139, 242
De Botton, Alain, 141, 242
De Graaf, John, 96

Denollet, J., 140, 242

Dhanurasana pose, 160

Diabetes, 83, 91, 177, 194, 205

Diamond, Jared, 88-89, 97, 205, 242

Diaphragm, 23, 25, 78, 105-107, 111, 113-116, 148

Dicke, Marcel, 151

Dillard, Annie, 212, 242

Diving Reflex, 137

Domestication

    Boids, 90

    Cows, 89-90

    Dogs, 90

    Humans, 88

    Of Elements, 103

    Seeds, 88

    Work as, 154

Donald, Norman A., 183, 242

Dopamine, 57, 64-65, 89, 145, 168, 184, 189

Dossey, Larry, 61, 64, 194, 197, 242-243

Dowling, Colette, 243

Drake, Michael, 215, 243

Dugatkin, Lee Alan, 16, 243

Dunbar, Robin 184, 243

DVT's (deep vein thrombosis). 23

Ears, 3, 6, 87, 117, 120, 150, 166, 177-178, 182, 218, 222

Earth, 19, 36, 44, 102, 131, 157, 159, 195, 210, 233

Edelman, Gerald, 6

Edison, Thomas, 7, 31, 60

Ehrlich, Paul R., 98, 241

Eickhoff, Hajo, 24

Einstein, Albert 48, 150, 163, 169, 172, 218, 234

Ekman, Paul, 94, 139, 170

Emptiness, 2, 36, 128, 150, 158, 229, 234, 242

Epidemics, 91

Everdell, William, 219

Evolutionary Medicine, 187, 204

Exercise, 21, 25, 39, 43, 51, 64, 69, 103, 105, 109, 134, 179, 181, 184, 203, 208, 233

Eyes, 6, 21, 40, 55, 57, 117, 119-120, 124, 150, 160, 164, 166-168, 170-171, 177, 190-191, 201

    In language, 8, 13, 158

    In thinking, 8, 95, 150, 156

    In television viewing, 54, 171

Faith, 5, 8, 10, 40, 79, 135, 145, 150, 155-157, 160, 163, 188, 212, 230, 247

Falling, 25-26, 40, 49, 56, 70

Faulkner, William, 148

Feet, 15-16, 22, 28, 31, 34-36, 41, 44, 46, 50, 56, 67, 73, 84, 114, 120, 123, 149, 201

Feldenkrais, Moshe, 37, 38, 78, 149, 180, 208, 230, 232, 243

Feng Shui, 98, 237-238

Feynman, Richard, 11, 89, 99, 243

Fingers, 24-25, 29, 76, 123-127, 136, 147, 158, 170, 172, 221

Fire, 12, 37, 42-45, 72, 74, 100-103, 109, 111, 130, 132, 159, 195, 210, 214, 221-222, 225-226, 234, 237, 239, 241

Flight or fight, 84, 95, 114, 118, 123, 138, 181, 206, 215

Flight, fight or bite, 138

Flight, fight or freeze, 138

Forgiveness, 33, 128, 131, 140, 163

Frattaroli, Elio, 156, 243

Friedman, Meyer, 94

Freud, Sigmund, 2, 10, 112, 184, 192, 204

Fulkerson, Mary, 148

Fuller , Buckminster, 77, 200

Furniture
Children's, 30, 237-238,
In schools, 24
Television viewing, 56
Fuzzy logic, 108-109, 244
GABA (gamma-aminobutyric acid), 64
Gage, Fred, 179
Game Theory, 140
Garudasana pose, 40
Gawande, Alul, 224
Gilbert, Christopher, 106
Gladwell, Malcolm, 175
Glover, Savion, 27, 243
Golden Handcuffs, 62
Goleman, Daniel, 64, 177, 233, 243
Gottman, John, 170, 181
Gould, Stephen Jay, 6
Granovetter, 175, 243
Gravity, 3, 10, 12, 25, 28, 35, 39, 49, 136,
150, 156, 163, 167, 201, 228, 235
Green decisions
Greening of religion, 73
Greenwashing, 73
Greenacre, Phyllis, 100, 243
Greenfield, Patricia, 146
Greenfield, Susan, 243
Gross, David, 214
Gunn, John, 144
Halasana pose, 234
Halfield, Elaine, 174, 244
Hamilton, William, 34
Hands
Grasping, 125, 127, 130, 132-133,
141, 172, 212, 221
Writing, 51, 158, 171
Hari Hara asana pose, 160
Hart, Mickey, 214-215, 244
Hatfield, Brad, 181
Hawking, Stephen, 152
Headaches, 52, 59, 120, 123, 167, 187

Heart
Broken heart, 107, 128, 209
Heart attacks, 85, 95-96, 106, 115,
139, 142
Hemispheres, Brain. 145, 166, 171, 176,
186, 215, 223
Hero, 37, 41-42, 44, 97, 129, 160
Heves, Gordon, 24
Hiatal Hernia, 103-104, 116
Hip, 23, 25, 28-29, 48, 50, 56, 66, 119,
142, 208, 215, 217
Fracture, 66
Replacement, 66, 202
Hiss, Tony, 19, 244
Hoffman, Eric, 181
Howard, Philip, 210, 244
Howlett, Allyn, 154
Hunter-gathers
In animals, 130, 169
Hurry sickness, 94
Immune System, 8, 15, 166, 91, 118, 151,
161, 173, 185, 194, 233
Incontinence, 29, 202
Ingber, Donald, 12, 86-87, 244
Jacobs, Diane, 244
Jathara Parivartanasana pose, 100
Janusirshasana pose, 101
Jaw, 115-116, 119, 136, 138, 141, 149,
157, 164, 180, 193
Jaynes, Julian, 192
Johnson, Mark, 62, 244
Jones, W. Paul, 156, 244
Jones, Steve 91, 203, 244
Jourdain, Robert, 236, 244
Juhan, Deane, 12, 25, 48, 62, 67, 110
Jung, Carl, 9, 199, 211, 222
Kabat-Zin, Jon, 132
Kandasana pose, 40
Keen, Sam, 70, 78-79
Keleman, Stanley, 45, 213

Kidder, Tracey, 200
King, Martin Luther, 9, 35
Kleinman, Ahtur, 60, 244
Knee, 22, 27-31, 55-56, 62, 101, 119, 201, 213
Kneier, Andrew, 85
Kornfield, Jack, 78, 94, 130, 162, 212
Korngold, Efram, 232, 241
Kosko, Bart, 108, 244
Krauss, Lawrence, 111
Kundalini, 46, 234, 239
Labor
    Drug use, 18, 52, 153-154
    Joy of, 61, 70, 238
    Obedience strike, 72
Lacan, Jacques, 10
Lakoff, George, 13, 62, 244
Language
    Acquisition, 4, 58-59, 139, 152-153, 158, 176
Laughter, 112, 149-150
LeDoux, Joseph, 177
Lenson, David, 153
Levine, Steven, 94
Loftus, Elizabeth, 45
Lotus pose, 34
Low back pain, 50-52, 54, 56, 81, 203
Lowen, Alexander, 112
Loyalty, 105, 107, 123, 127, 134
Lungs, 23, 93, 105, 107-108, 110-111, 113-114, 117, 122, 132, 139, 143, 151, 207, 234
Maha Banda pose, 71
Marijuana, 16, 63, 154-155, 189
Matricardi, Paolo, 151
Matsyendrasana pose, 101
Matzinger, Polly, 151
Mauss, Marcel, 200
May, Rollo, 4, 245
McAllister, James, 9

McLauhan, Marshall, 177
Mechovlam, Raphael, 154
Meditation, 35, 94, 130-132, 145, 156, 159, 188, 209, 228
Meme, 5-8, 11-12, 16-18, 43, 49, 53-54, 58, 68, 74, 146-147, 153-154, 169, 172, 175, 177, 188, 223-225
Memory, 77, 139, 169, 178
    Short-term, 31, 67, 155, 172, 188
Merudandasana pose, 40
Metaphor, 5, 13, 38, 43, 75, 121, 188, 191, 192, 195
Mikuriija, Tod, 171
Montessori, Maria, 24, 232, 245
Moore, Thomas, 149, 163, 229
Mosley, Nicolas, 39
Motor Development, 31
    In speech, 136, 147, 178
    Of thought, 5, 22, 59, 95, 97, 165, 176, 185
Mouth, 44, 104, 156, 136, 139, 141, 143, 144-146, 157, 163
    As sound cave, 213
Moyer, Bill, 156
Mulabandha pose, 234
Mullen, Brian, 176
Muscle spindle, 48
Music
    Body as, 9, 12-13, 36, 81, 100, 111, 124, 136, 147, 157, 181, 196, 200, 226, 245
    Drumming, 189, 214-215, 223, 243
Myss, Caroline, 119, 192, 245
Napier, John, 26, 245
Nash, John, 32-33, 188
Nataraj II pose, 100
National Freeway System, 17
Natural selection, 6-7, 21, 152

Neck, 25, 56, 79, 81, 105, 114, 116, 121, 142-143, 148, 150, 157, 162, 170, 182, 203, 206
Negative coping, 59-60
Nei Jing, 10
Nesse, Randolph, 245
Niralambana Paschemottanasana pose, 71
Ober sign, 28
O'Day, Vicki, 71
Opposites
    Bivalence, 108
    Polarities, 94
    Yin and Yang, 70, 107-108
Ornish, Dean, 231
Ornstein, Robert, 93-95, 245
Overeating, 1, 31, 91, 246
Oxytocin, 123
Pain
    Absence of, 5, 43, 62, 102, 106, 132, 156, 161, 203
    Referred pain, 116, 142
Palumbi, Stephen, R., 6, 245
Paschimottanasana pose, 100
Pauling, Linus, 89, 184
Pavighasana pose, 159
Pectoralis, 116-117
Piezo-electric charge, 217
Perkins, David, 16
Persinger, Michael, 215
Pert, Candice, 6, 207, 233, 245
Pestalozzi, Johann Heinrich, 171
Pinker, Steven, 21
Planck, Max, 16
Play, 4, 22, 39, 103, 161, 199, 209, 211-212, 220, 228
    Playgrounds, 209-210
Pollan, Michael, 155, 245
Porpora, Douglas, 129, 245
Posture

Basic, 13, 22, 68, 111, 131, 143, 185, 229, 244-245
    Cultural variants, 169, 201
    Moral Posture, 129
    Sleep, 106, 112-113, 158, 163, 168, 179, 187, 191, 201, 205, 212, 227, 235
    Stomach emptying, 65, 136, 163
    Supine, 182
Pranamasana pose, 71
Proust, Marcel, 1, 26
Psychoactive plants, 63, 153-154, 188-189
Pulse, 133, 137, 168, 214-215, 221, 223, 244
Qigong, 11, 83, 101, 130, 181
Quadratus lumborum, 28, 50, 67, 81, 105, 111, 142
Railroad, 17, 167, 219
Railroad Spine, 167
Ramachandran, Vilayanur, 185
Ratey, John, 21, 61, 91, 95, 145, 170, 245
Redefining Progress, 93
Reich, Wilhelm, 38, 112, 149, 232
Responsibility, 20, 35, 62, 69, 73, 99-100, 125, 145, 157, 188, 203-204, 209, 213, 226, 229, 237, 241
Rest and digest, 84
Reynolds, Craig, 90
Reznikoff, Iegor, 146
Rhythm, 64-65, 93, 127, 130, 138, 147-148, 168, 174, 176, 180, 189-190, 212-217, 220, 222-223, 227, 229-230, 235, 240, 243-244
Ridley, Matt, 34, 245-246
Rilke, 73, 131
Rinpoche, Sogyal, 22
Roads, 17-20, 24, 120, 155, 203
Robbins, John, 58, 104, 246
Robinson, J. P., 54
Rockwell, Irini, 98

Rolf, Ida, 208
Rosenman, Ray, 94
Rules of thumb, 220, 245
Rumi, 71, 192, 228, 231
Rybcyznski, Witold, 29, 246
Sachs, Curt, 214, 246
Sacrament
    As hinge point, 156
    Music as, 215
Sacrum, 28-29, 81, 156
Sagan, Carl, 5, 188
Sainting, 19
Savasana pose, 39
Sawaswati, Swami Ambikananda, 235, 246
Schueller, Gretel, 88, 92, 246
Schwartz, Jeffrey, 74-75, 214
Scurr, John, 23
Seligman, Martin, 193
Senses
    As rhythm transformers, 168
    As unreliable, 167
Serotonin, 145
Shavasana pose, 235
Shaw, George Bernard, 155
Shipman, Pat, 115
Shoes, 27, 31, 36, 201
Shoulders, 12, 40, 55, 105, 111, 117-119, 121-123, 125, 128-129, 131, 136, 142, 182, 200, 203, 207, 210, 220, 234
Simon, Hubert, 89
Simhasana pose, 159
Sirsha Angusthana Yogasana pose, 234
Sirshasana pose, 101, 159
Sivananda, Swami, 191
Skinner, B. F., 147
Skinner, Martin, 176
Smolensky, Michael, 246
Sobel, David, 245
Social stomach, 32, 92

Solar Plexus, 82, 84
Solar Time, 219
Space Shuttle, 7, 17
Speech, 65, 114, 136, 138-139, 146-147, 152, 162, 175-176, 178, 186
Spine, 15, 22, 24, 30, 48, 50, 52, 55, 66, 78-82, 85, 98, 101-102, 105-106, 111-118, 132, 136, 167, 170, 196, 206
Squatting, 25, 27, 29, 125, 201-202
Standing, 15-16, 22, 28, 37, 38, 42, 67, 80, 111, 202, 230
Sternocleidomastoid muscle, 142
Storr, Anthony, 223
Surface sanity, 43, 62-63
Survival of the fittest, 6, 33, 53
Swallowing, 136-137, 142
Symbiont, 8
Tai Chi, 83, 97, 130, 181
Taylor, Shelley, 246
Television, 1, 21, 25, 32, 53-58, 60, 64, 69, 75, 76, 79, 161, 171, 183
Tend and befriend, 84, 123, 181
Tensegrity, 86-87, 200
Theta waves, 95
Thirst, 207-208
Time, 219, 227
Tipping Point, 175, 231, 243
Tit-For-Tat, 33-34
Tittibhasana pose. 234
Todd, Mabel, 148
Toe Walking, 113
Toilet, 29-30, 103, 202-203
Tomoshok, Lydia, 85
Tongue, 2, 40, 135, 138-139, 141-142, 147, 170, 230
Tools, 104, 125, 144, 159, 173, 177-178, 196
Travell, Janet, 246
Trikonasana, 41, 196

Trivers, 34, 140
Tuberculosis, 90-91, 205
Twain, Mark, 60, 85
Type A personality, 85, 94-95, 129
Type B personality, 94, 140
Type C personality, 85
Type D personality, 140, 242
Typewriters, 125
Tyron, Edward, 150
Urdhra Bhujangasana pose, 71, 131
Ushtrasana pose, 132
Uttanasana pose, 100
Utthita Hasta Padasana pose, 40
Vagal nerve, 181
Vaillant, George, 233
Vajrasana Yoga pose, 100
Vertosick, Frank, 246
Virabhadra I pose, 160
Virabhadra II pose, 71
Virasana pose, 37
Vital exhaustion, 140, 241
Walker, Alan, 115
Walking
        Number of footsteps, 53
        Roaming charges, 44

Sauntering, 19, 21
    As pendulum, 49
    While talking, 137
Water, 30, 45, 68, 72, 77, 102, 103, 115,
    159, 195, 233
Watts, Alan, 222
Weather, 69, 72, 141, 215-216, 221, 233,
    242
Weick, Karl, 10
Weil, Andrew, 189
Whyte, David, 11, 42, 44, 73, 105, 225,
    246
Williams, George, 65, 187, 204, 245
Willpower Deficiency Syndrome, 96
Wilson, Edward, O., 91-92, 151, 246
Wilson, Frank R., 126-127, 146, 246
Working wounded, 43, 61
Yoga, 5, 9, 11-13, 34, 36-37, 40, 46, 74,
    83, 100, 122, 130, 181, 191-192,
    203-204, 211, 213, 227, 228, 234,
    235
    For the eyes, 176, 190
    Kundalini, 46, 234, 239
Young, Iris, 208

0-595-29551-7

Made in the USA
Middletown, DE
11 March 2021

35192601R00158